Globalization & Football

Theory, Culture & Society

Theory, Culture & Society caters for the resurgence of interest in culture within contemporary social science and the humanities. Building on the heritage of classical social theory, the book series examines ways in which this tradition has been reshaped by a new generation of theorists. It also publishes theoretically informed analyses of everyday life, popular culture, and new intellectual movements.

EDITOR: Mike Featherstone, *Nottingham Trent University*

SERIES EDITORIAL BOARD
Roy Boyne, *University of Durham*
Nicholas Gane, *University of York*
Scott Lash, *Goldsmiths College, University of London*
Roland Robertson, *University of Aberdeen*
Couze Venn, *Nottingham Trent University*

THE TCS CENTRE
The *Theory, Culture & Society* book series, the journals *Theory, Culture & Society* and *Body & Society*, and related conference, seminar and postgraduate programmes operate from the TCS Centre at Nottingham Trent University. For further details of the TCS Centre's activities, please contact:

The TCS Centre
School of Arts and Humanities
Nottingham Trent University
Clifton Lane, Nottingham, NG11 8NS, UK
e-mail: tcs@ntu.ac.uk
web: http://sagepub.net/tcs/

Recent volumes include:

The Body and Society, Third Edition
Bryan S. Turner

The Saturated Society
Pekka Sulkunen

Changing Bodies
Chris Shilling

The Media City
Scott McQuire

Globalization & Football

Richard Giulianotti and Roland Robertson

Los Angeles | London | New Delhi
Singapore | Washington DC

First published 2009

SAGE Publications Ltd
1 Oliver's Yard
55 City Road
London EC1Y 1SP

SAGE Publications Inc.
2455 Teller Road
Thousand Oaks, California 91320

SAGE Publications India Pvt Ltd
B 1/I 1 Mohan Cooperative Industrial Area
Mathura Road, Post Bag 7
New Delhi 110 044

SAGE Publications Asia-Pacific Pte Ltd
33 Pekin Street #02–01
Far East Square
Singapore 048763

Library of Congress Control Number: 2008940426

British Library Cataloguing in Publication data

A catalogue record for this book is available from
the British Library

ISBN 978-1-4129-2127-5
ISBN 978-1-4129-2128-2 (pbk)

Typeset by C&M Digitals (P) Ltd, Chennai, India
Printed in India at Replika Press Pvt. Ltd
Printed on paper from sustainable resources

Contents

Acknowledgements

We wish to thank the Editorial Board and the Journal Manager, Jacquie Gauntlett, at the *British Journal of Sociology* for publishing in 2004 our co-authored article on football and globalization. That paper provided the inspiration for the writing of this book. We would also like to thank the Economic and Social Research Council for funding our two-year project on Scottish football and globalization (award number R000239833). Much of the theoretical and empirical work for this book was facilitated through that project. In the course of the last few years, we have benefitted substantially from correspondence and conversations with a wide range of social scientists on the subjects of football, sport and globalization. We would particularly like to thank the contributors to our edited book on *Globalization and Sport* (Blackwell, 2007) – David Andrews, Gary Armstrong, Thomas Hylland Eriksen, William Kelly, Frank Lechner, George Ritzer, Chris Rumford, Barry Smart – as well as John Boli, Susan Brownell, Robert Holton, Paul James and Franciscu Sedda. We are also grateful to *Theory, Culture & Society* for publishing our new book in conjunction with Sage. Particular thanks are due to Chris Rojek, Jai Seaman and Katie Forsythe at Sage who have done a tremendous job in patiently and expertly guiding this project through to completion.

List of Abbreviations

AELFP – Association Européenne des Ligues de Football Professionnel (European Association of Professional Football Leagues)

AFA – Asociación del Fútbol Argentino (Football Association of Argentina)

AFC – Asian Football Confederation

ASEAN – Association of Southeast Asian Nations

CAF – Confédération Africaine de Football (Confederation of African football)

CAS – Court of Arbitration for Sport

CBF – Confederação Brasileira de Futebol (Brazilian Football Confederation)

CBO – Community-Based Organization

CONCACAF – The Confederation of North, Central America and Caribbean Association Football

CONMEBOL – South American football confederation (also known as CSF or Confederación Sudamericana de Fútbol)

CSR – Corporate Social Responsibility

DFB – Deutscher Fussball Bund (German Football Association)

EPL – English Premier League

EU – European Union

FA – Football Association (England)

FARE – Football Against Racism in Europe

FDI – Foreign Direct Investment

FIFA – Fédération Internationale de Football Association (International Federation of Association Football)

FiFPRO – Fédération International de Footballeurs Professionels (International Federation of Professional Footballers)

IFAB – International Football Association Board

IGO – International Governmental Organization

ILO – International Labour Organization

IMF – International Monetary Fund

IOC – International Olympic Committee

MEP – Member of the European Parliament

MLS – Major League Soccer (US)

NAFTA – North American Free Trade Agreement

NASL – North American Soccer League

NFF – Norges Fotballforbund (Football Association of Norway)

NGO – Non-Governmental Organization

NSM – New Social Movement

OFC – Oceania Football Confederation

OFFS – Open Fun Football Schools

PFA – Professional Footballers' Association

TNC – Transnational Corporation

TNS – Transnational State

UEFA – Union Européenne de Football Association (Union of European Football Associations)

UN – United Nations

UNHCR – United Nations High Commissioner for Refugees

UNICEF – United Nations Children's Fund

WADA – World Anti-Doping Agency

WHO – World Health Organization

WTO – World Trade Organization

WUSA – Women's United Soccer Association (US)

Prologue

This book is about the interrelationships of globalization processes and the sport of football (sometimes known as 'association football' or 'soccer'). As joint authors, we share a deep fascination with both 'the global game' and transnational processes, and these subjects would appear to have a similar allure across most societies throughout the world.

To clarify matters, our focus is on the diverse sociological aspects of football. We are committed to looking well beyond football *qua* game, to explore its social history and diffusion, and its cultural, economic, political, and social dimensions. The more specific, technical aspects of football – such as playing skills or technological developments – are certainly not ignored here, but we do locate these within their full sociological contexts.

In placing the game within its global context, we need to clarify our understanding of *globalization* per se. Here we follow Robertson's (1992: 8) opening statement, which defined globalization as a concept that 'refers both to the compression of the world and the intensification of consciousness of the world as a whole'. To put this statement in another way: globalization is characterized by increasing global interconnectedness, or *connectivity* (for example, through greater migration and digital communication); and by stronger forms of *globality*, as people are increasingly reflexive about the world per se.

If we think initially of globalization in this way, then it is clear that the investigation of football is far from a marginal, academic pursuit; obversely, the game must be understood as increasingly important to globalization processes. Football's biggest event – the World Cup finals – is an exemplar of worldwide connectivity and advanced global consciousness; it is a tournament which attracts tens of thousands of international spectators, is televised intensively and worldwide for an entire month, and initially organizes more than 200 national teams in the quest to qualify. Football events promote and normalize forms of connectivity that in alternate social realms have been deeply contested. For example, since the early 1960s, UK club and national sides have been increasingly committed to participation in European football competitions; yet, in England particularly, deep forms of antagonism towards European engagement or integration have constantly surfaced, especially during the 1980s and 1990s. Similarly, major football fixtures have been contested between nations at times of lingering diplomatic or military hostility, such as the USA–Iran game in 1998, or the England–Argentina clash in 1982.

Despite some recent important advances, mainstream social science and the specific field of global studies have rather overlooked the significance of football and general sport to globalization processes. Our aim in part, then, is to contribute towards filling that lacuna. We are further concerned to develop the field of global studies itself, notably in conceptual and methodological terms. Through focusing on globalization in regard to a highly salient substantive realm such as football, the field of global studies may mature theoretically, and help to reveal the intensively complex ways in which transnational processes impact upon particular domains of social life.

One preliminary observation is that football may be understood in anthropological terms, as illuminating globalization processes in different ways. Consider, for example, how the game may be understood as a metric, a mirror, a motor, and a metaphor of globalization; these are heuristic terms that are particularly apt for a cultural form that attracts an array of alliterations as well as a variety of vantage points.

As a *metric*, football may be used to measure transnational, political, and social connectivity. The game's world governing body (FIFA) has a larger membership than the United Nations (208 to 192, as at end 2008), and holds jurisdiction over thousands of international fixtures each year. As a *mirror*, football is used by different peoples as a global looking-glass, as a means of imagining and reflecting upon their appearance, status, and identity, in relation to changing transnational audiences. As a *motor*, football may be understood as accelerating particular global transformations. In the early twentieth century, for example, football advanced the participation of non-European societies, particularly South American nations, within the emerging international society. More routinely, new social relations are developed across participants at major international football fixtures and tournaments. Finally, as a *metaphor*, the 'global game' provides a benchmark for comparing the transnational popularity of other cultural forms, while figuratively depicting the making of global consciousness (such as when images of a football and the earth are blended). Metric, mirror, motor, or metaphor – whichever interpretative device is favoured, one result remains constant: that the football–globalization nexus is one of the most significant and indeed fascinating of quotidian subjects for social scientific investigation.

Developing the Global Studies Field

In social science, the emergence of globalization as an object of inquiry was presaged by early scholarship regarding, for example, 'international society' in the 1960s, the world economic system in the 1970s, and transnational religious movements in the 1980s (cf. Nettl and Robertson 1968; Wallerstein 1974; Robertson and Chirico 1985). The 'global turn' in social science was confirmed in the early 1990s, as benchmark texts on globalization were published, and as the emergent keyword itself was transmogrified into an *idée maîtresse*, and so accelerated the shift that was otherwise occurring towards greater interdisciplinary and transdisciplinary scholarship. The methodological impact of the global turn has been such that it is increasingly difficult to formulate plausible research programmes that do not at least account for transnational processes.

The field of globalization studies now has the opportunity to make some epistemological and methodological advances by locating its core concepts and diverse debates within specific research fields or subdisciplines. Substantive research fields such as football, health, food, sexuality, and work, offer scholars of globalization the opportunity to examine, and to account more fully, for the 'second-order' complexity and uncertain outcomes of global processes. These types of specific inquiry should also encourage analysts to discard the relatively oblique or sweeping statements – for example, on issues of cultural domination or autonomy – that may still loiter in discussions of globalization, and to explore instead how more middle-range explanations account for the complex manifestation of global processes within particular social realms. Certainly, there have been significant moves in this direction within social science in recent years, and this book is intended to contribute towards that broad transition.[1]

Book Context and Contents

The focus of this book on globalization and football effectively fuses our research strengths and interests. Robertson is one of the founding figures in the social scientific analysis of globalization; his work has explored in particular the theoretical and socio-cultural issues surrounding global processes (see Robertson 1990a, 1990b, 1992, 1995, 2001, 2004, 2007a, 2007b, 2007c; and White 2003a, 2003b, 2004; and Scholte 2007). He has been a leading analyst of international societies and modernization since the mid-1960s, and is also known globally for his work in the sociology of religion. Robertson was an enthusiastic footballer and, despite spending much of his academic career in the United States, has remained a lifelong follower and intensive observer of the game.

Giulianotti is a trained sociologist whose research specialism since the late 1980s has been in football and sport studies. In terms of both research focus and collaborative projects, his work has always been marked particularly by

---

[1]The sociology of religion, for instance, has been underpinned by some sophisticated arguments on globalization (see, for example, Robertson 1985; Beyer 1994; Lechner 2005). Anthropological research has connected everyday practices in developing societies to the global context (see, for example, Hannerz 1992; Ferguson 1999; Friedman 2003), while important methodological innovations emerging from 'global ethnography' are also noteworthy (see Burawoy et al. 2000). Journals like *Global Networks* and *Globalizations* have enabled scholars to explore global processes within specific sub-disciplinary fields.

its transnational interests and dimensions (see Giulianotti 1991, 1995, 1999a, 2002, 2004a, 2005a; Armstrong and Giulianotti 1997, 1998a, 2001, 2004).

While working together at the University of Aberdeen, our collegiate chats on football and globalization quickly transformed into full research collaboration on these subjects. Our main work to date has featured *inter alia* articles in English, German, and Spanish, a two-year research project funded by the UK ESRC, and a special edition of the journal *Global Networks*. This book extends our article in the *British Journal of Sociology*.[2]

In our joint work thus far, we have developed Robertson's earlier arguments to interpret globalization as a long-term, complex, and multi-phased historical process, underpinned by subtle and shifting interdependencies between the local and the global, or the universal and the particular. Thus, the global football field is characterized neither by the routine manifestation of cultural imperialism, nor by the imposition of autonomous individual actions across a transnational domain. We do not advance essentialist arguments regarding the innately appealing qualities of football. Rather, we demonstrate that the global football field reveals many complex patterns of convergence and divergence within varied settings; many ways in which the game's rules, ethos, techniques, and aesthetics are interpreted across time and space. In developing these arguments, we disentangle the interrelations of competing politico-cultural themes and discourses that shape the global game. Specifically, these themes and discourses relate to neo-liberalism, neo-mercantilism, international governance, and global civil society.

The book is organized into five main chapters and concludes with a short epilogue. We consider in sequence the five particular perspectives and dimensions – the historical, cultural, political–economic, political, and social – that are most salient to world football. We adopt this procedure largely for reasons of analytical and explanatory coherence. We should emphasize that we are not arguing that each of these aspects stands in splendid isolation from the others; rather, they are interwoven in highly intricate and changing ways.

We set out in Chapter 1 our historical perspective on the globalization of football. Our discussion is structured by Robertson's five-fold historical model of globalization, spanning the 1500s to 2000, which we modify partly to correspond with football's genealogy. We concentrate particularly upon the third, fourth, and fifth phases from the 1870s to 2000 that are shaped in turn by globalization's 'take-off', and by increasingly complex transnational struggles and power balances. Our discussion of each phase is built around the four 'elemental reference points' of globalization that are highlighted by Robertson, namely the individual, national societies, international society, and humankind. We conclude by exploring briefly the

[2]See, variously, Giulianotti and Robertson (2005, 2007a, 2007b); Robertson and Giulianotti (2006); and ESRC research grant award number R000239833.

implications for football of Robertson's later submission that contemporary globalization has entered a sixth, 'millennial' stage since 2000, distinguished in part by climates of fear alongside the intensification of surveillance and security across social settings.

We turn to the cultural dimensions of the football world in Chapter 2. Drawing strongly on Robertson's earlier work, we argue that football's globalization must be understood in terms of the highly complex interplay of the local and the global, or the particular and the universal. Robertson's concept of 'glocalization' has particular utility here, in revealing how globalization is marked by trends towards both commonality or uniformity *and* divergence and differentiation. These interdependencies are more fully captured by the broad opposition between 'homogenization' and 'heterogenization', which registers trends towards cultural convergence and divergence. To pick the most elementary illustration, while football's global diffusion points towards a worldwide convergence over the popularity of particular sports, many societies display divergence in how they organize, interpret, and play the game. We assess debates regarding the possible 'Americanization' of football with strong reference to the game's cultural history and contemporary condition across the United States. More broadly, we consider how football is pivotal to periods of 'exceptional nationalism' (in a cultural sense) within many societies; and more routinely to the transnational development of 'banal cosmopolitanism', as individuals and social groups increasingly experience the practices and styles of other cultures at the everyday level. Football's globalization in recent times has also harboured significant postmodern cultural influences, notably in the contemporary forms of nostalgia that are constructed within popular media coverage of the game.

In Chapter 3, we develop a critical, 'global-realist' analysis of the contemporary political–economic dimensions of globalization, exploring in particular the implementation and consequences of neo-liberal or 'free market' policies within football and beyond. We address the contribution of television monies, notably through transnational pay-TV stations, in multiplying revenues in the richest football systems, primarily Western Europe. We consider how economic deterioration has seriously blighted the game in South America, although free-market policies have also engendered economic turbulence and indebtedness in Western Europe. We explore how the world's leading clubs correspond to our global-realist analysis of transnational corporations, in sustaining strong economic and symbolic ties to their national 'homes', while displaying increasingly transnational characteristics in labour recruitment, marketing, and ownership.

The political dimensions of global football are examined in Chapter 4. Building upon the earlier chapters, we consider initially the status of the nation and the nation state, with substantive reference to the 'club versus country' struggles that increasingly arise in the world game. We turn then to consider the 'neo-mercantile' dimensions of football, particularly the role of national league systems and associations, as well as international governing

bodies, in globalizing their tournaments and representative teams by pene-
trating new markets, usually in competition with equivalent sporting bodies.
We explore how particular tensions between neo-liberal and neo-mercantile
strategies continue to be played out in regard to the UEFA Champions'
League, especially in struggles between specific clubs, national associations,
and governing bodies. We also focus on broader issues regarding international governance, noting the corruption and other pathologies that continue
to blight the current political frameworks and balances of power.
Subsequently, we assess some models that would reform football's global
governance, notably the Habermasian idea of a 'cosmopolitan democracy'
that is derived principally from the work of David Held.

In Chapter 5, we examine the social aspects of globalization, a realm frequently overlooked by many analysts of global processes. We argue that the
keywords of transnationalism and connectivity enable us to interpret the
complex diffusion and adaptation of football-related social practices, as well
as the different kinds of 'disconnection' endured by many groups and societies. Football supporter cultures provide particularly vivid and varied
instanciations of social transnationalism and connectivity. In recent years, the
broad and contested concept of the 'global civil society' has become integral
to the social dimensions of globalization. On one hand, football remains a
contested domain for the extension of particular transnational processes of
social inclusion, such as concerning gender and ethnicity. On the other hand,
many governmental and non-governmental institutions – including the UN,
UEFA, and national governments and numerous charities – have come to
understand football as a crucial medium for the making of particular kinds
of global civil society. Just as the game's governing bodies have sought to cultivate its social role in peripheral societies, so football is utilized by other
agencies to assist with human development, the promotion of peace, and the
resocialization of traumatized peoples. However, in line with the broad thesis of this book, we argue that the critical and creative contributions of local
peoples need to be recognized and fully engaged if such projects are to
maximize their potential social impacts.

1

History: The Global Sport and the Making of Globalization

Introduction

The historical interpretation of the world in general, and of global football in particular, raises specific problems regarding method and perspective. The writing of 'world history' became particularly prominent in the late nineteenth and early twentieth centuries, but inclined strongly towards a rather Western-centric perspective. From the 1970s onwards, as 'global history' developed as a counterpoint, greater attention was directed towards hitherto marginalized voices and non-Western societies (Robertson 1992: 29–30; Schafer 2006). Similar trends have arisen within football studies, wherein relatively national or Eurocentric histories have been displaced by studies that chronicle and indeed celebrate the historical diversity and socio-cultural complexity of the 'global game' (cf. Walvin 1994; Armstrong and Giulianotti 1997, 1998a, 2001, 2004; Goldblatt 2004, 2006; Lanfranchi et al. 2004).

The distinction between world and global history has noteworthy parallels in the way in which 'globalization' has been understood by particular analysts. Paralleling the 'world history' model, some analysts tie globalization historically to the emergence and international diffusion of Western modernization – notably capitalism, industrialism, and bureaucratization – from the nineteenth century onwards (cf. Giddens 1990; Scholte 2005). We might call this the 'world globalization model'. Conversely, and mirroring a 'global history' standpoint, other analysts view globalization as a longer-term, diverse, and multidimensional phenomenon. In this latter perspective, which we might term the 'global globalization model', the modern West figures prominently but not exclusively, for crucially we find also an appreciation of how ancient civilizations, Islam, south and east Asia, and Africa, for example, have constructed distinctive forms of globality and have contributed to particular kinds of transcultural interdependence (cf. Therborn 1995, 2000; Robertson 1998a; Hopkins 2002). For example, Pollock (2000) encourages reflection on ancient kinds of globalization, arguing that outward-looking, 'cosmopolitan' literary cultures predominated through much of the first millennium, followed by more inward-looking, 'vernacular' thinking through much of the second.

This is not, of course, to argue that the 'global globalization' model is at odds with the analysis of modernity per se. Indeed, we should note the apparent affinities that arise between the global globalization model and theories of 'multiple modernity'. This latter perspective posits in part that non-Western societies modernize in distinctive and selective ways relative to the West (cf. Rostow 1960; Arnason 2001; Eisenstadt 2003). For example, as we also note in Chapter 3, many East Asian societies have germinated particular kinds of capitalism or religiosity that are distinct from those dominant models within 'Anglo-Saxon' societies (cf. P. Berger 1986; Beyer 1994; S. Berger and Dore 1999; Dore 2000).

In line with these 'global' models, our discussion of football's history seeks to highlight the varied, complex, and reversible ways in which different societies have engaged with and interpreted the game. In clarifying this point, we should make three initial remarks. First, we need to bear in mind the categorical distinctions between the terms global history, global change, and globalization. Global history refers to a particular way of imagining and telling the past of the world. Global change designates specific modifications or transformations in the world that possess some kind of empirical or material referent. And, to reaffirm our statement in the introduction, we understand globalization as referring to the increased concrete interdependencies of societies and to the greater consciousness of the world as a whole (cf. Robertson 1992: 8).

Second, we are not advancing the view that globalization, whether in regard to football or to other socio-cultural forms, constitutes some kind of 'triumph of the West' over the rest. Rather, the game displays many historical instances in which the West itself is either socio-culturally divided or 'left behind' by other nations and regions. An analogous dispute has recently surrounded the ontological presumptions of the sociology of globalization per se: specifically, that the dominance of a so-called 'northern' theory of globalization serves to silence voices and to occlude competing interpretative frameworks from the Global South (Connell 2007). This critique itself builds upon a rather narrower, northern-focused position than that of our own, in defining globalization as 'the current pattern of world integration via global markets, transnational corporations, and electronic media under the political hegemony of the United States' (Connell 2005: 72). Nevertheless, and in accordance with our earlier separate works on globalization and football,[1] our focus here is quite clearly on both northern and southern hemispheres, on the fully 'global' aspects of the global game.

Third, we are advancing the view that football has been a highly important aspect of globalization processes; indeed, the sport's significance in this regard is arguably intensifying. To put this in another way, and as we shall see in this chapter and later, football has both reflected and advanced globalization processes in a variety of ways.

---

[1]For example, our books tend to have a global focus; see, for example, Nettl and Robertson (1968), Robertson (1992), Giulianotti (1999a), and Armstrong and Giulianotti (2004). Our works more generally have been translated into at least 20 languages.

Five Historical Phases of Globalization

In the following discussion, we examine in detail the football–globalization nexus across the *longue durée*. Our analysis is structured by Robertson's six-phase schema of globalization, which spans the fifteenth century to the early twenty-first century (1992: 58–60, 2007a, 2007b). Our main focus is on setting out briefly the initial five phases that Robertson had extended, before applying these in detail to facilitate a succinct 'global history' of football. We then provide an outline, followed by a football application, of the current sixth, 'millennial' phase of globalization, as recently advanced by Robertson. Many of the football–globalization processes identified in this discussion are elaborated upon in later chapters.

Robertson's five general phases of globalization may be summarized as follows.

The first, *germinal* phase of globalization is focused on Europe, and spans the early fifteenth century through to the mid-18th century. Through this period, voyages of 'discovery' occur and are the crucial precondition for early forms of transoceanic connectivity and colonial subjugation. National communities emerge (underpinned particularly by the Peace of Westphalia, 1648) and Catholicism expands internationally. Different kinds of mercantilist economic principles and political strategies come to prevail in Western Europe – for example, through the Colbertist system in France – and are manifested in part through struggles and wars between protectionist nations over available international markets. Contemporary time–space thinking is concretized through the Gregorian calendar, heliocentric thinking, and the proliferation of different geographic projections; ideas of the individual and humanity are accentuated.

The second, *incipient* phase remains largely European, and spans the mid-18th century to the 1870s. The French Revolution has a near-global and long-lasting impact in terms of concretizing themes of revolutionary transformation and human emancipation for industrializing societies. It also presages an embryonic world conflict, in the form of the Napoleonic wars, and the subsequent crystallization of the international system through the post-war settlement. The Lisbon earthquake of 1755, which effectively destroyed the city and killed up to 100,000 people, was a global 'moment' that undermined Portugal's colonial aspirations while impacting strongly upon Enlightenment thought. A near-global model of homogenous nation states is established, alongside advances in international relations, legal frameworks, and communication systems (for instance, the telegraph system). Conceptions of citizenship and humanity are concretized (notably through the Enlightenment), non-European societies are established, and early international exhibitions are staged.

The third, *take-off* phase marks the electrification of globalization, spanning the 1870s to the mid-1920s. The four 'elemental reference points' of

3

globalization are crystallized: *individual* selves, national (male) societies (*nation states*), the world system of societies (*international relations*), and *humankind* (Robertson 1992: 104). Thus, personal and national identities become more sharply thematized and defined. Modern national societies become more isomorphic in terms of their juridical, political, and institutional infrastructure. Non-European societies enter an increasingly complex international society – most notably, the USA and Japan. Forms of international culture become more diffuse, for example in the arts and sport. Rapid technological advances help to promote intensive international 'connectivity'. Ideas of global humanity are formalized, while the first global conflict occurs. Yet each reference point is also constrained by the other three.

Many national museums, international exhibitions, and major sporting events are founded or staged, such as the quadrennial Olympic Games from 1896 onwards. These institutions or occasions serve to construct a global looking-glass for nations while also implicitly enhancing the value of international contextualization and competition. Thus, national claims to being 'the best' in particular cultural realms are advanced on the basis of international and cross-cultural comparisons.

During this phase, there is a strong accentuation of principles of national self-determination and identification. The 'Wilsonian moment' occurs at the end of World War One, as the principle of the equality of all nations is set out on the global stage, inspiring anti-colonial politics that were to result in nationalist revolutions later in the 20th century (Manela 2007). Meanwhile, throughout this phase, particular national 'traditions' are invented, such as through artistic movements, dress, language, and sports. Such 'forgery in the forging of nations' connects to rapid social transformations, notably urbanization and mass education (Ascherson 2002: 264; Hobsbawm 1983: Chapter 7). 'Wilful nostalgia' also becomes more prominent, as the world is imagined in terms of historical decline, and through senses of loss, homelessness, estrangement, and alienation (Robertson 1990a: 46, 1995: 35; cf. Stauth and Turner 1988). Nostalgia is prominent in culture, through popular literature or the 'folk' tropes of European composers. On the other hand, the counter-movement of modernism is also very significant (Gay 2007).

The fourth, *struggle-for-hegemony* phase spans the mid-1920s to the late 1960s, and continues to be shaped by the elemental reference points. Rival political–ideological frameworks come into sharper and more global conflicts, notably between liberal capitalism, state socialism, and fascism. The League of Nations and then the United Nations reflect moves towards global governance, while concretizing principles of national self-determination and the *realpolitik* of Anglo-European hegemony (Manela 2007).[2] The old European

---

[2]Of course, the national self-determination movement, which peaked with the League of Nations, was a critical precondition for the establishment of international football.

empires collapse, the 'Third World' is established, and nation states are defined by their Cold War positions. The future of humanity is thematized across cultures, as new technologies of mass destruction are registered by the Holocaust, the A-bomb, and the international stockpiling of atomic weaponry.

The fifth, *uncertainty* phase spans the late 1960s up to the year 2000. Increased wealth, economic crises and 'post-materialist' values arise in the West. The global event par excellence – the moon landing – provides fresh ways of imaging and imagining the world. The world system of societies becomes increasingly fluid and complex, as the 'Cold War' ends and militant Islamism emerges as the West's radical other. An exponential growth occurs in new global and social institutions, notably international governmental and non-governmental organizations (IGOs and NGOs), transnational corporations (TNCs), and new social movements (NSMs). Cultural and social politics become more prominent as ethnicity, gender, sexuality, consumerism, and human rights are deeply politicized. Satellite and digital communication is established, the internet is globalized, and media TNCs are founded. The notions of a global 'civil society' and global citizenship are thematized, alongside the status and future of humankind in regard to contemporary 'risks' (cf. Robertson 2007a).

Football History: Five Phases

In applying this model to football's historical globalization, two initial points should be made. First, some empirical and temporal discrepancies inevitably arise between global and football histories, notably up to the mid-19th century. Nevertheless, we retain the terms 'germinal' and 'incipient' to describe football's prehistory, with appropriate amendments to the periodization; by the 'take-off' phase, football and wider globalization processes are in closer correspondence. In any case, this historical model of globalization was not intended to be applied in a rigid manner (Robertson 1992: 59).

Second, our analysis accounts for the *social* construction of football's history. The five-phase model appreciates the interplay of particular themes at relevant historical moments, notably in regard to the four elemental reference points, from 'take-off' onwards.

First and second phases: germinal and incipient – up to the 1870s

The first, **germinal** phase covers football's prehistory up to the early 19th century. We should begin by noting that some emerging disputes surround the origins of football. As expansion into Asian markets has become a major objective, FIFA literature and press releases tend to highlight the region's ancient football games.[3] One ancient ball-kicking game was *tsu-chu*, played

---

[3]See, for example, www.fifa.com/fifa/history_E.html and http://access.fifa.com/en/article/0,4151,106928,00.html

in China between the second and third centuries BC, while the Japanese game of *kemari* was practised from at least the 12th century AD (Goldblatt 2006: 5–9). The Florentine game of *calcio* has been played, particularly by those with social status, since at least the 16th century. Other *calcio* games were played across northern Italy, according to local rules, serving to maintain forms of civic and regional distinction (De Biasi and Lanfranchi 1997: 88–9). Elsewhere, other nationalistic claims to football's origin have been advanced, including Stalinist social history which stated the case for Georgian or northern Russian feudal games, named *lelo* or *shalyga* respectively (Edelman 1993: 29).

In contrast, while noting these ancient curiosities, most academic histories continue to prioritize direct evidence to emphasize the British origins of modern football (cf. Walvin 1994: 11–12; Murray 1996; Lanfranchi et al. 2004: 11). In Britain, different 'folk' or 'mob' football games were contested as early as the 14th century, and possibly extend back to the 8th century (Henderson 2001: 80). Participants were almost entirely male, notably from the lower classes. Games were played according to local customs and often as part of annual festivities such as Shrovetide (the British Mardi Gras), with rival teams differentiated according to village, parish, employment, age, or marital status (Magoun 1938: vii; Elias and Dunning 1986; Holt 1989: 14–15). Given the rudimentary rules and prior tensions between competing communities, broken bones and occasional deaths occurred during play. The authorities regularly sought to ban these games, usually to maintain work and public order (Walvin 1975: 16–17).[4] Some analysts have suggested that two main types of folk football were played, dating back to at least the late 18th century, with different rules that connect respectively to the modern games of rugby and soccer (Goulstone 2000: 135–6, 142). These pre-modern games and pastimes underwent general adaptation, notably during the early 19th century, as Britain underwent protracted industrialization and urbanization.

The second, **incipient** phase of football's globalization spans the early 19th century to the 1870s. Shaped by the crucial interplay between educational institutions and residual folk cultures, this phase culminated in the foundation of modern football. From the 1830s onwards, English public schools underwent a 'games revolution', as different sports were introduced to dissipate the rebellious, violent, and sexual energies of pupils, and to inculcate new masculine norms centred on leadership, obedience, hygiene, and Christianity, as encapsulated in the sporting myth of 'fair play' (Mangan 1981: 129–30, 1998: 182–3). Significant rule differences remained over the football games played by schools; for instance, Eton and Harrow prohibited catching and running with the ball, unlike Rugby. These games subsequently transferred to the universities, where hands-free football made particular headway at Cambridge.

---

[4]The English writer John Gay penned some verse on 'The Dangers of Football' circa 1720, based on his experience of 'the Furies of the Foot-ball War', in which various young tradesmen make up a 'throng' or 'crew' of eager players (see Gay 1974: 153).

We should also be wary of the way in which this public school story has rather overshadowed a hidden history of football's working-class origins and organization. Indeed, it has been argued that adapted 'folk' games were often more civilized than their public school counterparts, in being more sophisticated in the use of rules, umpires, and club systems, and also involved less violence among participants (Goulstone 1974, 2000; Harvey 2005).

It was the social elites, nevertheless, who were instrumental in establishing football's rules. As elite teams came into more regular contact, the demand for common rules had intensified. The 'Cambridge Rules' were agreed in 1848, regularly updated, and eventually published in 1863. A few days later, the Football Association (FA) was founded in London by various teams committed to a game that banned hacking and handling (Murray 1996: 3–4). The new game of 'association football' was sometimes known as 'soccer', notably where alternative 'football' codes were favoured. In the north, notably Sheffield, a vibrant football culture had initially eclipsed London but by 1877 the FA had secured its authority over the non-handling game (Harvey 2001).

The rulebook distinguished association football from other codes. Rugby's proponents stayed loyal to handling and hacking, despite player shortages (Birley 1993: 258–60). 'Australian rules football' was codified in Melbourne in 1859 by an old Rugbeian and his friends. (Indeed, a little mischievously, some commentators suggest reverse colonialism may have transpired, as the FA's rules reveal curious similarities to the older, Australian game (Grow 1998: 11–12)). In the United States, the leading colleges battled over football's rules: soccer-style (backed by Yale) or rugby style (favoured by Harvard). The Princeton–Rutgers fixture of 1869 was the first intercollegiate football contest. Six years later, several institutions agreed rugby-style rules, but distinctive American innovations, such as block-tackling and fixed sets of play ('downs'), were introduced to produce the unique 'American football' code (Gorn and Goldstein 1993: 131).

Aided by 'universal' rulebooks, the game's cult underwent different kinds of 'mini-globalization' through British influence overseas. Chief proselytizers of these games included schoolmasters and missionaries who were emboldened by a 'complacent and confident ethnocentricity', and were determined to cultivate a 'universal Tom Brown' in all imperial outposts; thus, 'in the most bizarre locations could be found those potent symbols of pedagogic imperialism – football and cricket pitches' (Mangan 1998: 18, 182).

Third phase: take-off – the 1870s to the mid-1920s

The third, **take-off** phase covers the 1870s to the mid-1920s, when football became embedded within the popular cultures of Europe and South America, and in 'Europeanized' parts of Africa, Asia, and North America.

Britain was first to generate many standard traits of contemporary football, in terms of working-class popularity, league structure, and professionalization.

7

The FA was dominated by southern elites, but working-class teams mushroomed in schools, parishes, and workplaces, abetted by increased leisure time (particularly Saturday afternoons), better public transport, and growing newspaper coverage of fixtures. As thousands of spectators were drawn to the leading fixtures, and as hidden payments became more widespread, the FA's old amateurist elites were forced to relent, and so player professionalism was legalized in 1885; the world's first league soon followed, in 1888.

The international diffusion of British games followed two trajectories. Sports like rugby and cricket were popularized through the 'colonial ecumene' across imperial outposts, while football spread through a 'trading ecumene' via business and industrial routes and in relatively informal social ways (Perkin 1989; Appadurai 1995: 25).[5] British maritime and industrial workers in the 1870s and 1880s played football matches in numerous ports across the Channel, North Sea, Mediterranean, Black Sea, South American coastline, and in Asian outposts such as Hong Kong (Edelman 1993: 29; MacClancy 1996: 192; Murray 1996: 24). Everyday social relations contributed massively to the incubation of football within these settings, as local people watched the British play and, in emulation, were inspired to found their own clubs.

Three aspects of modernization were prominent. First, new football hotbeds were typically undergoing rapid urbanization and industrialization; for example, in South America, Buenos Aires grew from 178,000 inhabitants in 1869 to 1,576,000 by 1914, and São Paulo expanded from 40,000 in 1880 to 800,000 in 1920 (Taylor 1998: 26). These and other cities – notably Rio de Janeiro and Montevideo – harboured large populations of European migrants for whom football was an accessible, enjoyable medium of cross-cultural socialization, and so the game was rapidly transmogrified into the urban, 'national sport'.

Second, young foreign pupils in British-led schools often returned home to teach football to their compatriots; for example, Anglo-Brazilians like Charles Miller and Oscar Cox founded clubs in São Paulo and Rio de Janeiro respectively (Del Burgo 1995: 52–3; Mason 1995: 1–11). Football was taught in many overseas British schools, but failure to sustain a foothold could damage the game's local diffusion, as transpired in New Zealand and other imperial dominions where rugby dominated elite education (cf. Little 2002: 40–5).

Third, modern social clubs enabled football's popular expansion. Across Europe, Anglophile locals founded sports clubs in which football teams blossomed. By 1900, in Italy for example, the Genoa, Juventus, Milan, and Palermo clubs had been established. In Japan, the modernizing Meiji period (1868–1912) enabled European residents to introduce football and other sports to local elites, mainly through schools and sporting clubs (Guttmann and Thompson 2001: 70–1).

---

[5]Nevertheless, some British colonists viewed football as another sport that embodied imperial manliness and Christianity (Mangan 2001: 41).

In line with Rogers' (1962) analysis of cultural diffusion, we may observe that football typically depended upon initial patronage by local elites before spreading through the population (Guttmann 1994: 43–4, 70), most obviously in South American nations like Brazil, Peru, and Uruguay (Carvalho et al. 1984: 21; Mason 1995: 13–14; Leite Lopes 1997: 56; Giulianotti 1999b: 136–7). In France, football spread among the Anglophile bourgeoisie and in port cities, then settled in multi-sports clubs, secular and religious institutions, and in the military when national service was established in the 1880s (Hare 2003: 16–18). Conversely, German elites prohibited football in schools and the military, as an alien British threat to the gymnastic *Turnen* movement (Eisenberg 1991; Murray 1996: 26; Merkel 2000: 169–71).

The British were highly active in football's civil society development. First, expatriates taught, organized and popularized the game, notably Scotsmen John Hurley (in Montevideo) and John Madden (Prague), and Englishmen Harry Welfare (Rio) and Jimmy Hogan (Vienna). Second, the British inspired the foundation of many clubs and governing bodies, as reflected in the 'archaic' names of leading South American sides such as Corinthians (São Paulo), River Plate (Buenos Aires), Newell's Old Boys (Rosario), Wanderers and Liverpool (Montevideo). Argentina's football bodies retained English as their official language until 1906, and only inserted the Spanish term *fútbol* into their title in 1934 (Mason 1995: 2–4; Archetti 1996: 203).[6] Third, illustrating modern linguistic transmission, many English football-related terms (such as offside and corner) were transferred directly into local languages or, as in Russia, creolized to fit local phonetics (e.g. *forvard, gvgolkiper*) (Frykholm 1997: 147–8; Okay 2002: 6–7).

Critically, British elites failed to formulate an internationalist political strategy to match the social efforts at grassroots level. Thus, FIFA, the body which would soon govern world football, was founded in 1904 by seven mainland European football nations, with belated and highly ambivalent British participation. Only through the IFAB, which governed the laws of football from 1886 onwards, was British long-term political influence secured.

We noted earlier that the 'take-off' period was shaped increasingly by the interrelationships of the four elemental reference points, namely individuals, national societies, international relations, and humankind. Football was no exception.

At the *individual* level, some players were venerated as local male heroes in communities and, through press reports, nationally. British professionals were typically working-class, but enjoyed notably better earnings, conditions, and far higher social status than other workers (Mason 1980: 103, 1996). Match reports in the 1900s often lionized individual exploits rather than team events; in turn, some top players like Billy Meredith and Steve

---

[6]The process of influence and emulation could also go the other way; for example, since their foundation in 1865, the English side Nottingham Forest has played in 'Garibaldi Red', in honour of the Italian redshirts.

Bloomer set out to entertain crowds and featured at times in stage shows and films (Woolridge 2002). Yet Britain's players faced two squeezes upon their autonomy. On the field, individualistic playing styles were tempered by more cautious and defensive playing systems. In England in the 1870s, the number of forward players was reduced from eight to seven, and 'combination' or passing football was promoted, particularly by Scottish professionals (Russell 1997: 20–1). Soon, two further forwards were withdrawn, giving the 2–3–5 formation (Lodziak 1966: 22–3). Off the field, the 'retain and transfer' system prevented players from moving freely between clubs, such that, in many cases, professionalization strengthened the industrial power of club officials (Mason 1980; Russell 1997: 25–7).

At the level of *national* societies, by the mid-1920s, football was the dominant sport, and contributed strongly to public life. In England, league crowds quintupled between 1889 and 1914 to an average 23,000 (Tranter 1998: 17). Cup final attendances of over 100,000 became common, surging to around 200,000 at the famous 1923 Wembley final. Many British grounds were often poorly equipped to support this popularization, sometimes with disastrous consequences: for example, 26 died and 500 were injured when a stand collapsed at Rangers' Ibrox stadium in 1902.

In Europe, football crowds and stadium development were markedly smaller: for example, by 1926, Milan's leading stadium only held around 35,000, while in Madrid the capacity was nearer 15,000 (Inglis 1990: 11, 210). More impressively, in France, the 1924 Olympic football final was held in the packed 60,000 Colombes stadium (Mason 1995: 31). In Latin America, crowds at fixtures featuring British teams reached several thousand, but in Brazil, larger stadiums only held around 20,000 until Vasco's 50,000 capacity ground opened in 1927 (Leite Lopes 1997: 62). Yet national interest in football was sustained by newspapers and magazines across Europe and South America. Several sport-focused publications emerged during this period – such as *La Gazzetta dello Sport* (Italy, in 1896), *El Mundo Deportivo* (Spain, in 1906), and *El Gráfico* (Argentina, in 1919) – and were soon dominated by football.

Football was structured along national lines. National associations and leagues were formally established in the four British 'Home Nations' by 1890. Mainland Europe followed, for example, with the Netherlands, Belgium, Switzerland, Italy, and Germany all hosting football associations and leagues by 1902. In South America, Argentina, Chile, Uruguay, Paraguay, and Brazil had all established national governing bodies by 1914, but league tournaments centred on major urban centres were the norm.

Major football fixtures helped to cement national solidarity, generating strong communities of sentiment that were sustained by nation-building narratives in the media. Football fixtures and tournaments graced significant national days, such as the 1916 independence celebrations in South America. As Latin Americans established their own teams, many were named in honour of national heroes and events. Overall, rather as other analysts have pointed to administrators and railroad workers, so we would emphasize the role of football players, coaches, teams, and tournaments, in connecting cities and towns with hinterlands, and building forms of national identity at grassroots level.

National 'traditions' in playing style started to emerge. In England, robust physical play was prominent alongside the residual, tricky spontaneity of some individualistic dribblers (Mason 1980: 208–13; Russell 1997: 25). Scotland's industrial heartlands produced numerous technically proficient players who excelled at the passing game, and subsequently transformed football methods in Britain and then in Europe. In Argentina and Uruguay, the concept of *fútbol rioplatense* was developed in the early twentieth century, 'based on a superb technique, keeping, with endless touches, possession of the ball, and on rapid changes of rhythm in the attack', while also playing at different tempos across the pitch (Archetti 1996: 204). Uruguay could also be rather more pragmatic, alternating between combative and passing styles with remarkable results to win the 1924 and 1928 Olympic football gold medals (Giulianotti 1999b; cf. Taylor 1998: 29).

The invention of traditions was stronger where teams represented particular publics and ways of life. In Germany, the club name Borussia (from the Latin for Prussia) became commonplace. In South America, many clubs reflected strong class-defined habituses, giving rise to subsequent rivalries between elites and the 'popular classes', e.g. in Peru, Universitario-Alianza Lima; in Paraguay, Olimpia-Cerro Porteño; in Rio, Fluminense-Flamengo; in Porto Alegre, Grêmio-Internacional, and so on. Similarly, in Europe, class-inflected derbies still underpin the game's popular folklore: in Milan, between Internazionale and AC Milan; in Lisbon, between Sporting and Benfica; in Seville, between Sevilla and Betis; and in Istanbul, between Fenerbahçe and Beşiktaş.

In Europe, more extensive 'ideologies of home' underpinned some club identities, with specific ethno-national and ethno-religious ingredients. For example, Basque national politics and identity rapidly crystallized in the late nineteenth century, and several clubs were founded soon afterwards. Athletic Bilbao became a leading team in Spain, and instituted *la cantera*, a policy committed to recruiting only 'Basque' players. In Scotland, the Rangers–Celtic 'sectarian' rivalry was well established by 1914. Celtic were founded as a charitable organization for poor Irish-Catholic immigrants while Rangers were staunchly Unionist, Protestant and refused to employ known Catholics.

Across *Mitteleuropa*, Jewish clubs were formed and embraced a strong ethno-religious identity, adorned in the blue-and-white colours of Israel and wearing the 'Star of David' on their jerseys. Jewish communities adapted the British colonial ideology of 'muscular Christianity' to sculpt 'muscular Judaism' as a strategy for combating 'Jewish distress' and wider anti-Semitism (Foer 2004: 69–70).

In colonial contexts, football matches could become sites of nationalist resistance towards occupying powers. In Korea, locals painted goalposts white to symbolize nationalist opposition towards Japanese occupation (Jong-Young

2004: 77–8).[7] In India, local victories against British sides symbolized the national potential for independence (Majumdar and Bandyopadhyay 2005: 124–41). Yet the myth of British invincibility and superiority was hard to deflate, whether among football's world officialdom or during international fixtures; beating England remained elusive for many national teams that were more technically accomplished (cf. Meisl 1955: 61–2).

The take-off phase witnessed early but recurring claims by local clubs to have the deepest football histories. In Spain, Athletic Bilbao, Barcelona, and Recreativo Huelva all claim to be the first Spanish club (Ball 2003: 43). In Germany, club names such as TSV 1860 München, FC Schalke 04, or Hannover 96 contain claims to their respective years of foundation, yet the dates typically allude to the start of sporting participation as a whole and not to the football team's establishment (Hesse-Lichtenberger 2002: 22).

Finally, it is important to consider the debates and evidence regarding contexts in which football's take-off was less obvious or rather circumscribed. First, there is the issue of social contact: indigenous populations in many parts of rural Africa or Asia had relatively little exposure to football, due in large part to their restricted everyday social relations with Europeans or with modern educational systems. Second, there is the issue of cultural differentiation or rejection of football: in many former British territories and New World societies – notably the Indian subcontinent, the United States, Canada, Australia and Ireland – particular sports other than football were embraced or developed, at least in part as a way of constructing distinctive forms of cultural nationalism, often across very dispersed and ethnically varied populations. This is not to say that football was entirely expunged from these locations; indeed, there were some significant pockets of strong football activity, such as St Louis in the United States, Calcutta in India, and Irish towns and cities where British barracks and emerging heavy industries were to be found. We discuss these issues in rather more depth in Chapter 2, notably regarding the United States.

Football's *international relations* underwent 'take-off' in five particular ways. First, the Home Nations established their own national championship in 1884, and founded the IFAB two years later. Second, formal international football relations intensified and were built upon nation state lines, notably within FIFA (cf. Beck 1999: 56–7). Thus, the organizational framework of the new governing body was strongly informed by Wilsonian principles of national self-determination, and would subsequently enable elites from non-Western and post-colonial societies to exercise major political influence in football from the 1970s onwards. During the take-off phase, international fixtures became commonplace, notably in South America, where Argentina met Uruguay 41 times between 1901 and 1914 (Mason 1995: 27). In 1910,

---

[7]The Korean FA's website states, 'During the decades of colonial rule by Japan, football contributed to alleviating the frustrations of the subjugated Koreans and fostering the hope of liberation'. See http://en.kfa.or.kr/kfa_history/history.asp

an early South American tournament was contested; six years later, the first continental governing body (CONMEBOL) was founded.

Third, football facilitated non-European participation within the emerging world system of societies. Many British clubs undertook overseas tours across Europe, Latin America and the Empire's colonies and dominions. The Oxbridge amateur side, Corinthians, was notably peripatetic, touring South Africa in 1897 and then making three trips to Brazil before 1914 (Walvin 1994: 110). Several English teams – notably Swindon Town, Everton and Tottenham – visited Argentina, attracting crowds of over 20,000.

Fourth, as global conflict loomed, most sports, including football, became theatres for the display of national virility and military capability. Despite regular internationals, Anglo-German relations inside FIFA became fraught. During warfare, troops on all sides played recreational football behind the lines, or discussed the game in the trenches. When called into attack, some British troops emerged from the trenches and charged across no man's land with a football at their feet (Birley 1995: 74). Inevitably, many club and national sides were decimated in the conflict: for example, the Heart of Midlothian team lost seven men in action, while Tottenham Hotspur lost eleven former players. After the armistice, the British nations resigned from FIFA rather than share membership with their former foes.

Fifth, football tournaments reflected the vitality of international society. Successful Olympic football tournaments, from 1908 onwards, confirmed the need for a separate global event. The 1924 Paris Olympics marked South America's football powers, won by the brilliant Uruguayans in a final against Switzerland for which 250,000 ticket applications had been lodged (Goldblatt 2004: 46).

Apropos *humankind*, political battles were contested regarding social inclusion and participation, notably along class, 'race' and gender lines. Class disputes took different forms. In Britain, the professionalism issue had underlined class and regional divisions between mainly southern amateur gentlemen and northern business interests (Hargreaves 1986: 68–9). Elsewhere, class antagonisms typically centred on status closure and resource denial. In pre-revolutionary Russia, working-class groups were persistently prevented from accessing clubs, league tournaments, match officials and playing fields. In response, 'outlaw' worker teams were gradually established (Frykholm 1997: 144–5). For those contexts in which working-class sides were established, we noted earlier the role of class-based rivalries in many club cultures.

Second, race and ethnicity were central to struggles for recognition or participation in non-European contexts. In Chile and Brazil, various authorities questioned the right of black players to play internationals (Taylor 1998: 81–2). Uruguay gained enormously from its greater tolerance of non-white players, notably the 'Black Marvel' José Leandro Andrade. In Brazil, white elite clubs were initially challenged by factory teams such as Bangú that fielded talented black and mulatto players (Leite Lopes 2000: 246–7). In 1923, Vasco da Gama won the Rio championship, being the only leading club to hire lower-class players, including non-whites, on a professional basis. Suitably piqued, Rio's sporting elites excluded Vasco from future tournaments and implemented spurious social rules such as literacy tests to eliminate non-whites (Leite Lopes 1997: 63–4). In southern Africa, sport participation was marked by increasingly inflexible racial stratification, with white colonists dominating rugby and cricket while other populations seized upon football (Nauright 1999: 190–1; Alegi 2004; cf. Giulianotti 2004a: 80–3). Across the continent, the game often symbolized forms of African indigenous pride and proto-nationalism; in Ghana, for example, the 'Hearts of Oak' side was founded in 1911 in memory of Accra's slaves.

Third, on gender, football typically reproduced patriarchal social values. In Britain, despite pressures to display only decorative qualities among spectators, some middle-class women did play as early as the 1890s in Scotland, while the 'British Ladies Football Club' later played matches before up to 8000 spectators (Williams 2003: 114; cf. Tranter 1998: 79). Women's wartime industry assisted the creation of football teams, most famously the Dick, Kerr Ladies club which subsequently toured Britain, France and North America (Newsham 1994). When Dick, Kerr teams attracted nearly 900,000 spectators to 67 fixtures in 1921, the FA effectively killed women's football by banning these matches from being played at its members' grounds.

Overseas, in some contexts, such as China (from 1915 to the 1920s) and Denmark, female corporeal exercise and emancipation were advocated, enabling radical physical educationalists to promote stronger participation in football (Brus and Trangbaek 2003: 97; Hong and Mangan 2003: 47–8). More commonly, women's football was viewed as curious entertainment and mocked by the local press, notwithstanding often sizeable crowds (cf. Marschik 1998: 71; Fasting 2003: 149–50; Hjelm and Olofsson 2003: 184–5).

Fourth, the possibilities of football in advancing peaceful co-existence were also explored. De Coubertin, founder of the modern Olympic movement, believed that international sporting contacts could advance cosmopolitanism and cultural tolerance (Morgan 1995). On the day that Archduke Ferdinand was assassinated in Sarajevo, setting off the chain of events that would produce the First World War, FIFA passed a resolution calling for all nations to 'substitute arbitration for violence' (Goldblatt 2006: 234–5). A few months later, the myth of the 'Christmas Truce' was born, as the story emerged in rather sketchy detail of how British and German troops had ceased their hostilities, met in no-man's-land, and played impromptu football matches to mark Yuletide (cf. Brown and Seaton 1999). In general terms, however, fraternal cosmopolitanism was one of many social values that transpired within football. We noted, for example, football's colonial and nationalist aspects which sought to enforce social harmonization through organized play. At the other extreme, some fixtures, whether in Europe or Latin America, could also occasion serious crowd disorder.

Fourth phase: 'struggle-for-hegemony' – the mid-1920s to the late 1960s

The **fourth**, '**struggle-for-hegemony**' phase spans the mid-1920s to the late 1960s. Two football 'moments' heralded this phase.

First, in 1925, bowing to English and commercial pressures, the IFAB amended football's offside law, making defensive play more difficult and increasing goal-scoring opportunities. All football nations were obliged to respond to the new rule. In Britain, a goal glut ensued, followed by greater coaching professionalism. Arsenal, under Herbert Chapman, dominated English football during the 1930s by creating the 'WM' team formation, producing 'safety-first', watchful, counter-attacking football that mirrored the decade's insecurities and anxieties (Meisl 1955: 17–25).[8]

The position of the centre-half varied across football regions: WM withdrew this player from midfield into defence, but elsewhere he remained upfield – notably in South America (until well into the 1950s) and most of the European mainland (such as in the brilliant Austrian *wunderteam*) (Lodziak 1966: 26–7). Italy, who won the 1934 and 1938 World Cups, advanced *Il Metodo* (the method), featuring a watchful centre-half and two withdrawn forwards to create a 2–3–2–3 formation. Even when Switzerland, under Karl Rappan, introduced a further defender, the 'sweeper' role remained relatively inventive.

Second, FIFA started to prepare its own international tournament. The first World Cup, hosted and won by Uruguay in 1930, drew only 13 nations, but was an enormous local success, with over 90,000 fans at the final. The 1934 and 1938 events were hosted in France and Italy respectively, thus the tournament became a fixed quadrennial event, interrupted only by global warfare.

The four elemental reference points of globalization acquired greater centrality during this phase. At the level of *individuals*, firstly, more top football players acquired local or national hero status. In Germany, the great 1930s Schalke team sustained close ties with local working-class communities. The brilliant Matthias Sindelar, 'the wafer', became a 1930s Viennese coffee-house hero (Horak and Maderthaner 1996). The 'Black Diamond' Leônidas was a national hero in Brazil, appearing regularly in popular media and endorsing everyday products (Mason 1995: 55). In England, players like Jackie Milburn (Newcastle United) and Nat Lofthouse (Bolton Wanderers) were typically loyal to their clubs and team-mates, and struck unassuming figures off the pitch. However, during periods of wider industrial emancipation, football's labour relations remained antediluvian; systems like the UK's 'retain and transfer' allowed clubs to keep, dismiss or transfer their employees like chattel (cf. Imlach 2005).

Uruguay's players became national heroes when winning the 1930 and 1950 World Cups. The latter win, against hosts and hot favourites Brazil,

---

[8]The playing system featured four lines of players, whose formation effectively traced the letters W and M on tactical drawing boards.

inspired national narratives along a *Bildung* theme (cf. Dallmayr 1998: 244). Indeed, some have stated that modern Uruguay was built by two Varelas: the first (José Pedro) was a nineteenth century President and educational reformer; the second (Obdulio, no relation) was the great World Cup captain of 1950 (Giulianotti 1999b). The mythology of football heroes also featured genuine tragedies, most obviously the air disasters that wiped out the brilliant Torino team in 1949 and which killed eight Manchester United players in 1958.

Second, elite player status was enhanced by the founding of national professional tournaments across Europe and South America during the interwar years.[9] Germany was the most prominent dissident, with the national professional league only founded in 1963. When England abolished its maximum wage in 1961, a cluster of elite players raised their earnings markedly, although football remained a part-time profession at most lower league clubs. Only when football was embraced by commercial popular culture, notably pop music and television, did players acquire 'star' or celebrity status, with off-field activities exciting the mass media, notably in the iconic case of the brilliant George Best (sometimes known as the 'Fifth Beatle').

Third, international player mobility was highly uneven, but occurred most visibly when South Americans moved to southern Europe. At least 118 professionals from Argentina, Uruguay, and Brazil held dual citizenship with Italy and so joined Italian clubs between 1929 and 1943 (Lanfranchi and Taylor 1999: 83). Post-1945, many leading central European and South American talents typically switched to Spanish and Italian clubs. British players seeking fortunes abroad ran into legal trouble when joining the breakaway *Di Mayor* league in Colombia, or commonly found their new environment too alien to settle in (e.g. Baker, Law, and Greaves in Italy in the early 1960s). However, in turn, national football cultures were often incubated by the banning of 'foreign' players, as a very definite response to wider globalization processes. In England, an effective ban stood for over 45 years until the European Community's intervention, and then Tottenham Hotspur signed the Argentines, Ardiles and Villa, in 1978. Spain banned the further importation of players from 1965 to 1973, as did Italy from 1964 to 1980. Less developed economies still established effective football systems with occasional high rewards. Brazil's *estrelismo* (star system) reportedly enabled Pelé to become the world's highest paid athlete, on around $340,000 annually, in the late 1960s (Lever 1969: 41).

Fourth, football coaches acquired an increasingly strong public persona, bringing 'science' to the game's organization, and often imposing playing systems upon players through quasi-militaristic methods. Autocrats like Herbert Chapman (Arsenal), Major Frank Buckley (Wolves), and Matt Busby (Manchester United) dominated club operations and instituted many tactical innovations. Internationally, Vittorio Pozzo (Italy), Otto Nerz

---

[9]For example, in Austria (1924), Hungary (1926), Spain (1929), Italy (1930), Argentina (1931), France (1932), and Brazil (1933).

(Germany), Karl Rappan (Switzerland), Helenio Herrera (Barcelona, Internazionale), and Alf Ramsay (England) successfully reshaped their teams, though often with a focus on risk control, to the detriment of highly skilled players like Fritz Szepan in Germany or Jimmy Greaves in England.

At *national* level, first, football helped to build national solidarity, but also disclosed forms of fissure and fragmentation. Many international fixtures were deeply nationalistic rituals that were intensively covered by national media. In the UK, the Home International championship dramatized sub-national rivalries while arguably strengthening the bonds between England and its smaller partners. In South America, international fixtures contributed massively towards the assimilation of immigrant populations, notably first- and second-generation Spaniards and Italians in major ports along the eastern coast. West Germany's 1954 World Cup win was viewed by many as a founding moment for the new Federal Republic (Hesse-Lichtenberger 2002: 125). Korean post-occupation independence was honoured by the national team's victory over Japan, to qualify for the 1954 World Cup finals.

In Europe and Latin America, military juntas and totalitarian regimes engaged football's populist appeal. Under Mussolini, Italian athletes were national 'warriors', while in Brazil and Argentina, populist dictators Getúlio Vargas and Juan Perón institutionalized the political manipulation of football (Lever 1983: 62–3; Mason 1995: 70; Scher 1996; Alabarces and Rodriguez 2000: 122–3; Bellos 2002: 38). In these contexts, and in Soviet states, vast modern stadiums were erected (cf. Inglis 1990).

The mass production and consumption of radio – then television – was integral to the nation-building process, in which football played a crucial part (cf. Anderson 1983; Gellner 1983). By the late 1920s, radio was broadcasting live fixtures in many European nations. As Hobsbawm (1990: 143) observes, when constructing national identity, 'The imagined community of millions seems more real as a team of eleven named people'. He recalled listening, with several Austrians, to radio coverage of the Austria-England fixture in 1929: 'I was England, as they were Austria ... In this manner did twelve-year-old children extend the concept of team-loyalty to the nation' (quoted in Beck 2003: 400). Subsequently, to illustrate television's rapid spread in the wealthiest Western nations, the FA Cup final in England drew around 10,000 viewers in 1938, one million viewers in 1950, and perhaps 10 million in 1953 when, to national celebration, Stanley Matthews finally gained a winners' medal (Banks 2002: 104).

Yet post-war nation-building, and the emerging consumer society, could also vitiate football's economic vitality. In England, for example, after a boom in attendances, crowds started to fall seriously in the early 1950s, and the Football League responded by banning match broadcasts (Walvin 1994: 161). In France after 1945, *les trentes glorieuses* (or 30 glorious years) of economic recovery and national modernization also witnessed the sharp *decline* of club and national football, as new urban citizens pursued alternative consumer lifestyles (Hare 2003: 43–4).

Inevitably, football enabled particular communities to contest forms of official nationalism. Most famously, in Spain, Barcelona symbolized Catalan separatism towards Franco; yet the dictator's personal association with Real Madrid may have been craftily manufactured to restrict autonomist political expressions to the cultural field of football (Ball 2003: 121–2; cf. Burns 1999).

Second, throughout this phase, further tactical innovations were instituted by particular national football cultures. In the early 1950s, Hungary perplexed opponents by playing a deep-lying (rather than advanced) centre-forward; according to team coach Gusztáv Sebes, this was a free-flowing, 'socialist football' style. Following earlier Paraguayan innovations, the Brazilian national team won the 1958 World Cup with the 4–2–4 formation that contained the first 'flat back four'; Brazil withdrew another forward in 1962 to produce the 4–3–3 formation. England's 'wingless wonders' sacrificed outside forwards to play an industrial 4–4–2 formation at the 1966 World Cup. Meanwhile, coach Helenio Herrera (born in Argentina but with French citizenship) had elaborated the sweeper system in Italian league football. Herrera's Internazionale team, often playing 1–4–4–1, posted a *libero* (free man) behind the defence to snuff out attacks; off the field, the players were subjected to rigid social controls, while club officials allegedly bribed referees to secure victories (cf. Goldblatt 2006: 435–6). However, national playing styles owed much to processes of innovation and cross-cultural creolization. In Germany, for example, varied influences abounded: southern clubs adopted fluid passing styles from Austria and southern Europe, northern teams borrowed the English 'Hussar' style, eastern sides favoured Danubian aestheticism, and working-class Western outfits yoked passionate commitment to tactical pragmatism, notwithstanding the technical artistry at Schalke 04 (Hesse-Lichtenberger 2002: 10).

The most intensive struggles for hegemony arose in *international relations*. First, during the 1930s, many sports were symbolically charged fields for the clash of nationalist ideologies. The four British football associations viewed football as 'their game' and, despite separately and reluctantly joining FIFA before 1914, had always displayed deep misgivings towards the governing body's status. The British associations disconnected themselves from FIFA's emerging international society in 1920, rejoined in 1924 after 'normal' relations were resumed with old war foes, but then resigned again in 1928 over the issue of 'broken-time' payments to amateurs (Goldblatt 2006: 238–40). Crucially, in a pompous and myopic forfeit of parentage, the British associations remained outside FIFA until 1946, just as the governing body helped to foster the game's exponential growth in international popularity and institutional development. In the interim, English political and football authorities exploited the game's ideological and diplomatic functions through tough contests against Germany and Italy during the 1930s (Beck 2003).

Prioritizing international glory, Mussolini's Italy assimilated top South American players like Orsi, Monti and Guaita as *rimpatriati* (the repatriated), to win the 1934 and 1938 World Cups (Lanfranchi and Taylor 1999: 76). The Soviet Union deployed football to promote domestic order and international diplomacy. Stalin's security chief, Beria, and other Party leaders actively assisted the State-favoured Dynamo teams. Spartak Moscow, the most popular side, was consistently victimized for 'bourgeois' practices; its star players, notably the Starostin brothers, were arrested and sent into exile (Edelman 1993: 58–68). In 1945, the crack Moscow Dynamo side were filled with top Russian talents, and played four matches undefeated in Britain before almost 270,000 spectators (Downing 1999). Cold War diplomacy underpinned the sporting rationale for other overseas football tours in the post-1945 period, notably when European nations on East and West enthusiastically hosted visits by African teams (Hanzan 1987: 256).

Post-1945, occasional violent outbreaks at international fixtures reflected ascendant, instrumental tactics and wider cross-cultural antagonisms. The 1962 Chile–Italy fixture – the 'Battle of Santiago' – was partly ignited by pre-match Italian press articles. Argentinian and European teams often contested brutal fixtures: Europeans castigated Latino 'dirty tricks', but South Americans believed they were implementing modern professionalism (cf. Alabarces et al. 2001).

Second, international football precipitated strong processes of 'relativization': as national societies came into increasing contact with each other, so they were inspired to differentiate themselves, to sharpen their identity-markers, in relation to others. Moreover, international football provided global looking-glasses for national societies. In this sense, football fixtures functioned rather like international exhibitions, in allowing nations to advance the claim to 'be the best' so long as a wide range of outside challengers were competing. On the other hand, international defeats could provoke much soul-searching about generalized national entropy vis-à-vis the rest of the world.

For post-war Britain, football mirrored the old Empire's global decline, feeding a broader national *antiquation anxiety*. England endured the heaviest blows, losing 1–0 to the USA in 1950, then thrashed 6–3 and 7–1 by Hungary in 1953; a year later, Uruguay annihilated Scotland 7–0. Up to Celtic's European Cup win in 1967, British club and national teams struggled to match continental sophistication.

Similar traumas befell Argentina. Little international engagement had allowed Argentinians to hold unrealistic confidence in the standards of their national team. When Argentina were thumped 6–1 by Czechoslovakia at the 1958 World Cup finals, furious public debates were sparked, with football functioning as a partial mirror for the dilemmas of national politics: should the nation continue on its unique, indigenous, *criollo* path, or should it embrace the modern, industrial, European way (Archetti 1998: 174–5; Alabarces et al. 2001: 237–8)? Notably, such disputes presaged more fundamental debates over 'underdevelopment' in Latin America during the 1960s.

Third, football's international framework was transformed. Initially, relations between neighbouring nations were the nuclei of international affairs. For example, British isolationism towards FIFA reflected the importance placed upon fixtures between the Home Nations. In Central

Europe, the Mitropa Cup was founded in 1927 and featured Austrian, Czech, Hungarian, Italian, and Yugoslav sides. The tournament's salience declined sharply from the 1960s, as continental and world competition gained stature (Marschik 2001).

Football's global system expanded dramatically. FIFA grew from 40 member nations in 1925 to 80 in 1954 and 133 by 1970; confirmed as the globe's premier tournament, the World Cup grew to 53 entrants by 1966. Continental governing bodies were established: UEFA (Europe) and AFC (Asia) in 1954; CAF (Africa) in 1957; CONCACAF (North and Central America) in 1961; and OFC (Oceania) in 1965. UEFA's foundation was partly intended to challenge South American influence inside FIFA, while AFC and CAF reflected the Third World's growing political relevance. Britain's role inside FIFA was preserved, with a shaky hegemonic bloc, by the presidency of the patrician Stanley Rous (1961–1974).

International club tournaments were established annual events and became hugely popular; the European Cup, founded in 1955, attracted at least 127,000 fans in Glasgow to the 1960 final. The Copa Libertadores, South America's premier club tournament, began in 1960, as did the World Club Championship, contested by European and South American champions.

In regard to *humankind*, football tensions intensified internationalist or universalist discourses, and continuing dynamics of social marginalization. First, aided by greater mediatization of key tournaments, consciousness of a global football 'family' grew sharper. Most European nations enjoyed live televised fixtures from the 1954 World Cup, enabling global audiences to identify 'world-class' players and teams. By 1970, over 250 million television sets were distributed globally, 50 times the 1950 figure (Whannel 1992: 165). Through regular replays, football provided some 'global moments' that were sedimented as 'world memories' – for example, Pelé's hat-trick in the 1958 World Cup final, or England's disputed 'goal' in the 1966 final (see Smith 1990). In turn, football crystallized particular aesthetic forms whose status became globalized. Brazil and Di Stefano's Real Madrid articulated 'the beautiful game' (a term attributed to Pelé), creating a highly refined style that humankind could witness on television, celebrate, and then endeavour to emulate.[10]

Second, systematic forms of social segregation were transposed into football, partly through the construction of rigid national solidarities. In Nazi Germany, Jews and Marxists were systematically excluded from the game from 1933 onwards. In Europe after 1945, players drawn from ethnic minorities typically endured racist or other discriminatory treatment. More broadly, players who sought to escape exploitative industrial control within their national football system endured strong dynamics of social exclusion. English recruits to the lucrative breakaway league in Colombia faced long domestic bans upon return. In post-war West Germany, players

---

[10]The popular romanticization of a balletic, fluent football style stands in major contrast to the cagey, highly instrumental, often violent play in Brazilian club football.

exiting national 'amateur' leagues to play abroad were typically ignored for international honours.

Football's class connections varied significantly by nation and region. In Britain and some other parts of north-west Europe, elite groups distinguished themselves by practicing sports other than football, whereas the game's cross-class appeal was evidenced in southern Europe and South America (Giulianotti 1999a). Supporter identities varied markedly between nations due to divergent club constitutions. In Iberia and Latin America, most clubs were private associations that allowed *socios* (members) to elect presidents and to use many sporting facilities. In the UK and Italy, private ownership prevailed, producing weaker owner–supporter bonds. Meanwhile, in the former British colonies and North America, football failed to dislodge rival 'national sports' – for example, American football, which was backed heavily by national education systems and mass media.

On 'race', non-white players and developing nations made some significant, albeit restricted advances. The small scattering of black players in European leagues encountered routine, unthinking racism across the football system. In the post-war era, South American teams, most obviously Brazil, widely recruited black and mulatto talents, but racial prejudices remained, notably in the coaches' reluctance to play black goalkeepers (Leite Lopes 1997; cf. Wood 2007: 130–1). Some European nations exploited their colonial ties to claim elite talents, such as the Mozambicans Eusebio and Mario Coluna at Portugal, or the Algerian Rachid Mekloufi with France. Meanwhile, developing societies struggled to gain full inclusion in global football: only one side (North Korea in 1966) from Asia or Africa was admitted to the World Cup finals until 1970, while battles ensued to expel the racially stratified societies of South Africa and Rhodesia (now Zimbabwe) from FIFA. More commonly, local battles were fought by the indigenous peoples in Africa through football, to secure greater political independence within and beyond the game in relation to their colonial rulers (Martin 1991; Stuart 1996; Mazwai 2003). Under the apartheid system of South Africa, political prisoners on Robben Island ran a football league from 1966 until the prison's closure in 1991. The league was mainly for recreational purposes, but also served to bring normal aspects of the outside world into the prison context, and to demonstrate the organizational capabilities of the prisoners (Korr and Close 2008).

Finally, all four elemental reference points were defined in masculine terms, reflecting the generalized marginalization of women. Individual identities and national cohesion were largely constructed through football according to masculine iconography and themes. In turn, across Western Europe, women's football was often systematically repressed by the football authorities, and only initiated its modern organization in the late 1960s, through the founding of national associations or leagues, in nations like Sweden, Germany, and England (Hjelm and Olofsson 2003; Pfister 2003; Williams 2003).

Fifth phase: 'uncertainty' – the late 1960s to the early 2000s

Football's 'uncertain', **fifth phase** spans the late 1960s to the early 2000s, and was heralded by two broad international developments. First, non-European football societies – particularly Latin America, but also Africa and Asia – exercised greater political influence, culminating in Brazil's João Havelange unseating of Sir Stanley Rous as FIFA President in 1974. Second, mass mediatization transformed international football, with the 1970 World Cup as the first finals widely televised in colour.

Throughout this period, intensified uncertainty marked interrelations between globalization's four 'reference points'. At *individual* level, vast differences and inequalities emerged between elite and grassroots football, in terms of the financial and symbolic rewards afforded players, coaches, officials, and journalists. Elite European Union players enjoyed the greatest benefits. During the 1980s, several European nations relaxed recruitment restrictions on overseas players, leading to the '3+2' system in club football from 1991 to 1995.[11] The 1995 *Bosman* ruling tied football to European law, destroying 'retain and transfer' systems by enabling out-of-contract European players to move freely between clubs. Significantly empowering elite players, *Bosman* helped to raise salaries and signing-on fees; thus, within a few years, many European clubs were directing over 80 per cent of annual revenues into wages. International player mobility was fuelled further by huge new television revenues in top European leagues, the emergence of sports agents with global contacts, and the greater prestige of continental rather than national club tournaments.

Some economists identified dual labour markets emerging in Europe. On one hand, a small pool of outstanding players (superstars) was pursued assiduously by many football institutions, from clubs to merchandise corporations and other TNCs (Pujol and Garcia del Barrio 2006; see Rosen 1981; Lucifora and Simmons 2003). From Pelé onwards, greater numbers of players experienced a status transmogrification, from hero to star, from sport-specific athlete to global signifier (cf. Andrews and Jackson 2001). Off-field earnings multiplied through diverse endorsement deals with TNCs that hypercommodified football's most accomplished artists, particularly forwards rather than goalkeepers (Smart 2005; Walsh and Giulianotti 2006). On the other hand, for the vast remainder of players, a monopsony situation pertained, wherein a large supply of comparative mediocrity was available to a limited number of clubs offering modest rewards.

World economic inequalities ossified the football systems beyond Western Europe. In the late 1980s, *perestroika* enabled Eastern Europe's decaying communist systems to lift bans on players moving West in return for hard currency (Edelman and Riordan 1994: 276). Players

---

[11]The '3+2' rule, agreed with the European Commission, enabled all UEFA-governed clubs to sign any number of European players, but only three non-nationals and two 'assimilated' players could play in each fixture.

in non-EU nations endured far less industrial emancipation: for example, in Brazil, the *passe* (player ownership) system was only partially reformed, and by 2000 nearly 90 per cent of 23,000 registered players still earned less than £100 per month (Bellos 2002: 21). More generally, various European football and legal authorities criticized the 'slave-trade' treatment of young African players by some European clubs and scouts.

The new pantheon of football celebrities enriched further circles of managers, directors, match officials, media figures, and player agents. In Western Europe, from the late 1980s onwards, patrician club owners lost ground to more commercially aggressive business figures (for example, Berlusconi at Milan, Tapie at Marseilles, Dein at Arsenal, Murray at Rangers). In Latin America, populist football officials (*caudillos*, or *cartolas* in Brazil) still exerted long-term political influence, notably Teixeira (at the CBF), Miranda (at Vasco da Gama), and Grondona (at the AFA). Some football analysts gained national prominence for their distinctive coverage of seminal fixtures on radio and television – prominent examples being Wolstenholme and Motson in England, Bjørge Lillelien in Norway, or (further back, in the 1950s) Herbert Zimmermann of West Germany. Player agents with global contacts increased the stream of clients into major European leagues.

Apropos the *nation state*, the game maintained its relevance to national vitality. First, football continued to ritualize national solidarity, particularly within new or emerging football nations, for example with semi-finalists Croatia at the 1998 World Cup finals (literally kitted in the national coat of arms), or the 1990 quarter-finalists Cameroon (cf. Nkwi and Vidacs 1997). Football assuaged the ingrained Japanese reluctance to celebrate national identity after reaching the 1998 World Cup finals. At international tournaments, supporters were increasingly committed to highly visual national differentiation, through team-scarves, shirts and face-paint. National pride was further invoked when rival nations competed furiously to host tournaments, or to win 'best behaved fans' awards at major events.

Growing consciousness of ethno-national differentiation was revealed in football's complex array of national referents. In the United States, millions of young, white, middle-class Americans came to play football, but at elite level the most committed followers tended to be first/second generation migrants with strong allegiances to 'home' nations. France's 1998 World Cup victory was celebrated in Paris by citizens of long French descent, as well as those of North African and other extraction, some of whom paraded alternative national flags to mark the winning players' multicultural background. Conversely, Germany's citizenship laws undermined football's multicultural potential by complicating opportunities to hold dual citizenship, with particular consequences for Turkish *gasterbeiters*.

In some contested settings, club rivalries stretched the ethno-national and ethno-linguistic divisions within nation states. In the former Yugoslavia, the violence at a fixture between Serbian and Croatian sides was one crucial 'tipping point' for the outbreak of civil war in 1991. In Spain, in 1976, a year after Franco's death, two Basque sides, Real Sociedad and Athletic

Bilbao, entered the field carrying the Basque flag and then observed the Basque 'national' anthem. Yet intense rivalries and ill feelings still existed *within* these regions, such as between Sociedad (of San Sebastian) and Bilbao, over the right to symbolize these submerged nations (cf. Walton 2001; Ball 2003: 33–7).

National solidarity was stretched by the frequent eruption of 'club versus country' conflicts. Many clubs criticized national football fixtures for exhausting players and producing injuries that were barely indemnified through insurance. Following the deregulation of labour markets, national associations complained that clubs were recruiting too many non-national players, undermining the development of indigenous talents.

Third, supporter movements in most European and Latin American nations underwent further differentiation through the creation of young 'militant' fan groups associated with varying levels of violence. In the UK, 'football hooliganism' was more consciously thematized as a social problem and as an identity embraced by particular supporter formations. English fan violence overseas was particularly prominent, notably at the 1985 European Cup final between Liverpool and Juventus, when 39 Italian fans were fatally injured inside the stadium after fleeing attacks from English fans, causing a wall to collapse. Elsewhere, the *ultrà* spectator identity – rooted in colourful, vocal, and sometimes violent backing for the club – spread from Italy across southern Europe. In Argentina, the militant *hinchadas* (supporters) were dubbed *barras bravas* by a critical media from the 1960s onwards (see Gil 1998, 2002). In Brazil, club *torcedores* (fans) had gained a distinctive, carnival identity through the *Charanga* groups (founded initially at Flamengo) in the 1940s, which were later supplanted by more critical and violent independent fan movements, beginning with the *Gaviões da Fiel* at Corinthians in 1969. National and regional differentiation occurred over techniques of social control at football matches. Relevant strategies included: proactive measures (notably intensive surveillance) and criminalization of violent fans in the UK; different community-work 'fan projects' in northern Europe (notably Germany, Holland, Sweden, Austria, Belgium); reactive riot-policing in much of Europe, notably Italy and Belgium; and the use of tear-gas, water-cannon and stadium moats in Latin America.

Fourth, football playing formations were less nationally defined and became evermore varied, for example 4–4–2, 4–2–3–1, 3–5–2, 4–3–2–1, 4–3–3, and 4–5–1. Moreover, football's public spheres also evidenced increasing reflexivity regarding the 'invention of traditions', particularly at national levels. Perhaps most notably, many Dutch football followers viewed the mythology surrounding the 1974 team, and its world-renowned 'Total Football' style, purely as that: a myth that had only limited basis in actual playing strategies (Lechner 2007).

Football's realm of *international relations* expanded with three particular consequences. First, FIFA's membership rose rapidly from 136 members in 1970 to 204 by 2000 (more than the United Nations). Growth was largely attributable to post-colonial independence in Africa and Asia, post-Communist revolutions and nationalist struggles in Eastern Europe and Asia, and greater integration of small Pacific and Caribbean states.

Second, as noted, the emerging nations gained political influence particularly through President Havelange, who reciprocated through the allocation of seats on important committees and the foundation of development projects. In 1998, Sepp Blatter succeeded Havelange, with strong support from outside Europe, amidst allegations of corruption and cronyism.

Third, emerging football nations enhanced their competitive participation in world football: allocated World Cup finals positions rose from two of 16 competing teams (including the first African one) in 1970, to four of 24 teams (with three African) in 1982, and 11 of 32 teams in 1998. By 2000, emerging football powers in relatively rich consumer markets – notably the United States, South Korea, and then Japan – were set to become regular qualifiers. A world rankings system established by FIFA in 1993 evaluated results over an eight-year period, and functioned to position the emerging nations highly, despite the rarity of their encounters with European or South American sides.

Fourth, football was a recurring theatre of struggle between rival ideologies. The extraordinary 1974 World Cup fixture between West and East Germany, won 1-0 by the East, was cross-cut by diametrically opposed political (capitalist vs communist), intra-national (German vs German) and football (favourite vs underdog) themes (cf. Hesselmann and Ide 2006: 41–3). The cynical *realpolitik* of football's elite engendered the toleration and occasional embrace of military regimes, notably in Latin America. The 1978 World Cup finals were awarded to, and hosted by, Argentina, then under a military *junta* that was 'disappearing' up to 30,000 people. The USSR were ejected from the 1974 World Cup for refusing to play Chile, where the Pinochet regime had been torturing and executing people inside football stadiums. In Brazil and Argentina, the military regimes sought to ingratiate the leaders with the game's most prominent players, notably the victorious 1970 Brazilian side (Levine 1980: 246–7).

Fifth, since 1990, football's political management became both more complex and more closely integrated within the broader international system. Political influence was pursued by a wider array of institutional actors, such as governing bodies (global, continental, and national), media and merchandise TNCs, organized labour (especially the professionals' world union, FiFPro), player agents, international federations (especially the EU), the world's top clubs, and supporters' organizations. Each participant category became increasingly reflexive towards both greater global interconnectedness within football and the complexity of competing interests across these stakeholders.

The reference point of *humankind* was thematized in cross-cutting ways. First, and in later years, the social marginalization of ethnic minorities and women was given some significant political focus. In the UK, for example, wider societal racism was routinely reflected through the abuse of black players by crowds and club officials. Institutional racism typically funnelled local black players out of academic education and into sport and then, when playing for teams, racial stereotypes saw Afro-Caribbeans allocated outside positions to exploit their 'natural' speed (Hill 1989; Giulianotti 1999a; Back et al. 2001; King 2004). From the late 1980s onwards, however, anti-racism initiatives gained strong ground, notably among non-white players and new social movements in football, and racist abuse inside stadiums was ultimately criminalized. Meanwhile, wider debates focused on broader forms of ethno-national abuse and exclusion, as affecting overseas players at UK clubs or Asian minorities (Finn and Dimeo 1998). Similar processes – entailing generalized racism, followed by anti-racism initiatives – occurred across Europe and with subsequent backing from the game's international governing bodies. Elsewhere, the game encapsulated wider political struggles centred on 'race'. The racist states of Rhodesia (now Zimbabwe) and South Africa were finally expelled in full from FIFA during the 1970s. Domestic football pointed to future societal transformations when, for example, in South Africa, the all-white league system finally collapsed in 1977, while the black national league boomed throughout that decade (Mazwai 2003).

Football culture in Europe and Latin America was slower than other commercialized public domains in softening its patriarchal codes and conventions to facilitate women's participation. Perhaps the strongest advances were made in Brazil where women's football had been banned by law until 1979, but by 1988 the national team had risen to third-placed position in the International Championship staged in China (Votre and Mourão 2003: 254). Through the 1980s and 1990s, grassroots women's football flourished in more socially democratic societies (such as across Scandinavia) or emerging nations (particularly the USA and China). Recognizing the social and marketing possibilities, FIFA inaugurated the Women's World Cup in 1991. Notwithstanding the old strategy (such as in Italy) of embedding telegenic female presenters on television's football shows, women gradually penetrated the game's mainstream culture as advanced commercialization, from the late 1980s onwards, inspired clubs and leagues to embrace a lucrative, untapped 'reserve army' of consumers. In some societies, such as Italy and Argentina, forms of gender emancipation enabled noticeable numbers of young women to join 'militant' supporter groups.

Second, the status and participation of established working-class supporter groups came under critical analysis in many football nations. Established football systems experienced significant drops in attendances, for example, in Germany from the mid-1970s to mid-1980s, in England and Brazil through the 1980s (Helal 1994; Goldblatt 2004: 106; Hesse-Lichtenberger 2002: 204). Explanations for these falls focused in part on declining ties between clubs and local communities, decrepit stadium facilities (particularly in England), and perceived threats of fan disorder.

The commercial reinvention of European football during the 1990s was viewed by some critics as exacerbating the social exclusion of working-class fans, through high ticket prices and growing intolerance of informal participatory fandom (cf. Conn 1997; Wagg 2004; Giulianotti 2007).

Third, football's universalistic possibilities have been explored through numerous development initiatives since the early 1970s. Governing bodies – notably FIFA and continental federations – developed partnerships with humanitarian NGOs and major corporations to supply football equipment, coaching clinics and other technical advice to developing football nations, particularly in Africa and Asia. These issues are explored more fully in Chapter 5.

Sixth phase: 'millennial' – early 2000s onwards

In recent articles, Robertson (2007a, 2007b) has identified a contemporary, sixth, **millennial** phase of globalization that dates particularly from September 11, 2001. The millennial phase takes the more pessimistic strains of the uncertainty phase into new realms, principally with reference to the transnational impact of religio-cultural forces. The apocalyptic declarations of Jewish, Christian and Islamic groups are prominent in millennial thinking, though there has been a more generalized spread and darkening of climates of fear across other socio-cultural realms, as expressed through anxieties over personal security, national identity, and the global environment. The millennial phase serves also to reverse old modernization arguments regarding the perceived remorseless advance of secularization across the world.

The sixth phase is defined largely through fresh constructions of the four elemental reference points. In regard to *individuals*, millennial thinking is evidenced through more intensive governmental regulation of hitherto 'private' or personal space. Personal concerns regarding risk encounters have been concretized, whether through the fear of identified hazards or, as in some forms of postmodern leisure, in the hedonistic pursuit of dangerous experiences. Millennial thinking is evidenced further in northern societies through the mass-market diffusion of ideals regarding the 'perfect body' or ultimate lifestyle, while the project of self- or identity reconstruction is promoted through the booming cosmetics and 'makeover' industries (Jones 2008).

The millennial phase is marked by the 'increasingly complex opening and closing' of *national societies* (Robertson 2007a: 413). Nation states are evermore concerned with 'managing' the perceived problems of security and alterity, at least with partial reference to increasing migration and transnational connectivity. On one hand, there has been a well-known boom in surveillance and 'dataveillance', at both public and private levels, in part (but far from solely) as a consequence of 9/11. The riskiness or failures of these information-gathering systems increase the temperature of climates of fear, for example when internet hackers break into online bank networks, or whenever stolen computer disks and laptops are revealed to contain intimate information on millions of citizens. On the other hand, there is a curious revelling in this culture of surveillance, a public and commercial celebration of 'being watched' across national societies, as reflected by the global popularity of 'reality television' shows. Websites such as Facebook or MySpace enable individuals to reveal themselves to the world, through kinds of 'reality self-mediatization', while building friendship or contact networks across the world.

International relations have been defined in recent times by the self-declared globalist 'crusade' of the American Bush administration against 'Islamic militants' or the 'axis of evil'. Some analysts are beginning to understand these processes in systemic terms, as a portent of global fascism or totalitarianism. Other impending crises may be identified in the chronic diminution of oil and water reserves.

Finally, *humanity* is a critical focus for global millennialism. Fears of impending ecological catastrophe and the obliteration of non-industrial ways of life have crystallized further in recent years. Greater consciousness of human–animal relations has contributed to concerns over the impending extinction of many endangered species. Millennial global politics are evidenced in the crystallization of a 'global civil society', and in the associated struggles involving IGOs, NGOs, NSMs, and the corporate social responsibility (CSR) divisions of TNCs, for example regarding human rights and development. Millennial thinking also underpins the proliferation and growth of ethno-national or religious fundamentalist movements which advance their own specific or absolute solutions to transnational problems and dilemmas.

Although the sixth phase is only in its preliminary stages, we may identify ways in which it takes root within football. In *individual* terms, personal lives are increasingly managed by state bodies or football's governing authorities, notably through the legal regulation and monitoring of behaviour inside and outside stadiums, and through the constant promotion of messages by public agencies and private corporations regarding good/bad types of supporter or player identity. More broadly, the game is a focus for the expression of millennial emotionality, for example as goals are celebrated in evermore joyous and choreographed ways by players and supporters.

On *national societies*, there have been greater debates over the impact of migration and transnational finance upon specific football cultures, for example regarding the possible diminution of national traditions (such as playing styles, or the psychology and professionalism of players), or the perceived need among nations to modernize their coaching infrastructures. On surveillance issues, the ubiquitous media coverage of the celebrity lifestyles of players aggregates into a form of reality television, and is typically played out before national audiences. Meanwhile, nations imbue leading football competitions such as the World Cup finals with increasingly millennial hopes and aspirations, if not in victory then at least in terms of participation.

In regard to *international relations*, there has been extensive apocalyptic talk regarding the 'inevitable' wholesale transformation of football, to create, for example, a European Superleague that will either deplete or destroy national competitions. Security issues surrounding major tournaments, such as the World Cup finals or European Championships, have intensified greatly since 9/11, engendering highly sophisticated techniques of spatial control and surveillance that often bypass or infringe established civil liberties. We may anticipate future concerns over the 'carbon footprints' that are imprinted by the global movement of peoples when attending these major championships.

Finally, in regard to *humankind*, sport is increasingly understood by many national and international bodies as having unique, universalistic qualities that both transcend civilizational differences, and which may even be harnessed to heal intersocietal wounds. Thus, for example, football and other sports have been engaged by the United Nations and numerous NGOs to promote the 'Millennium Development Goals', and to implement grassroots projects that foster peace and reconciliation between communities that have been divided by warfare. Such millennial thinking in regard to football is neatly instanciated by the global 'Football For Hope' programme which is driven by FIFA through partnerships with international NGOs. Millennial thinking is also instanced in the particular interaction of football and forms of transnational religiosity, for example through the centrality of evangelical Christianity among elite Brazilian players.

Concluding Comments

Clearly, football has been a significant component of globalization processes and, arguably, the game's relevance has intensified throughout the 'uncertainty' and 'millennial' phases. The game's genealogy is closely interwoven with broader globalization processes, from British international trading influences, through periods of intensified and militarized nationalism across the world, to the growing interpenetration of cultural realms like football by economic institutions and ideologies.

Moreover, if we briefly consider the elemental reference points, the game may be seen further to have contributed much to the making of the global field. Individual selves and social consciousness of 'the world' have intensified through, for example, the centrality of club allegiances or solidarities to the personal and collective identities of many millions of football followers. The changing crystallization and differentiation of national societies have been underpinned by the complex symbolism and contested discourses that are attendant upon national football teams. The concretization of international society has been assisted and, at times, accelerated by football, notably for example through the extensive participation of the Global South within the game's political and competitive realms. And, the thematization of humankind has been increasingly apparent within football, through mobilizations in regard to class, ethnicity, and gender, and also through discourses and policies concerning the game's unique universalism.

Through some adaptation, Robertson's six-phase model of globalization provides an appropriate framework for the historical analysis of football. The model departs in particular from alternatives that pin globalization to Western modernization processes. Thus, as a component of a 'global globalization' standpoint, the six-phase model highlights the historical complexity and transnational unevenness of global processes within football – from the reluctance of North American nations to embrace or adapt football, to the highly divergent legal and economic positions of professional players in Europe and South America. We consider such issues concerning cross-cultural matters more fully in the next chapter.

2

Culture: The Glocal Game, Cosmopolitanism and Americanization

Introduction

The cultural domain of globalization is highly debated within social science, primarily with reference to the question of agency and determination. Much debate concerns the analytical and empirical degrees of freedom that may be discerned in how local cultures engage with 'the global'. The arising arguments are often predicated upon conventional binary oppositions – notably between the local and the global, or the particular and the universal – and are flavoured by a critical preference for one perspective over the other.[12] On one side, 'cultural imperialism' arguments emphasize the determinant potency of global culture, particularly as manifested by Western (primarily American) institutions, which effectively circumscribes the critical agency of social actors at an everyday level (see, for example, Barber 1996; Latouche 1996; Ritzer 2004). Conversely, sociocultural and anthropological positions spotlight the creativity of social actors, including ways in which forms of local identity are purposively constructed 'in resistance' to perceived global processes (see, for example, Hannerz 1996; Watson 1997; Tomlinson 1999; Pieterse 2007). We argue here that the most plausible perspectives on cultural globalization involve the integration of *both* of these standpoints. That is to say, social scientists need to appreciate the intensive analytical and empirical *interdependencies* of the global and the local, or the universal and the particular, when seeking to account for the complexity of cultural globalization.

Culture has been, for social scientists, the most substantially examined of all the aspects of football's globalization. Some analyses in the late 1960s and early 1970s implied that instrumental rationalization, coupled with monopoly capitalism and militaristic nationalism, had come to dominate sports culture, creating an oppressive and alienating environment for all participants (cf. Vinnai 1973; Brohm 1978; Rigauer 1981). However, from the late 1980s onwards, much academic inquiry on the international aspects of football adopted a comparatively Herderian approach in exploring the distinctiveness of national football cultures, initially in Europe and Latin America, and

---

[12]We appreciate that the concepts of the local and the global, and the particular and the universal, are not identical binary oppositions.

subsequently at a more global level.[13] Particular transnational themes in football – such as the civic identities of clubs, or spectator-related violence – have provided highly fecund fields for comparative contrast and analysis. The spread of academic interest in football's international dimensions reflects a wider process of transnational exchange across the game, involving competitions, players, and finance. Most notably here, growing public and media interest in different football cultures has mushroomed, and has been reflected further in the transnational 'hybridization' of young supporter fashions.

Our discussion of football's cultural globalization requires us to address analytical and substantive questions. Universalism–particularism, 'relativization', and 'homogenization–heterogenization' represent our initial analytical concerns, and enable us to develop our theorizations of 'glocalization' and 'duality of glocality' (cf. Giulianotti and Robertson 2007b). Through this analytical prism, we consider more contemporary or substantive football themes, including Americanization, cosmopolitanism, postmodernization, and nostalgia. Throughout, in broad terms, we seek to sustain the argument that, in cultural terms, the football/globalization nexus is a highly varied one in which multipolar influences are at play.

The Universal and the Particular

The interrelationships of the 'universal' and the 'particular' are central to football's cultural dimensions and, more generally, may be understood as 'the elemental forms of global life' (Robertson 1992: 103, 1995). Any particular experience, identity, or social process is only comprehensible with reference to universal phenomena, and vice versa.

The 'globewide nexus' of the particular and the universal gives rise to two interrelationships: the 'universalization of particularism' and the 'particularization of universalism' (Robertson 1990a, 1992). First, the universalization of particularism 'involves the extensive diffusion of the idea that there is virtually no limit to particularity, to uniqueness, to difference, and to otherness' (1992: 102). A 'global valorization of particular identities' has intensified since the late nineteenth century, notably through principles of national identification that are underpinned by the international system. Major international football tournaments provide lively cultural arenas for the (re)production and interplay of national–societal particularities. Different national supporter groups converge and commingle, displaying their particularistic dresses, songs, and patterns of social behaviour.

Second, the 'particularization of universalism' involves the growing 'concreteness' of the world in socio-political or 'global-human' terms. This process is characterized by forms of global standardization and integration that differentiate societies along objective lines (Robertson 1990a: 51–2). For

---

[13]See, for example, Lanfranchi (1992); Giulianotti and Williams (1994); Sugden and Tomlinson (1994); Armstrong and Giulianotti (1997, 1998a, 2001, 2004); Brown (1998).

example, nations are positioned within global systems of time (or time zones) or communication (such as through international telephone codes or internet suffixes) (Robertson 1992: 102). International time-space categories were defined particularly during the take-off phase of globalization. In recent times, intensified social interconnectedness has accelerated the particularization of universalism, creating cultures of speed and immediacy wherein, for example, global communication networks enable financial markets or media TNCs to transmit information instantaneously (Tomlinson 2007).

In football, the particularization of universalism features the engagement of all institutions and actors within a pyramidal world system. FIFA (and the IFAB) sits at the apex, followed by the continental governing bodies, then national associations, regional and local associations, the various football clubs, and fans at the base, who literally 'support' the entire edifice. Global standardization is secured through FIFA-endorsed football associations that have jurisdiction over national teams and implement the game's rules and procedures. Each nation is also located within, and helps to authorize, a world calendar of tournaments and fixtures.

These preliminary comments enable us to focus critically on commonplace assumptions regarding globalization. For example, public and academic discourses typically present 'the local' and 'the global' as fundamental binary opposites, as a kind of alpha and omega in the ontology of globalization (cf. Rowe 2003). Anxieties commonly arise when this binary opposition is blithely accepted, over whether the 'global' is abolishing or subverting the 'local' (Robertson 1992, 1995: 35). Conversely, more nuanced standpoints highlight the complex interdependencies between the local and the global.

Certainly, it might be argued that football, as a global cultural force that has been backed by potent colonial or corporate interests, has served to obliterate many local, indigenous games. In Africa, for example, Western sports were purposefully inculcated among local peoples, to the chagrin of many elders (Haruna and Abdullahi 1991; Bale and Sang 1996). Similarly, in Latin American nations such as Peru, football's social spread often coincided with the decline of traditional games such as *bochas* (Escobar 1969: 75).[14]

Nevertheless, within football, cultural exchanges between the local and the global are not unidirectional. Host societies are not passive recipients of global cultural content. As we noted in Chapter 1, football's initial diffusion and subsequent popularization depended upon the positive reception by young males in diverse contexts. Indeed, football's 'humankind' conflicts have typically featured excluded people struggling for opportunities and resources to engage in the game. Football has also enabled 'local' cultures to explore fresh forms of particularity, for example through founding community clubs and developing specific styles of play.

Additionally, local cultures are not 'fixed' in time and space. Rather, we need to explore the routes and roots of any culture; its mobility and its

---

[14]Also, in Turkey, football's urban appeal has weakened traditional wrestling (Stokes 1996: 26–7).

senses of 'dwelling fixity' (cf. Clifford 1997), where, to borrow from John Cale, *homo sapiens* meets *hobo sapiens*. Over time, local cultures undergo processes of deterritorialization and reterritorialization. Deterritorialization relates particularly to the weakening spatial connections of cultural practices, identities, products, and communities. Strongly influenced by transnational migration and mediatization, deterritorialization processes are exemplified by Asians in Canada or Chicanos along the US–Mexico border (Canclini 1995; Appadurai 1998). Deterritorialization is accelerated in dromomanic developed nations, where national and transnational mobility is deeply entrenched. Yet, deterritorialized individuals and groups do not submerge themselves in a meaningless cultural mélange, but instead manufacture new 'homes' and senses of located cultural identity: in other words, *re*territorialization occurs, abetted by the crucial resources of electronic media.

In football, deterritorialization is historically problematic. Leading clubs are historically *rooted* in communities (through stadium location, civic engagement and regional symbolism), but the *routes* of team lore and allegiance are spread through migration and mediatization. For example, Liverpool football club is anchored in the eponymous city, with a cultural identity that claims to retain strong local 'structures of feeling', in deliberate contrast to more globalist rivals, Manchester United (cf. Williams et al. 2001).[15] However, deterritorialization processes are evidenced by Liverpool's national and worldwide following since the 1970s, the dominance of mainland European players and coaches from the late 1990s, and the club's ownership by two American sports entrepreneurs.

The increasingly complex and uncertain contours of support for national teams further reveal deterritorialization processes. Nations with large migrant populations inspire internationally diffuse support for their football teams; thus, Irish President, Mary Robinson, claimed in 1994 that she and the national football team represented 'the modern Ireland' which included Irish citizens and the children of the diaspora (Giulianotti 1996: 339). Similarly, among players, post-colonial and diasporic movements can highlight the complex ties between residency, nationality, and ethno-national identity. For example, in Paris, a friendly in late 2001 between France and Algeria reportedly saw the erstwhile 'visiting team' field more French-born players than the home nation.

The deterritorializing of national symbols is advanced by the international televising of some fixtures, and by football's interpenetration with other popular cultural fields. International tournaments attract wide interest across external nations and regions: for example, UEFA claimed that Euro 2004 was viewed by cumulative audiences of nearly 450 million in North America, 1 billion in

---

[15]While Manchester United have developed a potent mythology surrounding the club's history and its local connections (notably in regard to the 1958 Munich disaster, which killed eight players), supporters of local rivals, Manchester City, tend to claim a closer attachment to the city per se.

Africa and 1.1 billion in Asia.[16] Contemporary consumerism promotes diverse forms of national identification, such as through the transnational retail of replica shirts and kits. Since the late 1990s, UK fashion chains have produced many styles that imitate 'classic' national football attire, with 'Italia', 'USSR', 'Brasil' and other national signifiers emblazoned across clothing.

In these circumstances, 'reterritorializing' processes acquire particular salience. Through reterritorialization, claims of cultural ownership are formulated so that even transient or migrant groups inscribe geographical marks upon their identities. On occasions when clubs 'move home', reterritorialization occurs as supporters give fresh and intimate meanings to their new stadiums.[17] More potent reterritorializing occurs when supporters establish social clubs in distant settings. In southern Ontario, for example, leading English, Scottish, and Italian clubs have strong presences, with Celtic and Rangers fans boasting their own plush social clubs and memberships of over 400 (Giulianotti 2005a; Giulianotti and Robertson 2005, 2007a). More generally, the spectator cultures at leading clubs undergo continuing relativization and revitalization, typically attracting more fluid or 'cosmopolitan' followers to fresh forms of sporting diversity (cf. Cowen 2002: 134). Additionally, complex de-/re-territorializing processes underpin the pride that many nations have in regard to their foreign players. For example, imported talents such as Henry, Viera, Ginola (all France), and Zola (Italy) became national celebrities in the UK, were prized for legitimizing and enhancing the domestic game within the global context, and were lauded for their general acculturation (for example, in adapting to playing styles or building particular relations with media corporations).

Clubs endeavour to reterritorialize by claiming spatial meaning for themselves in distant settings. Consider, for example, the Asian 'club shops' opened by Manchester United or the summer tours of Asia and North America that are undertaken by leading European sides. Crucially, reterritorialization is not uncontested. The established, 'territorialized' supporters may object to the privileges granted to outside followers. Thus, Manchester United fans based in North-West England differentiate themselves from southern-based supporters; and even among Scandinavian fans of English teams, there are distinctions between long-standing and more 'touristic' supporters (Brick 2001; Heinonen 2005). Thus, different social groups contest the meaning of the 'local' within the global game.

Relativization

The concept of *relativization* illuminates further the local–global interrelationship, disclosing in particular the increasingly reflexive contrasts between

---

[16]See www.uefa.com/Competitions/Euro/Organisation/Kind=32768/newsId=332293. html

[17]For example, in Buenos Aires, the fans of San Lorenzo refer to their stadium as *Nuevo Gasómetro*, in collective memory of their old ground, the *Gasómetro*, which was torn down in 1979.

'local' cultures. Relativization reveals how globalization brings cultures into sharper reflexive and comparative focus, thereby compelling these cultures to respond to each other in an ever-amplifying manner across the universal domain. Indeed, in our view, it is comparison with others that makes reflexivity a possibility. Relativization also involves particular entities being shaped by the elemental reference points of individuals, national societies, international relations, and humankind (Robertson and Chirico 1985). Thus, any 'national' football culture will acquire particular coherence, as a relativized entity, from interrelationships between individual citizens, the international football system, and themes of shared (or variegated) humanity.

We may unpack the interrelations of these elemental reference points with reference to Brazil's football culture and the wider society. On *individuals*, we may connect Brazil's individualistic styles of play (notably dribbling and deception) to the streetwise *malandro* (or artful rogue) who survives in Brazilian *favelas* (DaMatta 1991), or to the political power of *cartolas* ('big hats') inside football personify the nation's dense patronage networks. In regard to *international relations*, we may tie Brazil's status in football competitions and FIFA to greater political coherence across 'Third World' societies, and to transnational connectivity through the mass media and long-distance transport. With respect to *humanity*, we might explore how Brazilian football successes symbolized a sporting 'pedagogy of the oppressed', showcasing the struggles of marginalized groups to participate, to express themselves, to represent 'the nation' (cf. Freyre 1963; Freire 1970).

The particular Brazilian context was infused by diverse, often conflicting, social forces. On one side stood a national history of brutal colonization, charismatic authoritarianism, and rigid 'racial' stratification. Beneath official discourses that have celebrated the 'multi-racial democracy', there lurks an elitist and statist commitment to 'whitening' the black population (Robertson 1998b).[18] Yet, on the other side, a populist ideology remains, which venerates 'racial hybridity', social informality, and the vibrancy of mass participation in national events. When considering the other three reference points, we gain a fuller understanding of Brazil as a *nation*, within football, as registered further by national styles of play and a fully national focus on the *seleçao* (the Brazilian national team). The nation is further revealed by football's role in constructing modern Brazilian identity, through mass media, education, language, and popular culture.

Reflection on Brazilian football also helps to challenge assumptions about uniformity and homogeneity in regard to national cultures. Brazilian football is instead a highly varied realm with complex, multidimensional relationships to the wider society. In terms of playing styles, significant

---

[18]Thus, leading football stars, notably Pele, were visibly integrated into elite/white society, while white players were notably more prominent in Brazil's national team during the 1980s. On the subsequent attempts to 'whiten' leading black athletes in the United States, notably Michael Jordan, see Andrews (2001).

variations arise between major cities, while national debates occur over the expressive *futebol-arte* or the physical *futebol-força* methods.[19] Additionally, Brazilian football does not passively reflect the national society, but represents an extraordinary domain of mass participation and global cultural success, in contrast to a painfully stratified and still-underdeveloped society.[20]

Analysis of specific football episodes helps to reveal the complex forces that are at play between the various elemental reference points within and beyond the game. Consider, for example, the visit to violence-torn Haiti by the Brazilian national team to play an exhibition match in August 2004. The event was promoted by the CBF (national elemental reference point, football institution), Brazilian government (national, non-football), UN (international relations, non-football), and FIFA (international relations, football). The billed 'Football for Peace' visit helped to promote the game's universalistic claims (international relations/humankind, football), carried a global humanitarian message (humanity, non-football), and advanced the standings of the Brazilian President, his government and the UN (individual/nation/international relations, non-football). Despite pressures from the President (individual, non-football) and governing bodies (nation/international relations, football), some European clubs (international relations, football) refused to release their Brazilian players (individuals, football) to participate. These players were then dropped from Brazil's side for the next fixture (individual/nation, football). The Haiti visit fostered Brazilian pride in the team's global status (nation/international relations, football), while enhancing Brazil's standing in the UN and specific pursuit of a permanent seat on the Security Council (international relations, non-football); yet, the visit also drew criticisms that the nation itself faced huge domestic problems (nation/international relations/humankind, non-football). All in all, this single match demonstrated the complex layers of relationship that arise between football and the wider social order.

The concept of relativization also facilitates a clearer understanding of particular 'defence of the local' or anti-globalist discourses. These arguments are deployed, for example, to challenge global influences upon indigenous playing techniques, such as when European coaches impose their methods upon African players (*FIFA News*, February 2002). But as definite cultural responses to transnational processes, these discourses emerge from relativization processes and serve to advance particular understandings of 'the local' per se vis-à-vis alternative meanings.

More simplistic 'defence of the local' discourses assume that global flows are largely unidirectional, from international society into particular nations or continents. Yet, even in settings where local identities are strongly sustained, complex matrices of relativization serve to mould and refashion 'the

---

[19]Indeed, even the 1970 Brazil team blended the two logics, through brilliant expressive play and rigorous training at high altitude.

[20]Similarly, outsiders typically discuss 'African football' as a uniform entity, thus ignoring enormous local, national, and regional diversity (cf. Armstrong and Giulianotti 2004).

local'. For example, to return to Brazil, it may seem initially that 'the local' (in this case, national) playing style is an uncontested concept, in being renowned globally as highly expressive, aesthetically pleasing, and indicative of a unique, 'Lusotropical' national society (cf. Freyre 1963). However, Brazilian football history reveals a rather more complex story, with the national team having long been influenced by European sides and tactical systems. In the 1970s, the Brazilians explored Dutch 'total football' (itself something of an invented concept), then switched to a 'native' style in the 1980s. Lack of competitive success then sparked a move to a cautious, quasi-Italian style in the 1990s; victories at the 1994 and 2002 World Cup finals thereby featured tactical caution, defensive solidity, and occasional improvisational brilliance. Thus, over three decades, the 'local' Brazilian style was recast and relativized in a variety of complex ways.

We should note too that relativization processes produce very different emphases on the assertion of the local, depending upon the particular societies or the social practices in question. In most nations, formidable relativization is apparent in the nationalistic rituals of football spectators, but is perhaps less apparent in regard to national styles of play. In South America, nations that understand themselves in terms of particular 'schools' of play include Argentina (*criollo* style), Brazil (balletic, spectacular), and Colombia (intricate short passing); conversely, Chile, Paraguay, and Uruguay tend not to advance these local-making assertions, although they tend to compensate by advocating strongly competitive virtues (such as the brave combative methods of Paraguay's *guaraní*).

Homogenization–Heterogenization

We turn now to an axial problem in the sociology of globalization, namely the homogenization–heterogenization debate. Homogenization arguments generally posit that globalization is marked by growing cultural convergence at the transnational level. Conversely, heterogenization arguments contend that global processes maintain or facilitate cultural diversity or divergence. The rival 'schools of thought' tend not to strike absolutist poses – for example, most homogenization theorists recognize significant instances of cultural diversification – yet the broad differences between the two sides remain intact. In the following discussion, we consider homogenization theories before exploring the heterogenization position.

Homogenization

Homogenization theories posit that social actors and their local cultures are orchestrated into passively absorbing or otherwise reproducing the cultural products, practices, and predilections of the world's most powerful corporations and nations. Perhaps ironically, these theories of global cultural convergence have produced a diversity of keywords and theories, such as cultural imperialism, synchronization, Americanization, Westernization, and grobalization (Schiller 1969; Hamelink 1983; Tomlinson 1991; Latouche 1996; Ritzer 2004).

Early convergence arguments emerged in the preliminary analysis of global mass communications. McLuhan (1964) is widely credited with initially exploring the possible genesis of a 'global village' through heightened forms of media connectivity. However, we should recall that McLuhan did appreciate the complexity of contemporary international politics by noting the magnitude of global conflicts and East/West cultural differences (McLuhan and Fiore 1989).

However, other writers on global communications have argued that political–economic rather than cultural-technological factors lie behind global cultural convergence. Schiller (1976: 9), for example, contends that Western media corporations are rapacious, culturally imperialistic forces that dominated international markets, such that, in Wallersteinian language, 'a largely one-directional flow of information from core to periphery represents the reality of power' (1976: 6). Hamelink (1983, 1994, 1995) highlights the global diffusion of Americanized consumer lifestyles and products through corporations like McDonald's and Disney (Hamelink 1995: 111). Thus, even in Mexican football, Hamelink reports the symbolic importance of Coca-Cola to pre-match rituals (noted in Tomlinson 1999: 109). Overall, he contends that Western corporations 'reduce local cultural space' by controlling negative information and obstructing indigenous initiatives.

Homogenization theorists argue that, when TNCs micro-market their products, little meaningful engagement occurs with local cultures. Thus, while Western media corporations translate their programmes into local languages, the substance remains alien to peripheral cultures, and must still 'bear the ideological imprint of the main centers of the capitalist world economy' (Schiller 1976: 10). Hamelink (1995: 113) argues that such adaptations merely ensnare 'consumers, particularly young ones, to watch programmes and in the process influence their tastes, lifestyles, and moral values'.

In turn, these theorists celebrate episodes and strategies of cultural resistance towards media imperialism. France and the European Commission have sought to protect indigenous film and cultural industries from the worldwide 'flood' of cheap, low-grade American media products (Hamelink 1994: 180–1, 1995: 114).[21] Schiller (1976: 106–9) advocates popular public participation in alternative forms of mass communication, which Hamelink (1994) understands as a contemporary human right.

Sports broadcasting provides some evidence for this strand of homogenization theory. Most obviously, television TNCs and powerful European football systems (such as Serie A, the EPL, UEFA) ensure that images of major continental tournaments are beamed remorselessly into developing

---

[21]Elsewhere, Canada has endeavoured to counteract perceived Americanization at economic, political and cultural levels (Smith 1994).

societies, notably Africa, East Asia, and even South America. The core-to-periphery flow of media content is very rarely reversed, for example through live UK screening of Latin American fixtures. In turn, TNCs advertise their standardized products, and the generalized Western consumerist lifestyle, to football audiences across developing nations (cf. Sklair 2002).

However, staunch applications of homogenization theory can stretch the cultural evidence. Importantly, some reverse flows do occur across global and 'mini-global' plains. For example, Argentinian and Brazilian leagues attract international interest, particularly across Iberia for obvious ethno-historical reasons. In non-core football nations, television stations add crucial contextualization and 'vernacularization' to their coverage of leading European or South American fixtures (cf. Appadurai 1998). Thus, for example, in South Korea, local television stations have their own studio discussions and commentators to interpret English Premier League matches; special attention is paid, wherever possible, to the performances of Korean players.

Some homogenization arguments might borrow from Wallerstein (1974, 2000) to differentiate 'core' (high-income), 'peripheral' (low-income) and 'semi-peripheral' (middle-income) societies, but it is problematic to translate these categories directly into world football. For example, core global nations like the United States and Japan have semi-peripheral football systems that rarely grace European television screens. Similar hazards surround the core/semi-peripheral classification of small Western European national league systems.

Where football does fit Wallerstein's categories, the vitality of 'peripheral' nations is still evidenced, for example by the state subsidizing of national teams or airing of local sports events on television. In football, as in the wider context, national groups are more focused on the challenge from neighbouring or historically significant 'others', rather than 'core' nations as a whole. For Argentinians, fixtures against Brazil germinate the strongest sentiments; for the Dutch, it is the German game; for the Chinese or South Koreans, it is the Japanese; and for the Scots, it is the English. Moreover, core nations have themselves become at least partly 'peripheralized' through the mass entry and settlement of peoples from developing nations. Thus, in football, we find Zimbabwean sides in England, or North African teams in France, playing friendly fixtures before thousands of local and migrant spectators.

We may ask, too, when elite European leagues are being watched by African or Asian populations, whether the homogenization thesis provides the most plausible explanation. To those with little football engagement, it may appear so. However, if we appreciate that viewers critically engage with television content, and that many will be inured in football's cultural complexities, then an alternative judgement is fairer: that these audiences have, quite rationally, chosen to view and to appreciate the world's most aesthetic, technically sophisticated displays of football skill. Indeed, young players actively seek to imitate and emulate these global talents, thus football's diverse aesthetic and technical qualities hold a stronger currency than its simple consumerist adjuncts.

Finally, the homogenization thesis is far less controversial when explaining aspects of the 'particularization of universalism' which, in short, gives rise to global similarities that structure national differences. Some insightful convergence arguments identify a transnational social isomorphism across nation states whereby national identities, practices, and structures are constructed according to universal standards and procedures (Robertson 1995: 30–1; Meyer et al. 1997). In football, such convergence is evidenced in the standardized structures of *particular* national football associations, league systems, and calendars of competition.

Heterogenization

Theories of cultural heterogenization pivot on a variety of keywords, notably 'creolization', 'indigenization', and 'vernacularization'. To begin considering these, the concept of 'creolization' describes the 'creative interplays' between cultural cores and peripheries, creating creole cultural forms and rhizomic identities, such as in language, cuisine, and film (Hannerz 1992: 264–6; Vergès 2001: 179). For Hannerz, creolization enables the periphery to 'talk back' to the centre, for example as Third World music becomes 'world music', or 'ghetto' phrases enter mainstream society.

In football, cross-civilizational exchanges fire intensive creolization processes. For example, Western observers are often struck by Asian football cultural values and practices that, in contrast to Europe and South America, emphasize consensus, orderliness, and politeness (see Moffett 2003). In Africa, Levi-Strauss (1966: 31) noted that the Gahuku-Gama people of New Guinea ritualized football in accordance with indigenous values, wherein the social humiliation of defeat was purposively alleviated by staging fixtures on consecutive days, thereby providing losers with further chances to win (Bromberger 1995: 299). Football's popular history has many wider instances whereby the periphery 'talks back' to the centre, for example when South Americans developed particular technical skills (for instance, the *chilena* or 'bicycle kick', or the swerving free kick) that were then mimicked in 'core' European nations.

Problematically, creolization implies that, prior to the making of creole cultural forms, there existed authentic and sharply distinctive 'core' and 'peripheral' phenomena. Alternatively, creolization features the interplay of already creolized cultural forms. Thus, in football, for example, it is impossible to trace the histories of playing styles back to particular, autonomously generated national techniques and philosophies.

For Friedman (1999), the alternative concept of 'indigenization' portrays centre–periphery relationships in more cultural political terms. Particularly for developed societies, indigenization registers 'an increasing fragmentation of identities, the break-up of larger identity units, the emergence of cultural politics among indigenous, regional, immigrant, and even national populations' (Friedman 1999: 391). In football, indigenization is evidenced in the strategic resistance of Western Europe's ethnic minorities towards their racial abuse, and in their intensification of ethno-nationalist or regionalist identities at clubs in southern Europe and Australia.

The idea of 'vernacularization' is deployed by Appadurai (1998) to explain the discursive 'domestication' that occurs within general cultural forms, including sport. Appadurai explores how Indians have 'vernacularized' cricket, 'hijacking' the quintessential English imperial sport, notably through television commentaries; meanwhile, 'the game is inscribed in particular ways upon local male bodies' to become 'an emblem of Indian nationhood' (1998: 103, 112). This conception of local–global processes has notable continuities with the Japanese concept of *dochakuka* (or 'glocalization'), discussed later in this chapter.

Similar observations may be advanced regarding football, notably in explaining how television has served to narrate and to popularize distinctive playing styles across nations, especially in South America.

For Pieterse (1995), 'hybridization' describes the mixing of cultures and the move towards translocal cultural forms that range from diasporic communities to cyborg beings and virtual reality. Cultural hybridity is identifiable in particular in the 'global mélange', for example through 'fusion food' or cross-cultural artistic ventures, and helps to foreground the shift from anti-colonial to postcolonial social orders (Pieterse 2007: 142–3). By way of criticism, we may note that the concept of hybridization harbours some potentially risky biological metaphors (Beck 2004: 26), and may promote the false assumption that phenomena which are 'hybridized' had been initially in a state of distinctive cultural purity. However, the concept of hybridization has been deployed most effectively by Archetti (1998a) to explain the construction of cultural identities in the New World, particularly in relation to football in Argentina, wherein the vibrancy of a hybrid society receives translucent expression in sport.

Evidently, each concept is persuasively founded upon substantial research, particularly in peripheral contexts, and encapsulates the agency of quotidian social actors in critically engaging with and transforming global cultural phenomena. However, we forward four caveats for utilization of these terms.

First, noteworthy differences in emphasis and position exist between these keywords – for example, indigenization foregrounds the centrifugal nature of cultural politics in developed societies, while vernacularization illuminates the linguistic and (by extension) corporeal aspects of cultural appropriation.

Second, we should dispute the assumption that societies which ground football are themselves homogeneous entities. Alternatively, for example, Latin American societies are highly variegated, mobile, and dynamic social formations that, in turn, formulate diverse and contested kinds of football-centred practices and beliefs (cf. Leite Lopes 1999: 89–90).

Third, emphasis upon processes of improvisation and heterogenization does not preclude consideration of socio-economic influences and themes. In football, for example, some commentators have interpreted the dribbling skills of lower-class Brazilian players to be both a sporting extension of the street-wise habitus, and a crucial component of public theatre within a highly stratified society, wherein the oppressed defeat their oppressors and so are acclaimed as heroes (*World Soccer*, June 2004). Similarly, albeit somewhat reductively, some European coaches attribute the individualism of African players to wider problems of daily survival in the poorest locales (*Sunday Herald*, 30 January 2000).

Finally, there are important regional and indeed 'civilizational' differences in the way in which these processes come into play. In historical terms, multiple modernities or multiple globalizations may be said to have occurred (see Arnason 1991, 2001; Wagner 2000). Therborn (1995), for example, has argued that modernity developed relatively autonomously in four major sites: in *Europe*, where revolution or reform involved 'endogenous change'; in the *New World*, where transcontinental migration, genocide, and independence occurred; in large parts of the *Middle* and *Far East*, where much modernization was viewed as an external threat or fit for selective importation; and, in most of *Africa, southern and south-east Asia*, where modernity brought conquest, subjugation, and colonialism. Thus, football's spread throughout Europe was symptomatic of the continent's endogenous modern development; the game's limited entry to the New World (specifically, North America) reflected the cultural differentiation of settler populations; its uneven penetration of the Middle and Far East reflected selective cultural importation strategies; and its highly localized relevance in Africa and southern Asia reflected the subjugated position of the indigenous peoples. Thus, at least in the early twentieth century, creolization, vernacularization, and indigenization functioned in different ways within these contexts: for example, with little impact in the Middle and Far East, but with rich vitality in Europe and in South America.

Glocalization

Ritzer: the grobal and the glocal

The homogenization–heterogenization debate has made a significant advance through the work of Ritzer (2003, 2004) on the globalization of culture. Ritzer's thesis is largely built around his binary opposition of the keywords 'grobalization' and 'glocalization'. 'Grobalization' describes a sweeping process of homogenization, wherein the powerful sub-processes of 'capitalism, Americanization and McDonaldization' overwhelm the indigenous cultures of local individuals and social groups (2004: 73). Conversely, the idea of 'glocalization', for Ritzer, encaptures an increasingly heterogeneous world, wherein individuals and social groups are intensively innovative and creative in their dealings with global culture.[22] Ritzer's

---

[22]Cohen and Kennedy (2000: 377) adopt a similar stance, defining glocalization in terms of the selective and adaptive capacities of local actors in relation to global culture. They contrast this definition directly with the machinations of powerful companies in 'customizing' products to suit local markets.

binary opposition has significant continuities with earlier theories, notably the Jihad/McWorld couplet advanced by Barber (1992, 1996).

Ritzer's grobal/glocal binary represents the two extreme poles on an ideal-typical continuum; in reality, most cultural commodities fall somewhere between the two ends. He concludes, pessimistically, that local cultures typically fail to resist grobalization processes. He accepts too that his standpoint is 'both elitist and incurably romantic, nostalgic about the past' in its veneration of particular local cultural commodities (2004: 213).

Ritzer's analysis does benefit from its succinct case studies of cultural production and consumption, and its critical empathy for struggles against dehumanizing rationalization processes. However, we identify four particular differences between his position and our own. First, while his grobal/glocal continuum has significant continuities with our position on universalism/particularism, we adopt a longer-term view of globalization's impact upon, and construction of, 'the local'.

Second, Ritzer's analysis may underplay the highly varied ways in which McDonald's restaurants, or other paragons of rationalization, have originated or been introduced within different historical and cultural contexts. The modus operandi of McDonald's restaurants was in significant part inspired by the White Castle fast-food chain founded in 1921 (Steel 2008: 233–6). Moreover, different social practices and cultural impacts obtain in McDonald's restaurants in Asia compared to North America; for example, in terms of unseated customers 'hovering' at tables, or promoting hygiene standards across all local restaurants (cf. Watson 1997).

Third, Ritzer's analysis is restricted to cultural *commodities*, and so omits to explore fully cultural *meanings* and *institutions*. Indeed, we might argue that his emphasis on cultural commodities may itself be understood as a distinctively American interpretation (or 'glocalization') of the homogenization/ heterogenization debate.[23] Football highlights some of the analytical limitations to this focus on commodities. As we have noted, any football-playing social grouping will produce varied cultural innovations – most obviously in playing styles – that reflect its particular 'ethos', and which are more generally indicative of the *multidimensionality* of globalization.[24]

To substantiate this criticism, we may begin by noting that club football reveals a continuing cross-cultural diversity of institutional frameworks and practices. For example, traditional match-days fall on Sundays in much of southern Europe, but on Saturdays in the north. In Spain, football matches frequently kick off far later in the evening than would be permissible in

---

[23]Ritzer could clarify more precisely his conception concerning the 'nothingness' of grobalization. In our context, it would seem to imply that 'grobal' football is simply 'nothing', a point that is difficult to sustain given the political and economic impact of the professional, commercial game.

[24]For Cowen (2002: 48), an ethos refers to the 'special feel or flavour of a culture', providing 'the background network of world views, styles, and inspirations found in a society, or a framework for cultural interpretation. Ethos therefore is part of an implicit language for creating or viewing art'.

northern Europe. Since the late 1990s, many South and Central American nations feature two league championships inside one season, usually with play-offs to determine the overall champions. Conversely, in Europe, the standard one-championship season remains intact, although nations differ significantly over their format (for example, teams may play two, three, or four times each season) and calendar (for example, many European nations have winter breaks of varying length). In Europe, the team coach is responsible for training senior players, team selection, and tactics, while the general manager conducts player negotiations and other organizational business. In the UK, by contrast, both roles have traditionally fallen to the team manager, although assistant managers and coaches provide back-up. In southern Europe and Latin America, autocratic club presidents can produce extremely high turnovers of managers and players, whereas in northern Europe, managers have tended to be more secure.[25] UK and South American players (most obviously Brazilians) are more renowned for significant drinking or party cultures, unlike Scandinavian or southern European talents. In Italy and Latin America, the entire team typically spends the eve of fixtures together, in practices known as *ritiro* or *la concentración*, but in northern Europe, players only tend to congregate on match day. These and numerous other diverging institutional frameworks and practices are integral to football's culture, but would be overlooked if analysis were restricted to commercial issues.

Fourth, crucially, we differ with Ritzer on the meaning of glocalization. Whereas Ritzer associates glocalization with processes of heterogenization and critical social agency, we understand the term as featuring the possibility of *both* homogeneity and heterogeneity, as we explain below.

Glocalization and the 'duality of glocality'

It is useful to consider the historical and social-scientific development of the concept of glocalization. The word glocalization itself may be traced to the Japanese term *dochakuka*, meaning 'global localization' or 'localized globalization', which was widely used in business circles in the late 1980s to describe the micro-marketing techniques of Sony and other companies, whereby generic products and industrial practices are adapted to suit local conditions (cf. Dicken and Miyamachi 1998: 73; Rothacher 2004: 185, 189).[26] Subsequently established as 'one of the main marketing buzzwords of the beginning of the nineties', glocalization appeared in recent times to underpin the advertising discourses of TNCs like HSBC, which projected itself as 'the world's local bank' (*Oxford Dictionary of New Words* 1991: 134, quoted in Robertson 1992: 174; cf. Gertler 1992: 268).

---

[25]For example, during his 17-year presidential reign at Atlético Madrid, the mercurial Jesus Gil disposed of 39 coaches and recruited 141 players (*World Soccer*, July 2004).

[26]The co-founder of Sony, Akio Morita, understood this as involving the meeting of 'local needs with local operations while developing common global concepts and technologies'. See www.sony.net/Fun/SH/1-29/h1.html

In football, this original form of glocalization is evident in club and league marketing. For example, some European clubs recruit players from the United States or East Asia in part to build consumer/fan bases in these regions. In the United States, Major League Soccer (MLS), which controls the professional club system, has sought to boost crowds by micro-marketing to Latinos in California, notably by having the popular Mexican club Guadalajara open a US 'franchise' (*The Economist*, 30 April 2005).

The social scientists Robertson and Swyngedouw developed the concept of glocalization at around the same time in separate and different ways in the early 1990s. For urban political economists, glocalization has come to describe the rescaling and intensified complexity of networks and systems, notably in the interrelationships between institutional actors at subnational, national and supranational levels (Swyngedouw 1992, 2004; Brenner 1998, 2004). Despite complaints that glocalization is inconsistently defined and applied within this field, the 'scalar' approach certainly chimes with related arguments on the 'cascading' and 'turbulence' of global politics (Rosenau 1990; Jessop and Sum 2000). We consider these points more fully in Chapter 4.

In socio-cultural theory, Robertson (1992, 1994, 1995, 2007c) introduced the concept of glocalization in part to update the old anthropological theory of cultural diffusion by allowing for the intensification of social connectivity and stronger forms of global consciousness. Capturing the broad interplay of the universal and the particular, glocalization registers the 'real world' endeavours of individuals and social groups to ground or to recontextualize global phenomena or macroscopic processes with respect to local cultures (Robertson 1992: 173–4, 1994, 1995). Thus, 'glocalization projects', as practiced by different cultures, represent 'the constitutive features of contemporary globalization' (Robertson 1995: 41). Long-running processes of transnational commingling and interpenetration have resulted in a profusion of 'glocal' cultures, such that the old binary distinction between 'here-it-is' local and 'out-there' global cultures becomes increasingly untenable.

Both socio-cultural and urban political–economic theories of glocalization have significant continuities with Rosenau's (2003) concept of 'fragmegration', which notes the simultaneously fragmenting and integrating forces of globalization. Moreover, our interpretation of glocalization has strong elective affinities to the theorization of relativization set out above (see Robertson 1992, 1995; and White 2004).

In some contrast to Ritzer, our socio-cultural reading of glocalization allows for the production of both cultural divergence *and* convergence, or homogenization *and* heterogenization (Robertson 1995; cf. Ritzer 2004: 73). In other words, a *duality of glocality* is apparent, which foregrounds the societal co-presence of sameness and difference, and the 'mutually implicative' relationships between homogenizing and heterogenizing tendencies (Robertson and White 2003b: 4; Giulianotti and Robertson 2007a, 2007b). Notably, Ritzer (2004: 73) himself recognized that, in earlier work, Robertson 'is certainly interested in both sides of the local–global, homogenization–heterogenization continua'. We recognize, of course, that much social-scientific discussion on glocalization has focused hitherto on the heterogenization side, partly to rebut more reductive arguments regarding cultural homogenization. Yet, as Miller et al. (1999: 19) put it, glocalization is an important term 'because global forces do not override locality, and because homogenization and heterogenization are equally crucial'. Hence, we concur with Cowen's (2002: 16, 129) observation that 'cultural homogenization and heterogenization are not alternatives or substitutes; rather, they tend to come together' and frequently produce cultures that are 'commonly diverse'.

Duality of glocality and football

Football provides a rich substantive field for exploring the complex 'duality of glocality' in regard to convergence and divergence. If we examine the game historically in regard to the five phases, we may identify how football's global diffusion has been underpinned by different interrelationships between the universal and the particular.

During football's *germinal* and *incipient* phases, football's initial diffusion was facilitated through social contacts with the British and its cultural appeal to Anglophile local elites. In more extreme circumstances, some cultures marginalized football to develop alternative national sports.

During the *take-off* phase (the 1870s to the mid-1920s), upon its favourable cultural reception, football was glocalized through a universalization of particularism. Specific local cultures worked inside the game's universal rules to establish their own football 'traditions', as illustrated by distinctive corporeal techniques, playing styles, aesthetic codes, administrative structures, and interpretative vocabularies.

During the *struggle-for-hegemony* phase (the 1920s to the late 1960s), football's glocalization also featured a particularization of universalism, as international tournaments and governing bodies were established, and as standardized national football institutions were created across the world, notably through affiliation to FIFA.

During the *uncertainty* phase (the 1970s to the early 2000s), glocalization processes were accelerated by intensified transcultural flows of labour, information, capital, and commodities, all of which may engender non-national forms of cultural identity. Glocalization registered stronger forms of global compression, thus the world appears as a kind of cultural switchboard, as different identity forms come more frequently into mutual co-presence.

Football provides many specific case studies for unravelling the 'duality of glocality' in regard to homogenization and heterogenization. Here, we provide four illustrations of such interdependency in regard to laws, belief systems, media framing and interpretation of matches, and playing styles.

First, homogenization is evidenced in the global diffusion of football's *laws*, and in FIFA's endeavour to synchronize the interpretations of different national referees, for example by running intensive courses for officials before each World Cup finals. As one English official concluded, 'There is no such thing as an English, Italian or French football set of rules. There is one football and one set of rules' (*FIFA Magazine*, June 1998). Similar convergence strategies have been evidenced by FIFA's 'Fair Play' slogan, which appeals globally to the ethical consciousness of football participants. According to Sepp Blatter, the Fair Play 'catchphrase' is 'a welcome intruder into all languages and cultures', and has 'succeeded in building bridges across communication and cultural gaps' (*FIFA Magazine*, August 1997).

However, significant pressures towards cultural divergence remain intact. On rule interpretation, UK referees, for example, continue to permit robust challenges that central and southern European officials tend to penalize. FIFA's own research revealed significant differences among European players over the parameters of 'fair play': German and French players disagreed over the moral status of 'revenge fouls' or 'professional fouls' that prevented goals being scored, while English players were particularly intolerant of players who faked injuries (*FIFA Magazine*, June 1997).[27]

Second, *religious and supernatural belief systems* display significant forms of convergence and divergence. Players, teams, and fans in many cultures utilize religious divination to help secure their goals, but there are obviously significant cultural differences on this matter. In Europe, many players have their own distinctive pre-match superstitions, such as eating particular meals, wearing lucky amulets, or being last onto the pitch. In Latin America, notably Brazil, the remarkable growth of evangelical and Pentecostal religious movements has directly impacted upon grassroots football culture. The 'Athletes for Christ' movement in Brazil has an estimated 7000 members, most of them footballers, including *seleção* stars Kaka, Jorginho, Mazinho, Lucio, Edmilson, and Taffarel (Bellos 2002: 219). Members of this movement celebrate goals and victories with the display of proselytizing messages, such as 'God Loves You'.

In some contrast, in sub-Saharan Africa, witchcraft or *juju* practices are more prominent, as teams seek to deflate the energies of opponents, or to ward off malignant spirits, for example by wearing certain amulets, carrying human or animal bones to games, casting spells on the pitch before kick-off (for example, by burying sacrificed animals or urinating on markings), and spreading *muti* (magic medicine) around the ground (Igbinovia 1985: 142–3; Leseth 1997). African football authorities sought to 'modernize' their international image by comparing these practices to cannibalism and banning 'juju-men' from fixtures, but with little success (the

---

[27]Nor do these observations require us to accept uncritically the lofty self-proclamations of particular nations regarding their football ethos. Brazilian football may be typologized as the 'beautiful game', but domestic fixtures are typically blighted by brutal and persistent fouling. For example, in one weekend, at the 2003 Paulista (São Paulo) championship final, there were three red cards, ten yellows, over fifty fouls, and assorted brawls; a day later, at the 2003 Carioca (Rio) championship final, there were 78 fouls, three red cards and a ten-minute fight between players and coaches.

Observer, 10 February 2002). Thus, while the transnational existence of divination practices confirms cultural homogenization, the very varied forms and contents of these religious belief systems point to heterogenization.

Third, *media framing and interpretation* of major football events harbour both cross-cultural convergence and divergence. At the game's international mega-events, most nations share the same television images from fixtures, yet different national broadcasters employ their own journalists, commentators, summarizers, and analysts to narrate and interpret the game in distinctive national ways (Hafez 2007: 26). Television audiences may show strong convergence in terms of the global teams and players that they prefer to watch (Brazil, for example, are particular global favourites); yet, like players, significant cultural differences remain in how viewers interpret the crucial incidents, such as free-kick and penalty decisions (cf. Katz and Liebes 1993).

Fourth, the convergence/divergence debate is especially lively in regard to football's *playing styles, techniques and tactics.* Some pessimists lament the perceived worldwide influence of technocratic, instrumental coaches who impose standardized, sterile, and disenchanting tactics upon games. As noted in Chapter 1, historical changes in playing formations have tended to be defensive and, through successful implementation, have spread internationally.

'Football science' too has undergone international diffusion since the 1980s. The world's best teams are increasingly prepared and organized according to identical principles, while individual performances are measured according to performative criteria, such as pass completion or tackle rates, shots on- or off-target, and distances run during matches. Unpredictable clashes of playing style rarely occur at international tournaments since the world's elite players now play in the same leagues, compete regularly against each other, and are drilled in similar tactical thinking (cf. *Toronto Star,* 10 July 2006).

On the heterogenization side, the very criticism of standardization in football points to its contestation by coaches, players, and fans. Players who receive the greatest adulation and richest rewards are renowned for transcending standardized forms of play, for redefining the technical and geometric possibilities of football, for their stunning unpredictability. Some clubs – like Ajax, Real Madrid, Celtic, or Manchester United – have constructed potent 'traditions' of highly fluid, entertaining, even spectacular styles that resist regimentation. These discourses sometimes acquire a strong national inflection, for example Spanish football followers dismiss the Italian penchant for such cautious, inflexible tactical systems as 'anti-football'.

Additionally, playing formations still continue to display much variation in form and implementation. Some nationally distinctive line-ups do appear, such as Argentina's 3-3-1-3 formation in the early 2000s. More commonly, even where a standardized team formation like 4-4-2 is favoured, major cultural differences arise over its implementation, as illustrated by the titles of coaching videos and DVDs, such as *Coaching the Dutch 4-3-3, Futbol! Coaching the Brazilian 4-4-2, The Italian 4-4-2, Coaching the English Premier League 4-4-2,* and *Coaching the European 3-5-2.*

Team formations may be similar, but the national or regional flavour defines how the team actually plays.

However, we should avoid advancing an over-simplified version of the heterogenization thesis in two senses. First, it may be argued that we should beware of slipping into a simple essentializing or 'Orientalizing' of cultural difference in terms of playing style. Although the theory of Orientalism needs to be considered with caution, we may consider how Orientalism is evident in the way that Europeans tend to classify African and Latin American playing styles in rather ethnocentric ways, as anti-modern, rhythmic, expressive, flamboyant, unpredictable, inconsistent, magical, and irrational, in contradistinction to the self-congratulatory Western qualities of consistency, reliability, and rationality (cf. Said 1995). Evidence of Orientalist discourses may also be identified in the media stereotyping of football regions and nations, and in the language of some leading football officials who have, for example, complained that the 'natural juice' of African football is being 'squeezed out' by European coaches (cf. O'Donnell 1994; *FIFA News*, February 2002).

Second, we should remind ourselves that heterogenization in peripheral contexts is typically marked by creolization processes, through diverse kinds of engagement between core and periphery. For example, African football has long been influenced by other football cultures through forms of colonial, post-colonial, and media-centred social contact, thereby engendering different playing styles across the regions. East African nations such as Uganda and Kenya were weaned on British styles of play, emphasizing highly energetic, combative, long-ball methods. The recruitment of European coaches, such as Yugoslavs in west Africa, produced better passing games and stronger organization. Alternatively, some nations such as Zambia and Zaire were more directly influenced by fluid and artistic Brazilian styles, in large part through watching videos of great South American players.

The convergence–divergence debate on playing style acquires additional layers of complexity through the intensive reflexivity of different societies on this very subject. In Latin America, the playing style debates become particularly polarized over the extent to which nations should homogenize towards employing scientific, 'European' methods, or retain and advance their cultural diversity. Some analysts suggest that, when confronted with strong global competition, Brazil and Argentina have tended to adopt markedly different glocalization strategies. From the 1960s onwards, Brazil looked strongly to scientific rationalism and organization, emphasizing physical preparation and elaborate medical support. Conversely, Argentina emphasized cultural differentiation through a veneration of a highly technical, *criollo* style (*World Soccer*, Summer 2005). Yet in Argentina itself, a fundamental ideological division between convergence and divergence strategies is understood to be embodied by two World Cup-winning coaches: the pro-improvisational, leftist, divergent César Luis Menotti (in 1978); and the ultra-pragmatic, convergent Carlos Bilardo (in 1986) (Archetti 1998a). Various Latino writers, coaches and football analysts have lent support to the divergent position, by castigating football's over-theorization by 'pseudo-scientists'. The renowned

Uruguayan writer Eduardo Galeano celebrates football as 'the art of the unforeseeable', while former Real Madrid and Argentina star Jorge Valdano insists that in popular football culture, a 'seduction by the sphere' occurs wherein 'you can't interrupt emotion' (quoted in Arbena 2000: 88).

Overall, we might observe that, in regard to the homogenization–heterogenization debate, football games themselves serve to narrate or to dramatize the dilemmas of standardization and differentiation. In broad terms, matches continually pit the technical efficiency of homogenization against the mould-breaking divergence of improvisation and innovation. While standardization is more associated with defensive play, differentiation is more commonly identified in attack. As Guillermo Stábile, Argentina's manager during the 1940s and 1950s, once insisted, 'you can organize a defence, but you had better not try to organize your attack' (Lodziak 1966: 13). In defence, organization is paramount, with players tutored to fulfil set roles and duties that usually correspond to global coaching manuals. In attack, while set plays (such as free-kicks and corners) may be studiously rehearsed, building attacks in open play is best achieved through creativity, improvisation, and the outfoxing of opponents. In this way, in the shifting balance between calculated defence and improvisational attack, the football match itself becomes a potent and unresolved dramatization of the duality of glocality.

The USA and Americanization: Succor for Soccer?

The subject of 'Americanization' is an important, wide-ranging strand of the general homogenization heterogenization debate. Theories of Americanization advance a particular kind of cultural imperialism thesis, in interpreting the United States as effectively globalizing and imposing its culture upon other societies (cf. Crothers 2007: 22–5). Cultural Americanization is understood to penetrate other regional, national or local cultures, and to be advanced particularly by American corporations such as McDonald's, Disney, Coca-Cola, Nike, and Microsoft. Cultural Americanization may be understood as functioning at two levels of intensity: *hard* Americanization involves the destruction of local cultural practices and products, and their substitution by American alternatives (for instance, US fast food); *soft* Americanization involves the everyday influence of specific Americanisms upon local cultural practices and products (e.g. cheerleading and majorette displays at local galas).

A *prima facie* consideration of football's historical globalization seems to refute the hard Americanization thesis, pointing instead to separate spheres of sporting development between the USA and most other nations or regions. First, the United States has played little role in football's global diffusion and cross-cultural flows, such as administrative leadership, tournament successes, coaching techniques, or player mobility. In turn, despite strong backing from US-based TNCs, the leading American sports have failed to dislodge football from its dominant global status (cf. Katz 1994; Kelly 2007).

Second, more substantively, US sport provides a prodigious illustration of the broad 'American Exceptionalism' thesis, of a national *sonderweg* (or 'special path') relative to cultural trends in other parts of the world (cf. Markovits and Hellerman 2001; Pieterse 2004). In the late nineteenth century, the old folk football games of Britain – with their highly localized and rather amorphous rules – were adapted in unique ways in the United States, to create the distinctive 'American football' code. Since that time, for most Americans, the word 'football' has referred to a particular, indigenous game, while the global game of 'soccer' connotes a rather 'non-American' pastime.

Moreover, American sportspeople sustained and advanced their own sporting models, in part by consciously rejecting modern European games redolent of the Old World's colonialist, nationalist, and socialist cultures. Whereas association football became the 'national sport' across Europe, Latin America and much of Africa, sports like American football or baseball received potent support throughout the United States' civil society, notably the education system, mass media, and consumer industries. For the tens of millions of migrants entering the United States through the twentieth century, the adoption of these American sports was an important symbolic means of abandoning the old Europe, and assimilating and showing patriotic commitment to the new society. To add everyday impact, American popular culture has tended to ignore association football or, particularly in local and regional media, to poke fun at major events such as the World Cup finals (cf. Foer 2004: 240–6).

It may be added that, somewhat remarkably, the globalization of sport is unlike other popular cultural forms (such as film, music, and food) which, in contrast, have been heavily influenced or even inspired by the United States (Cvetkovich and Kellner 1997; Ritzer 2004). Sassoon (2002) argues that the globalization of US culture was facilitated in part by the multicultural diversity of the domestic market, which enabled American corporations to test their products at home before pursuing international consumers. However, unlike other cultural forms, US sport was never so geared towards international diffusion, but tended instead to satisfy itself with domestic engagement, in part through a 'solipsistic' celebration of the 'American way' (cf. Martin and Reeves 2001). Such cultural introspection ensured that, beyond North American shores, and unlike other popular forms such as pop music or film, football had a relatively clear and unchallenged run across the emerging global sports field.

Moving beyond these initial observations, we do warn that the keyword 'Americanization' itself has some inherently problematic aspects. On one hand, the term misleads us into viewing the United States as a homogeneous and unitary entity, particularly at a time when North America is becoming increasingly heterogeneous through the influences of migrant groups and new forms of identity differentiation (Robertson 2004: 261–3). Indicatively, across the United States, football is particularly popular among migrants born in Europe and Latin America, providing Latinos in particular with a rare cultural opportunity to celebrate publically and en masse a form of distinctive identity, as manifested by the foundation of 'ethnic' teams, or by cheering for their 'home' national sides inside American stadiums or while viewing on television.

On the other hand, the term *USAmericanization* may be more accurate in denoting the intended meaning of the process in question, as it separates Canada, Mexico, central and South America from the United States (cf. Robertson 2004: 257). In football, it may be argued that the game has really undergone long-term *SouthAmericanization* processes, given the aesthetic, technical and political influences of Brazil and Argentina at a global level. Here, we continue to use the term 'Americanization' to denote the perceived spread of US culture, but with these caveats firmly in mind.

If we turn to examine the specificities of US influence upon football, it is possible to identify some soft and selective types of Americanization as occurring at transnational levels. Reflecting the wider influence of 'technical' aspects of US culture, American marketing methods and television production techniques have been copied in European football, such as to 'makeover' the Champions League (cf. Marling 2006; the *Guardian*, 15 February 2007). Some economists identify a business shift in European professional football from the old sports model of 'utility maximization' (emphasizing club success and status over profit) towards the more Americanized model of 'profit maximization' (see Chapter 3). European football leagues also show various kinds of financial and juridical convergence with American sports, such as in the sharing of national revenues across teams, the linking of television revenues to market size, the retention of gate-money by home sides, the role of agents in player contract negotiations, the advent of free agency, and the massive rise in media involvement. Football may yet consider following the American path in establishing salary caps (Andreff and Staudohar 2000). Moreover, there has been a significant penetration of European football, notably in England, by American capital. By spring 2008, three of England's top six sides (Manchester United, Liverpool, Aston Villa) were owned by US sports entrepreneurs.

One intriguing matter concerns the role of quantitative data in sport and its possible relationship to Americanization processes. Historically, there have been strong cultural differences: while US sports like baseball and American football are traditionally packed with statistical information for understanding performances, many football societies have long refused to reduce the game to number-crunching.[28] However, since the mid-1990s, data analysis has been increasingly prominent in professional football across the world, for example through the *ProZone* system which tracks and measures the performance indicators of all players. Thus, it is difficult to determine whether football's quantification represents a diffusion of American sporting culture or a parallel development in sport's rationalization.

---

[28]For example, distinguished football journalists like Brian Glanville lambasted the statistics-based tactics of English coaching gurus Charles Reep and Charles Hughes, who insisted that most goals are scored from less than three passes and inside so-called 'POMO' areas (Positions of Maximum Opportunity).

We need to consider too the critical reflexivity of social actors in regard to perceived processes of Americanization. In some circumstances, resistance towards perceived Americanization may be framed as a sporting 'clash of civilizations' (cf. Huntington 1993), as European football cultures actively differentiate their sporting ethos (expressed through senses of deep solidarity and belonging) to the perceived American emphasis on commerce (wherein clubs are mere 'franchises' that may be bought, sold, and transferred regardless of community ties). These kinds of discourse were evident in England during and soon after the takeover of Manchester United by the Glazer family in 2005, and following Liverpool's purchase by two US sports entrepreneurs in 2006; indeed, Liverpool fans held demonstrations to demand the club's sale to a Dubai business group. Of course, this sporting clash of civilizations was overlain by the strengthening of anti-American political sentiments in Europe, particularly after the Iraq War.

Other forms of perceived Americanization in football are also criticized by many of the game's close followers. The entry of cheerleaders and pre-game 'razzmatazz' into football is mocked by some 'traditionalist' forces, including longstanding US-based followers of the game.[29] Prior to the 1994 World Cup finals, intense criticisms were inspired by rumours that serious changes to the laws of football were being mooted – such as extending goal-sizes or replacing halves with quarter periods – to attract US television stations and audiences. Even in the United States, American sports marketing techniques may fail to ignite public interest in football: for example, the short-lived women's national soccer league (WUSA) alienated many prospective spectators through promotional exercises that normalized middle-class family audiences and emphasized top-down strategies for stage-managing crowd 'atmosphere' (Jones 2007: 243–4).

However, we should note that, despite a reflex, critical association of Americanization with commodification in sport and beyond, the real influence of market principles is rather more complex and varied. It may be argued that, like the entry of quantification, football's wider commodification from the late 1980s onwards would have occurred without any mimicry of US sports marketing techniques (cf. Sklair 1995: 153). Moreover, European football is in many ways rather more free-market than US sports, where league 'cartels', salary caps, and revenue-sharing are crucial economic features. Additionally, unlike the vast majority of elite football clubs, US sports teams do not carry sponsor logos on their shirts.

Football cultures across the world sustain major differences from the American sports model. Football typically generates more partisan atmospheres and rivalries in most US sports; most elite US sports fixtures have tiny representations of 'away' fans, unlike most top football games; and elite football players contest more vigorously the decisions by officials than do their US sporting

---

[29]Perhaps indicatively, in Germany, Bayern Munich are sometimes known, somewhat critically, as FC Hollywood, for their players' celebrity lifestyles.

counterparts. Thus, rather than being sucked ineluctably into basic convergence with US sport, football continues to display strong forms of cross-cultural, cosmopolitan diversity. Some analysts have argued that American foreign policy should be more attuned to exploiting these cosmopolitan aspects of football. For example, US military commanders were deemed to have missed a major diplomatic opportunity to exercise 'soft power' when they failed to screen the 2006 World Cup finals during the disastrous occupation of Iraq.[30]

Pace the Americanization thesis, football points to three kinds of 'reverse colonization' or *Americolonization*, whereby the 'global game' penetrates the USA. First, football does have a complex, submerged social history in the United States. In the late nineteenth century, soccer-style games were played at Yale while American teams contested representative fixtures (Gorn and Goldstein 1993: 130–1). Between the world wars, European immigrants developed local US football systems while many European and South American clubs regularly toured North America. In the post-war period, national soccer leagues were established. The North American Soccer League (NASL), founded in 1968, was laden with highly-paid senior world stars – such as Pelé, Beckenbauer, Neeskens, Chinaglia, and Carlos Alberto at New York Cosmos – but the tournament expanded too rapidly, failed to sustain national interest, and collapsed in 1984 (Wangerin 2006).[31] A modest but relatively successful indoor league system then maintained the national presence of professional football through the 1980s and 1990s. Plans for the foundation of a new national league system received a major boost when FIFA awarded the 1994 World Cup finals to the United States, and fixtures were played before very strong crowds, often in extremely hot conditions. The United States has also notched up some noteworthy football achievements, competing in all but one of the World Cup finals, defeating England in 1950, and reaching the later rounds for the first time in 2002.

Second, it is clear that US soccer has not usurped the financial and national-cultural power of the 'Big 4' sports – American football, baseball, basketball, and ice hockey. However, US soccer has made massive international and grassroots progress since the early 1980s, becoming the most popular youth team sport with an estimated 17.6 million listed players, over 40 per cent of them female, and around two-thirds aged under 18.[32] Football is particularly strong among white, middle-class, suburban school-children and college students, whose participation is often aided by family-oriented 'soccer moms', a distinctive socio-political category dating from

[30]As argued by Nicholas Cull, of the Center for Public Diplomacy at the University of Southern California (see *The Times*, 24 June 2007).

[31]The Cosmos' name, short of course for Cosmopolitans, was inspired in part by the New York Mets (short for Metropolitans) baseball team; the former title reflected the (for that time) exceptional international diversity of players in the team.

[32]See www.ussoccerplayers.com/resource_center/for_parents/basic_info_for_youth_parents/447864.html

the early 1990s (cf. Andrews et al. 1997). The US women's soccer team won the FIFA World Cup (1991, 1999) and 1996 Olympic gold medal at the Atlanta Games before national television audiences of over 40 million. Star players like Mia Hamm, Michelle Akers, and Brandi Chastain have received greater national accolades than their male counterparts.

Third, US soccer established a new professional league, the MLS, in 1996, with ten 'franchise' teams, growing to thirteen by 2007, following various expansions and contractions. MLS follows the US monopoly sport model, wherein a franchise league is controlled by a cartel of permanent members with no promotion or relegation. Television contracts were established with Univision/Telemundo and ESPN/ABC, and high profile TNC sponsorships with Honda, Budweiser, Kelloggs, and Yahoo, followed by a $100 million, ten-year deal with adidas in 2004. Learning from NASL's disastrously rapid expansionism, the MLS has controlled growth strategies and restrictive salary caps (just over $2 million for each club's roster of players in 2005). The entry of a Toronto team in 2005 highlighted MLS's pan-continental possibilities, but the most ambitious measure saw the LA Galaxy team sign the world's most famous and commercially successful player, David Beckham, in 2007, in a five-year $250 million deal. Reports initially surfaced that Beckham's future team-mates – some of whom earned $12,900 annually – resented his salary, although this issue disappeared when the player landed in LA (*Sport Illustrated*, 4 May 2007).

While its survival and expansion points to the US game's underlying strengths, the full development of MLS has been hampered by financial, political, and cultural problems. First, in its opening five years, MLS lost $250 million, and revenues from crowds and sponsors declined. By 2003, six of the ten teams were owned by one corporation (Phil Anschutz's AEG Group), confirming the limited football interests of other US corporations and sports behemoths. The salary cap – which saw over 80 players earning under $55,000 in 2004 – restricted MLS's competitiveness in international labour markets. In response, MLS introduced a 'designated player' rule in 2007, enabling each club to sign an elite player whose first $350,000 in wages would only count against the salary cap; the remainder would be covered by outside sponsors.[33] At the same time, efforts to broaden club ownership had been successful, with ten different parties controlling the thirteen clubs.

Second, MLS struggled to appeal to the established football-supporting public, primarily first- and second-generation migrants from Europe and Latin America, who tend instead to maintain allegiances to clubs 'back home'. Many subscription television networks serve these migrant audiences, such as GolTV with Iberian and Latin American games, or Setanta Sports which covers Scottish fixtures. MLS is often a net loser when foreign clubs travel to play summer exhibition fixtures in the United States. For

---

[33]Similarly in Australia, each A-League club is allowed two 'marquee players', whose wages are privately financed and do not count against the annual salary cap (set at AU$1.8 million for 2007–8).

example, on the same day in 2004, the MLS's All-Star game (with 21,000 spectators) was seriously overshadowed by the Manchester United–Milan friendly in New York (which drew 74,000 fans).

Third, MLS's financial travails have been mirrored elsewhere in US soccer. The Championsworld corporation that organizes summer tours for foreign clubs filed for bankruptcy protection in 2005 after accruing £5 million debts. WUSA collapsed, in part due to large losses ($80 million over three years) and national television audiences of below 100,000.

Fourth, the Latino influence is met with some ambivalence by US soccer. Latinos comprise around half of all MLS followers and 40 million of all Americans (*The Economist*, 30 April 2005; cf. Jewell and Molina 2005). To capitalize, MLS awarded a franchise to the Mexican team Guadalajara, to be sited in LA, for 2005, while senior executives ruminated on a possible merger with the Mexican First Division. Yet MLS tends to repeat American corporate and media misunderstandings of Latinos as a homogeneous, 'pan-ethnic' community rather than as a diverse category in terms of nationality, language, age, class, and gender (Delgado 1999). US soccer is still largely dominated by European-style rather than Latino coaches, and so tends to privilege white college players.

Overall, MLS and the strongest US sports continue to face analogous problems in different contexts, in attempting to dislodge more powerful competitors in the domestic or global marketplaces. US soccer faces a broader challenge in attempting to mould a popular national sporting identity from a relatively niche base across an increasingly diverse social landscape.

Cosmopolitanism

A further crucial debate on globalization and culture, and on the problem of homogenization/heterogenization, concerns the issue of cosmopolitanism (see, for example, Breckenridge et al. 2002; Vertovec and Cohen 2002; Beck 2006; Delanty 2006; Fine 2007; Rumford 2007). It is important to begin here by differentiating general and social-scientific understandings of the cosmopolitan. Commonsensical, essentialist positions tend to imply that cosmopolitans hold an innate superiority or greater moral value – as relatively bourgeois, liberal, and cultured global citizens – compared to the perceived chauvinism and parochialism of geographically fixed 'locals' (cf. Hannerz 1990; Eagleton 2006). Historically, at least in Anglophone societies, this latter division between cosmopolitans and locals may incline towards a dismissive view of 'uncultured' football players and other professional, usually 'lower-class' sports people. While this type of labeling has always been sociologically questionable, we might note in passing that in world football in recent years, increasing numbers of elite players, often aged in their early 20s, have become fluent in two or more languages, thus displaying an important form of cultural cultivation that remains rare among the professional classes, including academics, in the Anglophone world.

Conversely, we understand cosmopolitanism in more sociological terms in three broad senses. First, cosmopolitanism registers heightened degrees of experience and awareness of cultural variety and interplay, as partial consequences of increasing transnational connectivity through telecommunications and travel. Second, cosmopolitanism does not necessarily involve a fundamentalist opposition to 'the local'; indeed, without local cultures, the cosmopolitan is out of business. A 'rooted' or 'patriotic' cosmopolitanism may arise wherein social groups simultaneously engage with their 'home' society and other peoples, places, and cultures (Appiah 1997: 618). Third, particular types of cosmopolitanism may also be understood in normative or ethical terms, as advocating greater recognition or openness towards other cultures.

In many ways, contemporary cosmopolitanism is a mundane or banal characteristic of everyday socio-cultural life. Billig (1994) employs the idea of 'banal nationalism' to describe how images, symbols, and other references to national identity are routinely encountered in any nation. We consider that the concepts of 'banal cosmopolitanism'[34] or 'banal relativization' may also be advanced to register the quotidian, everyday experiences of cultural diversity, such as in food, language, nationality, dress, and popular tastes.

In Western European football, banal cosmopolitanism is evidenced by the multiplicity of international players in local teams, and the array of foreign clubs and tournaments that may be watched on television. But, in some contrast to Billig's original concept, we would add that football crystallizes periods of *exceptional nationalism*, as well as its banal variant. For example, it is increasingly the case that, for the duration of major international tournaments, symbols of national allegiance become suddenly ubiquitous in relatively unusual places, such as when flags adorn homes, offices, car windows, and major thoroughfares.

In regard to banal cosmopolitanism, broader knowledge of diverse football systems is facilitated by diasporic groups, satellite television, and the cultural valorization of fresh and diverse experiences. Leading European football divisions are presented in their distinctive national-cultural languages: initially, UK fans were familiarized with the *Bundesliga* (Germany), *Serie A* (Italy) and *La Liga* (Spain), but latterly we have *Ligue 1* (France) and *Eredivisie* (Holland). In passing, we may note the considerable continuities here with the duality of glocalization: everyday cosmopolitan tastes are attuned to experience and to absorb different grassroots football cultures and league systems, while sporting competitions are formulated and sometimes rebranded to appeal to diverse audiences.

A further aspect of contemporary cosmopolitanism concerns the proliferation of sporting crossovers. Certainly, we appreciate that there have long been individual, group, and institutional ties between football and other sports. For example, many leading football teams on the European mainland and in Latin America emerged from multi-sport clubs during the take-off phase of globalization. Several leading football clubs in Spain, Greece, Turkey, and the wider Balkans region have elite professional basketball sides. Moreover, many individual players are embedded within the established sporting and body cultures of their wider society, hence the continuing links

---

[34]Beck (2004: 21) also employs this concept.

between Brazilian players and capoeira, English players and sports like cricket or boxing, Irish players and 'Gaelic football', or Brazil's supporter associations and the 'samba schools' that compete during *carnaval*.

However, as major football clubs and competitions become increasingly transnational, so more diverse kinds of sporting crossover start to emerge. In terms of club ownership, US sports entrepreneurs have bought several leading football teams, especially in England. In terms of training methods, team formations, and tactics, football coaches have started to borrow more from US and other sports such as basketball and American football. In terms of technical skills, some elite players utilize their expertise in other disciplines on the football field; for example, the acrobatic Swedish star Zlatan Ibrahimovic is adept in taekwondo, a Korean martial art. Greater levels of transnational migration also contribute to this cosmopolitan complexity; for example, the Italian forward, Christian Vieri, is a renowned cricket fan, due to spending part of his childhood in Sydney, Australia.

Returning to Appiah's insights on 'rooted cosmopolitanism', football provides some of the strongest historical illustrations of this process on a mass scale, pitting teams and their representative communities against each other across national and transnational terrains. Most supporters are socialized into a cosmopolitan appreciation of the aesthetic possibilities of the game itself, even if these qualities are manifested by opponents during fixtures. In playing football, technical development and improvement are only possible through watching and learning from other cultures.

In more recent times, forms of 'virtually rooted cosmopolitanism' arise in football, through a movement beyond old 'national' forms of solidarity and into the creation of collectives that share preferences for particular world players, managers, clubs, and playing styles. For example, among the millions watching the World Cup, we find global 'neo-tribes' of cosmopolitans that identify with, for example, the counter-attacking guile of the 1982 Italians but not the 'pressing' Italians of 1992–4; or that scorn the 'European' Brazilians of 1974, but not the highly expressive 1982 Brazilians; or that admire the flamboyant 1978 Argentinians under Menotti, but not the 1986 or 1990 team under the dour Bilardo (notwithstanding Maradona's brilliance) (cf. Maffesoli 1996). In this way, heightened cosmopolitanism engenders, not an indiscriminate universalism, but fresh modes of cultural differentiation and particularization.

Cosmopolitanism may carry significant forms of particularity that are, for example, rooted in social class, such as through the habitus of new middle-class cosmopolitans (Giulianotti 1999a); cultural aesthetics, such as through favouring certain styles of play or sporting culture; and also ethno-cultural similitude, such as when Argentinians watch Spanish league fixtures. Even extreme forms of chauvinistic localism – such as the display of fascistic symbols inside stadiums – are only sociologically intelligible when contextualized with regard to universal or transcultural processes. We deal with these matters more fully in Chapter 5, but here our preliminary observation is that specific cultures tend to embrace more universalistic and humanistic forms of cosmopolitanism in rather uneven ways. For many cultures, the shock of banal cosmopolitanism engenders cultural introspection and societal self-inquiry, setting in motion a generalized 'search for fundamentals' which *may* at times be manifested through forms of xenophobic behaviour (Robertson 1992: 164–6).

It is useful, therefore, to differentiate between *thick* and *thin* cosmopolitanism. Thick cosmopolitanism features a relatively universalistic engagement with or embracing of other cultures. Thin cosmopolitanism involves a more pragmatic orientation towards other societies, adopting an 'equal-but-different' stance while instrumentally borrowing aspects of the outside culture in order to sustain the host culture. Thus, for example, thick cosmopolitanism is evident in football magazines and newspapers that discuss and explain in detail the game in different societies. Thin cosmopolitanism is more apparent in newspaper stories that report only on foreign players or teams that local clubs are set to encounter (cf. Giulianotti and Robertson 2007b). The relative balance between thin and thick variants of cosmopolitanism provides a broader mirror of the socio-cultural relationship between football and specific societies. In general terms, without further embellishment, banal cosmopolitanism is more closely connected to the thin variant. Both thick and thin variants are apparent in different kinds of rooted cosmopolitanism.

Finally, contemporary cosmopolitanism has been more generally implicated within the 'postmodern turn' and the structural transformation of football in Western Europe since the early 1990s. The postmodern, cosmopolitan aspects of football are evidenced in the blurring or collapse of modern broad categorical and aesthetic boundaries, such as in the de-differentiation of low (football) and 'higher' cultural forms (the performing arts, literature). In the UK, BBC television's wider framing of major football tournaments has been illustrative. In the 1980s, UK football had been derided by many as a 'slum sport for slum people', yet the BBC added a strong cultural theme to the 1990 World Cup finals in Italy through the musical accompaniment of classical music, notably Pavarotti's *Nessun Dorma* (cf. Taylor 1987). These forms of de-differentiation continued, appealing particularly to thick cosmopolitanism, and culminated in the 2004 European Championships, for which BBC television ran a short trailer that visualized leading international players in the style of their most celebrated national artists: hence, visual editing enabled England's Beckham to appear in the fleshy tones of Lucien Freud, Holland's Van Nistelroy in the vivid contrasts of Van Gogh, France's Zidane in the blurry lens of Monet, and Spain's Raul through the cubist prism of Picasso. In this way, the national icons of the world game are brought into playful, postmodern correspondence with the national masters of global art.

Nostalgia

We noted earlier that, since the nineteenth century, nostalgia has been a strong counterpoint of modernism. The 'nostalgic paradigm', according to Stauth and Turner (1988: 47), has four main components: the imagining of history in terms of decline; the sense of a loss of wholeness; the sense of loss of expressivity and spontaneity; and the sense of loss of individual autonomy.

We noted in Chapter 1 that nostalgia has taken two historical forms. First, during the third, take-off stage of globalization, 'wilful nostalgia' enhanced the invention of diverse modern traditions and identities. Wilful nostalgia was apparent in the amateurist and aristocratic values of football's British custodians, and among the overseas protagonists who forged close educational and commercial ties to 'Home'.

Second, since the 1960s, a 'somewhat different and diffuse kind of wilful, synthetic nostalgia' has arisen which is 'incorporated – for the most part capitalistically – into consumerist, image-conveyed nostalgia' (Robertson 1990a: 53–5; cf. Appadurai 1998: 76). This 'postmodernized nostalgia' is highly transnational, 'democratically' cultural, and highly simulated.[35] In football, this postmodern nostalgia centres particularly upon the great players and teams of the recent past, and in the senses of loss that are expressed when contemporary international sides fail to match their predecessors' exalted standards.

Brazil's World Cup-winning team from 1970 provides the example par excellence of such postmodern nostalgia. Burnished by brilliant individual talents, Brazil's triumphs were filmed in colour for global audiences. The stunning last goal in the 4-1 final victory against Italy is constantly replayed by television stations across the world, to become deeply embedded in the collective memory of global football followers. Through replaying such global moments, the transnational mass media has played a crucial role in converting Brazil into the 'second nation' of millions of football fans across the world (cf. Ritzer 2004: 90).[36] Moreover, it should be added that nostalgic constructions of this Brazilian team are typically counterpoised to representations of contemporary, modernist styles of play as functional and machine-like. Media discourses on football wax nostalgically on Brazil as the supreme exponents of *futebol arte*, therein conveniently forgetting some of the team's more robust methods or unsuccessful moves. Contemporary consumerism is further evidenced in postmodern nostalgia, for example as retro versions of the Brazilian team shirt (notably Pelé's number 10) and tracksuits became standard commodities in sports retailers across Europe in the early 2000s.

Other forms of nostalgia are evident in football. Football marketing constantly activates nostalgic themes. When England hosted the 1996 European Championship finals, the national media constantly recalled the 1966 World Cup victory, and the song 'Football's Coming Home' became a tournament anthem, although such nostalgia rather marginalized 'other' British nationals, such as the Scots, Welsh, and Northern Irish, and those of direct immigrant descent (cf. Carrington 1998). Elsewhere, a vast market in football nostalgia has mushroomed, as old stadiums open museums and long-retired players publish their autobiographies.[37]

---

[35]For an analogous differentiation of 'primary' and 'ersatz' nostalgia, see Appadurai (1998: 76–8).

[36]Hence, when their opponents outplay Brazil but lose (as did Spain's team at the under-17 world final), they may claim to be 'the real Brazilians', to claim the aesthetic high ground.

[37]In the UK, we may consider the various biographies and autobiographies of Billy Meredith (who played during the 1900s), Raich Carter (1930s), Tommy Taylor (1940s), Wilf Mannion (1950s), Bobby Moore (1960s), Giorgio Chinaglia (1960s and 1970s), and Alan Hudson (1970s).

Nostalgic football television shows draw upon an enormous reservoir of film from the 1960s, but particularly the 1980s, onwards. The timespan for nostalgia is compressed, such that television shows 'relive' events from the previous year, month, or week. Postmodern, instant nostalgia is precipitated by advanced digital technology and editing techniques that dissolve team histories, interweaving images of past and present players, to become team-mates in some timeless simulated game. Past and present are 'dedifferenti-ated' in real ways too, as indoor football tournaments feature teams of players from yesteryear, to inspire the armchair reminiscences of satellite television viewers. In this way, contemporary mediatization processes are pivotal to the diverse ways in which postmodern nostalgia is underpinned by both local and transnational forms of identification and collective memory.

Concluding Comments

Evidently, the cultural globalization of football is not a straightforward process. Revealing its complex making and contemporary condition requires us to unravel the mutually implicative relationships within the old antonyms of global thinking.

The universalism–particularism problem interrelates with relativization processes, and underpins the worldwide normalization of identity–differentiation through football and other cultural forms. This process has become increasingly complex as diasporic groups undergo de- and re-territorialization in terms of football and wider cultural identification. Similarly, processes of homogenization *and* heterogenization are evidenced in the cultural globalization of football, for example as nations share similar league systems, but interpret the game in varied ways. The concept of glocal-ization, containing the 'duality of glocality', reflects the mutual interrelations of these tendencies. In turn, football provides a potent refutation of the more routine variant of the Americanization thesis, to the extent that some signs of reverse colonization are apparent. Themes of social and normative cos-mopolitanism are also spotlighted, as football intensifies everyday forms of socio-cultural connectivity and varied kinds of engagement with 'other' social groups. Finally, the social construction of nostalgia has contributed signifi-cantly to the consecration of the 'local', and to the making of a global con-sciousness through postmodern ways of remembering within football.

Our arguments here have been underpinned by the introduction of new or modified concepts within the field of globalization studies. Relevant concepts here include duality of glocality, banal cosmopolitanism, exceptional nation-alism, thin and thick cosmopolitanisms, hard and soft Americanization, and Americolonization. The utility of these fresh concepts extends well beyond football and into a host of other cultural domains. As we shall see, these con-cepts and other arguments should not simply be located in abstract isolation from other dimensions of global processes. Rather, they have a direct and highly complex impact upon the economic, political, and social dimensions of globalization.

3

Economics: Neo-Liberalism, Inequalities and Transnational Clubs

Introduction

Since the 1970s, the global football field has undergone rapid commercial transformation. It is increasingly common to hear the game described as 'the football industry', thereby reflecting the remarkable growth and scale of its commercial revenues. Annual football-related business was estimated at around €250 billion by the year 2000 (Walvin 2001). In the season 2006–7, Europe's football market was valued at €13.6 billion, while the 'Big 5' leagues (England, France, Germany, Italy, and Spain) generated annual revenues of €7.1 billion. In England, the 20 Premier League clubs accrued over €2.3 billion in 2006–7, a rise of over 200 per cent on a decade earlier, and around nine times higher than the figure of 1991–2 (Deloitte 2007a, 2008). More broadly, in economies such as Spain, by 2004, football generated €8 billion in yearly turnover, contributing 66,000 jobs and 1.7 per cent of GNP (Robertson and Giulianotti 2006). Football's mega-events – most notably the World Cup finals – are claimed by some to provide huge economic impacts for host nations, for example the alleged US$12.5 billion boost to Germany's economy in 2006.[38] Moreover, football's commercial connectivity has expanded to encompass a broad variety of 'stakeholders', including clubs, supporters, players, agents, governing bodies, nation states, and other governmental institutions, NGOs, media and merchandise TNCs, and the full gamut of corporate sponsors and commercial 'partners'. Thus, the game's penetration of many commercial spheres means that it is also possible to talk of the 'footballization' of national and global economies.

Our discussion here seeks to map and to analyse football's major political–economic changes. Inevitably, we draw heavily upon the substantial body of economic evidence and analysis that is now available on elite football. However, we do advance a *political*–economic account of the global football field, by locating commercial issues within broader sociological contexts that concern politics, culture, and social relations. Our analysis also refers directly to core arguments in earlier chapters, for example regarding issues of sociocultural homogenization and heterogenization.

---

[38] See www.associatedcontent.com/article/46140/world_cup_2006_economics.html

To begin here, we need to recognize that football's economic expansion is not an isolated process but has been underpinned, particularly in Europe, by the general worldwide ascent of free-market or neo-liberal political–economic policies (Bourdieu 1998; Robinson 2002: 223; Harvey 2005; Ferguson 2006; Stiglitz 2006).

Neo-liberalists utilize the economic theories of Friedrich von Hayek, Milton Friedman, and (more selectively) Adam Smith to advocate the creation of a global 'free market', which is to be realized by withdrawing 'sclerotic' state intervention in the economy, privatizing public assets, 'rolling back' welfare programmes, and 'freeing' the transnational circulation of goods, services, capital, and investment. The so-called 'Washington Consensus' – driven on by the United States, its Western allies, the World Bank, the IMF, the WTO, and numerous TNCs – has advanced the global diffusion of neo-liberal poli-cies. 'Structural adjustment' policies have been imposed upon developing nations, principally through slashing public programmes and repaying long-term debts that had been amassed by previous regimes. Neo-liberalism has had many nefarious social consequences: the decimation of local industries, high unemployment, and the collapse of welfare services. In many cases, notably in Latin America, neo-liberalism has inspired popular political resistance, reflected by the subsequent election of left-wing governments that directly challenge market fundamentalism (Stiglitz 2002; cf. Johnson 2004: 266–9).

As we shall see, economic liberalization has had major consequences for football. Let us consider three examples at this initial stage. First, player labour markets have become increasingly liberalized, largely through EU pressure upon football's governing bodies to observe European law, which guarantees the free movement of labour. Since the early 1970s, UEFA was aware that existing national quotas (such as those in Italy) on foreign player recruitment were legally problematic. We noted in Chapter 1 that the 3+2 rule on foreign players was introduced by UEFA in 1991, but was with-drawn after the 1995 *Bosman* case, which allowed out-of-contract players in Europe to move freely between clubs. The position of non-EU players is rather more varied. Some EU nations (notably the UK) restrict the alloca-tion of work permits, while others such as Belgium and Spain are rather more favourable on employment rights or dual nationality (cf. Kapur and McHale 2005). However, once established in the EU, non-EU players receive the same legal status as their European team-mates.

Second, the old motives for financial investment in clubs – combining senses of 'custodianship' with the egotistical lure of local or national status – have been increasingly supplanted by the pursuit of profit. In England, for example, the FA had long restricted the opportunities of club directors to rake off profits from their involvement in football. These regulations were widely ignored as clubs floated on the stock market from the mid-1980s onwards, and were then abandoned in 1998 (Conn 2005). Elsewhere France, Germany, and many South American nations have relaxed their club owner-ship rules to enable commercial investors to acquire greater sharcholdings.

Third, we have witnessed the infusion of new volumes and types of capital within the game, notably through interlocking global relationships between football and business institutions (such as clubs and media corporations), and the growth in elite club ownership by foreign nationals. The most obvious beneficiaries of neo-liberal reforms are football-related TNCs, such as global media networks, which have mushroomed through their exclusive access to elite sport, particularly European football tournaments.

In general terms, it has been argued that the free-market ethos has become normalized as *la pensée unique*, to the extent that alternative political–economic models are obliquely dismissed as unfit for the modern global age (cf. Bourdieu 1999; Lane 2003: 326). However, despite its ideological potency and 'one size fits all' packaging, the record is rather more complex; indeed, it is possible to discern evidence of a 'duality of glocality' in regard to the varied way in which nations implement pro-market policies.

First, Bourdieu's assertion about neo-liberalism's absolute ideological power rather ignores the political debates and conflicts surrounding free-market policies – struggles in which he had engaged personally until his untimely death. As we shall see, in this chapter and afterwards, it is useful to contrast neo-liberalism with other influential political–economic models such as 'neo-mercantilism'.

Second, modern capitalism is not homogeneous but is typically adapted or 'glocalized' to fit with particular cultural contexts (Dore et al. 1999; Dore 2000; Amable 2004). For example, Asian capitalist models have far stronger state engagement than those in North America. More specifically, neo-liberal policies over the past two decades display significant variations both *within* and *between* nations. In the United States, for example, the Bush administration adopted a far more militaristic or imperialistic model of neo-liberalism than Clinton had attempted. Other nations, such as China or Mexico, have modified and advanced particular variants of neo-liberalism while safeguarding much of the old political system (cf. Harvey 2005).

Third, despite waxing over its vicissitudes, most advanced industrial societies owe their historical successes not to free-market policies but to an economic protectionism that enabled national corporations, industries, and financial systems to emerge and to flourish (Chang 2002). Thus, industries in developing nations tend to be severely undermined by the insistence of Western political–economic institutions on the early imposition of free-market policies.

Fourth, we should note that, without close regulation, neo-liberalism does not in itself maximize market competition; indeed, it may engender forms of *cartelization*, such as where small clusters of leading TNCs operate collectively to insulate themselves from the threat of 'normal', external, market competition.

To explore the political–economic aspects of elite football, our discussion is separated into two broad parts. First, we examine the game's major economic transformations and inequalities, focusing particularly upon three realms: television revenues, the theme of financial crisis, and the parlous economic condition of South American football. Second, we address football's strongest institutional embodiment of neo-liberalism, namely the world's leading clubs, which are understood as TNCs with reference to their transnational ambitions, corporate structures, player recruitment, and branding. Throughout this discussion, we advance a broad 'global-realist' rather than 'globalist' analysis, which is appreciative of the political contestation and cultural diversity of the 'free market' in football and beyond.

Part 1   Inequalities, Turbulence and Cultural Divergence

Television revenues

New broadcasting revenue streams, particularly from subscription television networks, have driven the stunning economic acceleration of European and world football. The major governing bodies have gained enormously from this economic expansion. FIFA income has grown exponentially, from around US$70 million, covering the period 1979–1982, through to US$1.2 billion for 1999–2002, and on to US$3 billion for 2007–10, primarily through television revenues and related income from advertising-focused corporate 'partners', generated mainly at the World Cup finals.[39] Television revenues for the 1978 finals were only around US$40 million, but rose rapidly, reaching US$1.7 billion for the 2002 and 2006 finals combined (*The Economist*, 30 May 2002). For 2010, the European television rights alone were set to earn over US$1 billion, twice the figure for 2006, after FIFA pressed the 'Big Five' nations into individual deals rather than collective purchase through the EBU.

UEFA's earnings have multiplied through the 'hyper-commodification' of television rights to major tournaments. Revenues for the European Championships multiplied from around €39 million in 1992 to €840 million in 2004; two-thirds of the latter figure came directly from television rights, and a further fifth from media-fuelled advertising revenues.[40] UEFA's major club competition, the European Cup (rechristened the Champions' League in 1992) earned around €8,000 in television rights for the first final in 1960. Over €400 million was earned from television and sponsorship packages for the 2005–6 tournament, enabling over €290 million to be distributed across competing clubs – seventeen times the level of finance in 1992–3 – with the Big 5 league teams dominating the share (Deloitte 2007a).

At club level, Europe's Big 5 leagues have gained enormously from the media policies of market-focused governments. Media deregulation from the late 1980s onwards helped to accelerate the development of

---

[39]In the early 2000s, football events, particularly the World Cup, accounted for over 95 per cent of FIFA's income. See www.loc.gov/rr/business/BERA/issue3/soccer.html

[40]See http://euro2008.uefa.com/newsfiles/491990.pdf

subscription-based satellite, cable, and digital networks, notably BSkyB in the UK. Meanwhile, the status of viewers shifted, from cultural 'citizens' served by free-to-air public broadcasting, to entertainment 'consumers' paying premium fees for live football (Boyle and Haynes 2004: 20; Rowe 2004).

The Big 5 leagues enjoyed huge new pay-TV revenue streams from the late 1980s onwards. In Germany, television money rose from DM20 million with free-to-air stations in 1987, to DM55 million for 1991, then DM700 million for five seasons (1992–7), to the equivalent of DM3 billion for four seasons (2000–4), and up to around DM840 million for the 2006–7 season (Hesse-Lichtenberger 2002: 218; Mikos 2006: 148; the *Independent*, 6 May 2006). In Italy, television moneys more than doubled to €500 million in 1999–2000 when clubs were freed to strike their own television deals. In Spain, through the 1990s, television money rose from around €40 million annually to approximately €300 million. In France, television money quadrupled over 1991–5 and rose steadily to the 2005 three-year €1.8 billion deal with Canal+ which, upon signature, became world football's most lucrative media contract (Hare 2003: 147). Despite the French League's relatively modest appeal, the investment enabled Canal+ to weaken and then absorb its rival, TPS, and to raise its pay-TV revenues by almost 25 per cent.

English football experienced the biggest change. In 1984, English club football earned around €2.6 million annually from free-to-air television contracts, rising to €44 million in 1988 over a four-year period. When BSkyB arrived, the value of domestic league television rights catapulted to €214 million (1992–7), €743 million (1997–2001), €1.46 billion (2001–4), and €1.2 billion (2004–7, plus €320 million in overseas rights); the subsequent €2.7 billion deal (2007–10) covered both domestic and international rights (Dobson and Goddard 2001: 81–4; Banks 2002: 110–18; Smart 2005: 93–4).[41]

The opportunity to secure rising television revenues had encouraged and underpinned the broader commodification and entrepreneurial transformation of English elite club football. In 1992, the top division of English clubs broke from the four-division Football League to form the Premier League under the FA's auspices. Whereas in the 1980s, the top division had been limited to 50 per cent of all television money, the new deal freed EPL members to seize virtually all of this rapidly expanding realm of income (Banks 2002: 108–9; Conn 1997). In turn, television contracts equipped football clubs to further commodify other spaces, notably tracksides and team shirts, to inflate sponsorship revenues.[42]

---

[41]See http://news.bbc.co.uk/1/hi/business/6273617.stm

[42]Germany offers a particularly strong illustration of the television–advertising relationship. The Bundesliga's biggest earnings in 2005–6 came from advertising (€418 million) rather than media income (€400 million), but the former is effectively dependent upon television deals that enable corporate messages to reach millions of households. See 'The Bundesliga – A Growth Industry', at www.bundesliga.de/misc/download/04_dfl_report2007_en.pdf

The avalanche of fresh television revenues has been distributed in highly uneven ways, thus intensifying inequalities within and between league systems. First, for example, in season 2006–7, the average EPL side generated €75 million in revenues, over 80 per cent more than sides in the next division (the Championship). In 2007, promotion to the EPL was worth an extra €60 million in revenues, while relegation slashed income by €35 million. By 2005–6, skewed revenues from television and related sources meant that the 'Big Four' sides (Arsenal, Chelsea, Liverpool, and Manchester United) were earning on average around three times more than other clubs, and so went on to win all league and FA Cup competitions between 1996 and 2007. In Spain and Italy, clubs negotiate their own television deals, hence the divisions are starker: for example, in 2006–7, Real Madrid and Barcelona had budgets that were more than 20 times that of the league's smallest sides. In Italy, collective selling of league television rights is scheduled to return in 2010, thus offering the possibility of some reduction in revenue inequalities between clubs.

Second, Europe's Big 5 leagues have left their continental counterparts trailing in financial and competitive terms. In the mid-2000s, average EPL clubs could earn over €30 million annually from domestic prize money and television, while leading Belgian or Scottish clubs struggled to earn €1–2 million (Giulianotti 2003; Dejonghe and Vandeweghe 2006: 109). In Russia, Eastern Europe's largest market, the national league earned around €25 million from two television deals over an eight-year period. UEFA's club competitions distribute television revenues largely according to national 'market size', hence clubs in the Big 5 leagues earn the lion's share. In turn, top clubs from outside the Big 5 have struggled to compete in UEFA's Champions League, with only Porto (Portugal) and Ajax (Netherlands) featuring as finalists between 1993 and 2007.

The resulting 'disconnection' of these smaller European football systems is neatly illustrated by Scotland. Up to the early 1990s, Scottish players held important and frequently dominant roles in English club football, and several were sprinkled across leading teams in mainland Europe during the 1980s. The Scottish national team also qualified for all World Cup finals between 1974 and 1990. From the early 1990s onwards, Scottish players were gradually disconnected from the international club game, as leading sides (including Celtic and Rangers in Scotland, and most English teams) developed more cosmopolitan (and non-Scottish) playing squads. In turn, the status of the Scottish national team fell into a long decline, qualifying for only one World Cup finals (1998) and two European Championships (1992, 1996) between 1992 and 2008.

Third, more extreme financial divisions separate European and other league systems. In North America, the MLS started to earn around US$20 million annually from its various television deals from 2007 onwards. In South America, the Brazilian national league received around US$70 million from Globo TV for 2007 television rights; the São Paulo state championship gained around US$30 million. In 2007–8, Argentina's top-division clubs pooled around US$50 million for blanket television coverage of league fixtures, with the leading two sides (Boca and River) sharing around US$10 million. In Africa, record-breaking television deals might net clubs a share of US$2 million (such as the Nigeria contract in 2005), while the South African league gained around US$40 million from its five-year deal with state broadcasters from 2002 onwards.[43] In Japan, in 2005, the J-League earned around US$40 million from television rights; its wealthiest club, Urawa Reds, grossed around US$48 million, less than one-eighth of Real Madrid's revenues. In Australia, the national federation signed a seven-year deal for league and national team fixtures worth around US$95 million.[44] In China – the largest and most prized long-term target market for European clubs – broadcasting revenues still constitute only around 5–10 per cent of club income, with the monopoly broadcaster CCTV controlling television rights. Though many of these television deals represent huge historical advances, the financial gulf still widens between these football systems and the Big 5.

Media-dependent revenues, such as in advertising, underscore the continental divisions. The blue-chip event, the 2006 World Cup finals, cost US$30–50 million for sponsorship rights; Euro 2004 was around half that, the 2004 Copa America was US$0.5–2 million, the 2004 Asian Cup was US$1.5–6 million, and the 2004 African Cup of Nations was only US$0.2–0.5 million.[45] Blanket global television coverage is the key to advertising income: for example, UEFA claims that the Champions League is widely viewed in over 220 nations, which tournament sponsors could access in 2005 in exchange for an estimated US$36 million.[46]

We should also underline the critical financial divisions that arise *within* Europe's Big 5. By 2007, the EPL was generating around €900 million more than its nearest competitors, primarily from television. The EPL has earned more than double its nearest competitors from overseas television contracts; in 2007, it began earning €900 million over three seasons for coverage across 208 nations.[47] Additionally, market surveys reveal the UK as the world's most commercialized football nation. In 2002, around 38 per cent of UK households subscribed to football-dominated pay-TV, and business analysts projected a possible 80 per cent take-up; conversely, only around 8 per cent of Italian households had pay-TV, where 'piracy' (illegal

---

[43]When African nations seek to compete in the global labour market, their expenditures can appear grotesque within the national context. In South Africa, the national team coach Carlos Alberto Parreira (of Brazil) earned US$3 million per year, ten times the salary of the president Thabo Mbeki, in 2007, in a nation where half the population live in deep poverty.

[44]Data from *World Soccer*, April 2007.

[45]Business analysts support these associations. For example, Hyundai reported that brand awareness rose by around 10 per cent through sponsorships at the 2002 World Cup finals, generating around US$5 billion in terms of advertising impact from an initial investment of around US$80 million (Miles and Rines 2004: 34).

[46]See www.bloomberg.com/apps/news?pid=10000102&sid=afdL2upf5WfE&refer=uk

[47]Asian audiences alone for the English Premiership were expected to grow to around 400 million by 2013.

access) was a major problem. Fans of leading English clubs also spend more when attending fixtures: in 2003–4, they averaged €48–73 for each game, Spanish fans €34–37, Scottish fans €31–32, and Italian and German fans only €18–24. In turn, the UK media have noted that German clubs attract the largest attendances in European football, in part through the cheapness of attending fixtures (the *Guardian*, 7 March 2007).

Inflated television revenues have contributed to the significant growth in player transfer fees and wages. Fresh television revenues enabled EPL clubs to increase summer spending in 2007 by 60 per cent, to €500 million, with half of all expenditure going outside England (Deloitte 2007a). Overall, 2007 summer transfer expenditure in Europe's Big 5 leagues totalled around €1 billion, with Spain's top few clubs also listed among the highest spenders, again largely from television income. Increasing television revenues equip average clubs in the Big 5 leagues – particularly in England – to outbid top sides from smaller leagues, such as in the Netherlands, Belgium, or Scotland. EPL clubs tend to spend double that of Spanish sides, and more than the combined expenditure of the German, French, and Italian leagues.[48]

It is worth noting too the role of indulgent owners and heavy borrowing in inspiring costly labour investment. Since the 1950s, Italian then Spanish clubs dominated the world's highest transfer fees, which rose nine-fold over 17 years, from €5 million in 1984 (for Maradona, to Napoli), to €8 million in 1990 (Baggio, Juventus), to €23 million in 1998 (Denílson, Real Betis), culminating in €37 million in 2000 (Figo, Real Madrid) and €46 million in 2001 (Zidane, Real Madrid). Indeed, from 2000–3, Real Madrid spent over €130 million on four *galácticos*, including these two world record deals. Subsequently, Roman Abramovich's transfer spending at Chelsea – estimated at €440 million from July 2003 to November 2006 – inflated much of the European player market (the *Observer*, 26 November 2006).

The wage costs of the Big 5 leagues show significant forms of divergence and convergence. From 1995 to 2007, the annual wages-to-turnover ratio varied significantly between the Big 5 leagues, with Italy hitting 90 per cent in 2001 while Germany never rose beyond 56 per cent; but by 2007, strong convergence had occurred, with England, Spain, Italy, and France all at 62–4 per cent, while Germany was most parsimonious at 45 per cent.

From 1995 to 2006, Big 5 wage bills rose hugely, but in markedly different ways. In 1995, the leagues harboured annual wage costs of around €170–€250 million apiece. Wages in the Spanish, German, and French leagues climbed steadily to 2006, reaching figures of €820 million (Spain) and €620 million (Germany, France). The English and Italian leagues expanded rapidly, with both reaching €1 billion in wage expenditure by 2001. In Italy, financial problems struck and wages dropped to €720 million by 2006, while in England, salaries continued to rise, albeit more gradually to over €1.4 billion by 2006 (Deloitte 2008).

---

[48]In Germany, for example, peak expenditure occurred in 2001, at around £90 million.

Thus, in 2006, the English Premiership's average player salary was over €670,000 per year, almost double the figures from France and Germany; the best-paid players, notably at Chelsea, earned marginally more than their peers in Spain, almost double that of Italy and Germany, and over three times the figure for France. Such skewed revenues led Bayern Munich's chairman, Karl-Heinz Rummenigge, to argue in 2005 that German clubs would need to double domestic television income in order to compete against their European counterparts.[49] Salaries and transfer fees will be further inflated by continued growth in European television revenues, and by the entry of some billionaire investors who are willing to run up large annual losses.

In turn, many leading international stars inflate their earnings by at least a further 50 per cent through product endorsements; for example, in 2007, around half of Cristiano Ronaldo's €9.5 million income came from advertising work. According to *Forbes*, the world's best-paid 20 players in 2007 earned an estimated total of US$3.7 billion, with the exceptional Beckham (US$49 million, of which only one-quarter came from his actual team salary) well ahead of Ronaldinho (US$32.6 million) and Henry (US$25.1 million). Excepting US-bound Beckham, the highest 18 earners were to be found in only three leagues (England, Spain, Italy) and at only nine clubs; Chelsea (5) and Barcelona (3) provided the most players.[50]

Other stakeholders – notably player agents, coaches, and football officials – have benefited from football's financial growth. For example, despite intensive secrecy surrounding FIFA's finances, Sepp Blatter eventually stated in 2007 that he received annual 'compensation' of US$1 million; others allege far higher bonus payments. In the UK, Gordon Taylor, head of the players' union, was earning €1.15 million annually in 2007, almost ten times more than the next best-paid labour leader in the country (the *Guardian*, 16 July 2007).

One critical cultural difference across the Big 5 concerns the legal freedoms of clubs to sell their media content. English, German, and French leagues have practised the collective selling of broadcasting rights, hence sizeable slices of these revenues are shared equally among all participating clubs while the remainder is apportioned according to television appearances and league performances. Conversely, in Spain and Italy, clubs negotiate their own television contracts, leading to the widening of competitive inequalities between teams. The latter system encourages the foundation of strategic class alliances between weaker sides. In Spain, for example, in 2003, most top clubs divided themselves into two camps – the G-12 (most of the richest sides) and G-30 (the rest) – to negotiate television deals. The

---

[49]He followed this in 2006 by noting how, in the Champions League, the German club Werder Bremen earned around one-sixth of their opponents, Barcelona, from domestic television revenues.

[50]See www.forbes.com/business/2008/04/30/best-paid-soccer-biz-soccer08-cx-cs_0430 players_ intro.html

G-30 gained around €93 million annually from their main television rights, while nine of the G-12 shared €140 million, including Real Madrid's €54 million slice. Club inequalities were later exacerbated as Barcelona and Real Madrid signed separate seven-year television deals with the Mediapro agency in 2006 for €1 billon and €1.1 billion respectively.

While weaker clubs may combine politically to challenge this process, it is difficult to achieve long-term success. In Italy in 2002, after a law in 1999 had freed clubs to barter with television companies, the TelePiù network offered large clubs such as Juventus up to €55 million for television contracts, but smaller clubs were offered less than one-tenth of that figure. The league was delayed by two weeks while a compromise was worked out, wherein the top six clubs forfeited around €5.5 million each to assuage the differences (Baroncelli and Lago 2006: 18). Clubs like Inter Milan went on to earn nearly €100 million in media revenues, while smaller teams drew barely 10 per cent of that sum.

Significant national differences arise in the vertical integration of media corporations and league clubs. In some nations – notably France and, to widen the comparisons, Mexico – media corporations exercise strong influence through club ownership. In the UK, media-ownership of clubs was restricted in 1999 when the Labour government eventually acceded to strong fan pressure and blocked BSkyB's bid to purchase Manchester United. Yet many media companies did establish small shareholdings in various UK clubs during the late 1990s. In other European contexts, some media corporations have paid additional fees to win favour among big clubs: for example, the Kirch group secretly paid Bayern Munich €21.5 million; in France, Canal+ paid the top six clubs around €160 million.[51]

Overall, the political economy of elite club football highlights two broad processes. First, free-market policies have facilitated the rapid growth of the pay-TV sector, which in turn has multiplied the revenues within elite football, most particularly in the Big 5 leagues. Vast inequalities have been magnified within these national leagues, across European football systems, and between Europe and other regions. We may thus speak of a critical 'disconnection' arising in global terms, as some nations which had been deeply embedded within the football world system have become increasingly peripheral in competitive and participatory terms. In Europe itself, smaller national football systems and modest clubs in the larger leagues have also endured processes of disconnection.

Second, there remain significant differences between national football systems in how they balance market fundamentalism and collectivist policies in the game. For example, English football has gained most from active participation in the commodification of television rights, while small European or

---

[51]In Latin America, the situation is similarly unequal. In Argentina in 2001, the TyC television firm offered around one third of revenues to the top two clubs (Boca Juniors and River Plate), around one half to the remaining clubs, and the remainder to be apportioned by merit (going to the top six league teams).

developing nations are disadvantageously placed in the game's new global economy. Additionally, some nations allow clubs to negotiate television contracts independently (Italy, Spain), while others emphasize collective negotiations (England, Germany, France). These national–cultural divergences are directly relevant to the issue of financial 'crisis' in European football.

European football and economic 'crisis'

In the early 2000s, substantial millennial discussion arose about an economic crisis in European and world football. The move towards economic liberalization and deregulation seemed to have made the game more financially volatile, with significant slumps and bankruptcies to go with the booms. FIFA provided perhaps the most devastating illustration, after incurring US$300 million in losses when its marketing agency, ISL/ISMM, collapsed with debts of over $1.2 billion (*Sports Illustrated*, 27 January 2002; *Business Week*, 1 April 2002).[52] More broadly, FIFA's General Secretary, Michel Zen-Ruffinen, reported that up to US$500 million had been squandered under President Blatter (cf. Jennings 2007).

Much discussion of a football crisis concentrated upon European clubs, which were estimated by the German *Kicker* magazine to share a combined debt of €7 billion in 2004. The evidence was certainly apparent. Italy's Serie A sides owed almost €2 billion, following losses of €950 million in 2003; two leading teams, Fiorentina and Napoli, were declared bankrupt and forcibly relegated. Spanish sides owed €1.625 billion by 2002, set against only €1.257 billion in annual revenues; debts rose to €2 billion a year later (Ascari and Gagnepain 2006: 86). Clubs like Atlético Madrid, Valencia, Real Sociedad, and Valladolid delayed wage payments, while Athletic Bilbao slashed salaries by 15 per cent in 2004. Barcelona's debt for 2004 approached €200 million, with Deportivo La Coruña at €178 million, and Atlético Madrid (a year later) hitting €101 million. In Germany, Bundesliga debts neared €550 million in 2003, rising to around €900 million for the top two divisions by March 2005.

Despite such headline problems, an international 'crisis' did not endanger European clubs in homogeneous, uniform ways. Indeed, the 'crisis' label might have fitted Italy, Spain and, to a lesser extent, England, but probably not France and Germany (Lago et al. 2006). Large 'national' league debts were often attributable to a few clubs: in Germany, Dortmund and Schalke were chief debtors; in Portugal in 2001, Benfica accounted for over 40 per cent of league debts, and Porto soon added another hefty slice (Barros 2006: 97); in Scotland in 2003, the collective debts of the top dozen clubs stood at €186 million, with Rangers accounting for over one third (the *Scotsman*, 18 January 2005).

---

[52]In a private letter to FIFA's Executive Committee, Blatter reckoned the loss at around US$340 million; he revised that figure down to US$42–46 million in public statements on the case.

Significant national differences arose over the causes of club indebtedness. These factors included:

- Excessive expenditure on player transfers, notably in Spain with Real Madrid and Barcelona, in Germany, and in England with Leeds United (Frick and Prinz 2006: 67). Chelsea lost world record figures of around €300 million over three years (2004–6), principally on transfer fees, but were bankrolled personally by their billionaire owner.
- Player wages, rising to 90 per cent or more of club turnover, notably in Italy, topping 125 per cent of Serie A club revenues in 2001, falling to 85 per cent by 2003, although around one third of players boasted salaries of €1+ million.
- The collapse of broadcasting groups. The Kirch group's demise cost Bundesliga clubs around €250 million between 2001 and 2003 (*Sports Illustrated*, 16 April 2003). ITV Digital's demise led to the cancellation of a €315 million contract with English lower league clubs; thus, between 1999 and 2006, 22 of these 72 clubs had entered administration (Lago et al. 2006: 7).
- The collapse of parent companies that owned clubs, notably in Italy at Parma and Lazio.
- Weak stock market performance, notably in England, Scotland, Italy, and Germany, provided one key index of economic decline. By August 2005, of the 22 floated UK clubs, only a dozen remained on the main market. Other European clubs (such as Borussia Dortmund and Juventus) followed British clubs into flotation, but endured falling share prices.

Overall, we can see that significant variations arose in the extent to which each of these factors impacted upon specific nations.

The different kinds of national regulations on club finances also affected the game's stability. For example, French football had learnt painful lessons from the widespread indebtedness of the late 1980s, and so introduced regulations on club expenditure on players while prohibiting stock-market flotation.[53] Consequently, total club losses in France for the season 2002–3 were rather modest, at only €36 million; or, put another way, around 3 per cent of the total losses incurred by Italian clubs (Gouguet and Primault 2006: 51–2). In Germany, clubs have restricted borrowing capacities, and must forward annual budgets (mainly regarding wages) in order to safeguard their Bundesliga membership (Frick and Prinz 2006: 64, 68); a second audit of club finances each year was introduced in 2007.

Conversely, in Spain, clubs seem to spend profligately on players, but supplementary resources may be provided by regional authorities. For example, Real Madrid sold its training ground to the local authorities for €475 million,

---

[53]Yet even France is not immune. Monaco accumulated exceptional debts of almost €90 million but survived enforced relegation after restructuring and earning cash injections of around €33 million (*World Soccer*, August 2003)

thereby eradicating massive debts and funding a €342 million transfer kitty, with €547 million going on wages from 2000 to 2005. Real Oviedo were set to be closed down in 2003 due to debts of €28 million, but after public pressure, the local mayor resumed the council's backing a year later, thus ensuring survival (Lago et al. 2006: 8). In further differentiation, Italian and English clubs have less legal regulation and political involvement; the possibility of bankruptcy is greater, though Serie A sides have long relied on indulgent owners.

These national–cultural factors have continued to impact upon the debt levels of national leagues. For example, in 2007, the top 36 German clubs carried combined net debts of just under €600 million, compared to around €3.15 billion for the twenty-team Premier League.[54] The latter figure fell to around €2 billion upon the removal of 'soft-loans' from club owners or shareholders, to become roughly equivalent to one single year's revenue (*Daily Telegraph*, 29 May 2008).

Overall, significant variations arise between European football nations in the scale of club indebtedness and the mixture of causes behind these financial problems. Despite greater reflexivity and caution over club finances, indebtedness constitutes a stronger potential risk within a liberalized football economy. In the late 2000s, further concerns were widely voiced regarding the effects on football of the credit crunch and the impending financial crisis. The biggest consequence lay in the credit squeeze, and its football-related effects upon banks, sponsors, stock-markets, and consumers. For example, English clubs owed a reported €3 billion in late 2008, and faced tougher future credit arrangements with banks. Many club owners suffered large financial losses during the economic crisis, placing their football-related investments in jeopardy. Corporations were less likely to spend freely on football, and some clubs saw their main sponsors go bust. Many governments sought to save imperilled financial institutions, particularly banks, through partial or full nationalization; one side-effect has been that, in cases where these institutions have been sponsors within football, nation states suddenly acquired significant financial interests within specific clubs, national associations, tournaments, and league systems. Meanwhile, those teams listed on stock exchanges saw their share-prices tumble, while the collapse in property prices closed off the option of selling land to secure extra revenues during hard times. From 2007 onwards, some clubs did not raise annual season-ticket prices or experienced drops in attendance as a reflection of the economic crisis. However, overall, in the game's favour, many European leagues and clubs were relatively insulated from the crisis by long-term television deals and strong subscription bases for pay-TV networks. Thus, the biggest risk would lie with the possible collapse of a major television network. While these threats hovered in European football in the late

---

[54]See www.dw-world.de/dw/article/0,,3192224,00.html

2000s, deeper structural crises have been identifiable over a much longer term in other continents, notably South America, where fundamentally weaker sporting and economic systems are in place.

South American football

The economic and competitive inequalities between South American and European leagues have become more extreme since the early 1980s. South American football has been severely affected by the major financial problems and crises of national governments since the 1960s. In Argentina, for example, the economic crises of 2002–3 may have helped to reduce club debts through devaluation of the national currency, but unemployment, poverty, and social turmoil have impacted very negatively upon domestic transfer markets, match attendance figures, illegal practices among football officials, and public order in stadiums (cf. Crolley and Duke 2007: 177).

South America's weakness in the global economy has long been a significant *problemstellung* within social science. From the 1960s onwards, various theories of underdevelopment have argued that the political–economic machinations of northern states and corporations have functioned to retard modernization across the global South (cf. Frank 1967; Wilber 1970; Kay 1975). Alongside the painful everyday social consequences of these inter-regional inequalities, underdevelopment, sometimes understood as *atimia*, is marked by strong critical reflexivity within economically marginalized communities and nations.[55] As we explain here, the underdevelopment of South American football is partly connected to longstanding forms of economic dependency upon the North, notably Europe; similar arguments may be extended to explain the African game (Giulianotti and Armstrong 2004: 10–12; Gilbert 2007). Yet some research indicates that South America faces more severe inequalities in global football than in other economic realms (De Melo 2007: 200).

South American football struggles to escape an underdevelopment cycle that conspires to institutionalize debt, to haemorrhage elite labour resources, and to minimize capital returns. In short, chronically indebted South American teams sell their best players, typically to Europe; transfer fees are then squandered or sequestered by corrupt club officials, leaving debt burdens largely intact; crowds at domestic matches decline due to the loss of star performers; national teams then struggle to qualify for major tournaments, due to player burnout and lack of team cohesion, hence little prize money is left for distribution across league clubs; to source new revenues, clubs turn to the sale of young players, and so the cycle is completed and repeated. Thus, for example, in little Uruguay, over 600 players were transferred abroad in the late 1990s, crowds for league games remained low, and the national team qualified for one World Cup between 1994 and 2006.

---

[55]On atimia, see Lagos (1963: 22–5) and Nettl and Robertson (1968: 29).

Confirming the role of external earnings, in Argentina, transfers accounted for half of all club income in 2006 yet debts remained high (Miller 2007: 12). For example, five years earlier, the River Plate club generated US$115 million in player sales, but still sank into US$48 million worth of debt.[56] In Brazil, the CBF reported that international transfers netted clubs US$500 million from 1989 to 1997 yet club indebtedness remains massive (Andreff 2004). In turn, in the leading nations of Argentina and Brazil, dwindling attendances have touched averages of 10,600 and 12,000 respectively. Unlike Europe, where bankruptcies are more likely to strike below the top tier of clubs, this cycle of underdevelopment afflicts all levels of South American football. Leading teams like Colo-Colo (Chile), Universidad de Chile, Millonarios (Colombia), and Racing Club (Argentina) have been declared bankrupt in recent years. In many instances, the national treasury is a leading creditor. By 2006, Brazilian clubs owed an estimated US$500 million in unpaid taxes, with Rio's Botafogo accounting for 11 per cent of that debt (Miller 2007: 12).

The reflexive aspects of underdevelopment are intensified by banal cosmopolitanism, which is itself underpinned by global football television. South American audiences regularly encounter, through television coverage, their leading national players competing in distant European leagues, knowing that local clubs cannot match the salaries or transfer fees of the world. Hence the forlorn comment, 'He is a European', which one of us overheard among supporters during a club match in Montevideo in 1997, after Álvaro Recoba had scored a brilliant solo goal for the local Nacional team; within a year, the young Uruguayan had been duly transferred to Internazionale of Milan.

Many European club directors extol the benefits of the deregulation and neo-liberalization of transnational labour recruitment: South American or African players are cheap, pliant, and expendable compared to Europe's equivalent talents. Weak market positions and questionable management ensure that many South American sides typically undersell their prime assets. For example, Ronaldinho was sold by Brazil's Grêmio for only US$4.5 million in 2001, then by Paris St-Germain to Barcelona two years later for a fee of up to €30 million.[57] Across South America, to cash in their assets prematurely, clubs have turned to selling the 'registration' of players to agents or corporations. When these assets join European sides, South American clubs receive only a proportion or nothing in transfer fees. Thus, in 2003, Rosario Central earned nothing from the foreign moves of three players. Latterly, private corporations such as Traffic in Brazil have bought up the 'economic rights' of many young players; professional clubs are then used as *de facto* 'shop windows' to

---

[56]A further report indicated that the club had an annual turnover of US$40 million but losses of US$28 million (Rachman 2007: 165).

[57]Flows of transfer revenues are also volatile. In Argentina, the fees from the export of players fell from US$92.6 million for 2004 to US$57.7 million for 2005.

display these football talents to European audiences, with the goal of securing highly profitable transfers into the Big 5 leagues (*International Herald Tribune*, 6 July 2008).

Lack of economic regulation opens the door to corrupt business practices. The movement of 'skimmed' transfer monies into secret accounts mirrors broader South American business practices, where for example two-thirds of all Brazilian foreign investments are stashed in tax havens (*The Economist*, 8 April 2005). Large corporate investments in clubs can often disappear: in Brazil, two TNCs put a combined sum of US$180 million into the Flamengo and Vasco clubs respectively, but the money was gone within a year without proper financial trace (Landau 2007: 210). Thus, a corrupt symmetry arises between free-market 'reforms' in football and national governance. According to one football analyst, in Argentina, 'companies were privatised, and yet a lot of the money would disappear into Swiss accounts and never reach the government. It's the same when football clubs sell players. The money never reaches the clubs. This is a country that likes to break the rules' (Ezequiel Fernandez Moore, quoted in *The Economist*, 30 May 2002). South American players also deploy law-evading strategies when pursuing employment: in 2001, police investigations revealed that many exported players held fraudulent European passports and work permits.

Significant socio-cultural factors often shape the patterns of player migration, although some diasporas, notably Brazilian ones, are globalized. For example, around one fifth of Brazilian exports moved to Portugal, often to play at semi-professional level. However, other destinations have included former Communist states, Scandinavia, the Far East, the Indian sub-continent, and Africa.[58] By 2007, Japan's J-League hosted over 40 Brazilian players – more than any other national league. While Brazil imported around 500 players in 2004, almost all were ageing native talents close to retirement (*The Economist*, 20 January 2005). In 2005–6, the 32 teams in the Champions League shared 67 Brazilians and 45 other South American players; Brazilians were particularly prominent at Portuguese clubs (eight each at Benfica and Porto), while Internazionale and Villareal hosted many Argentinians.[59] Brazil provided the highest number of registered players (107) among *all* teams competing in the 2007–8 Champions League, with footballers from the 'Big 5' European nations much further back (France, 72; Italy, 55; Spain, 54; Germany, 49; England, 30) (PFPO 2008).

At grassroots level, South American players live with the everyday consequences of economic decline. The term 'Brazilianization' has been used to describe the social reality of a highly stratified, free-market society,

---

[58]Elsewhere, the owner of Polish team Pogon Szczecin also controls a football academy in São Paulo, and imported over two dozen Brazilians over two years to improve his side's performances.

[59]For the 2006/7 season, 129 Argentinians were scattered across 18 European leagues, with over one quarter (36) located in the Spanish league (*World Soccer*, November 2006).

where the poorest 40 per cent earn less than 7 per cent of the national income (Perkins et al. 2001, quoted in Westad 2005: 151; cf. Beck 2000: 161–3). In Brazil, most footballers earn under €100 per month, yet most clubs claim to be hugely indebted, hence player payments can be highly volatile (for instance, the great Romario was understood in 2007 to be owed over US$8 million in unpaid wages by his club Vasco da Gama). In Argentina, Chile, and Uruguay, players have gone on strike to improve conditions and to claim their outstanding earnings.[60]

Retarded modernization is evidenced further in the poor football infrastructure across South America. Great football theatres, such as the Maracanã in Rio or El Cilindro in Buenos Aires, have been closed or had their capacities slashed for safety reasons. South American players develop particular technical skills by playing on tricky landscapes (such as the *potreros* or 'wastelands' in Argentina), yet better surfaces would enhance individual development (cf. Archetti 1998b).[61] In Bolivia, the Academia Tahuichi, on the fringes of Santa Cruz, has produced many fine players, but its grassless playing surfaces are described as *la luna* (the moon) by children. The next generation of players is threatened by poverty and malnutrition – the direct social product of startling economic decline. In Argentina, two-thirds of boys hail from poor homes, and half (around two million) are classified as 'dangerously undernourished'. Some clubs must provide the most basic meals to enable these young talents to complete simple training routines (*World Soccer*, Summer 2003).

Other symptoms of spiralling economic decline include increasing crime, corruption, and financial insolvency. In Argentina, over 180 football-related deaths are reckoned to have occurred since the 1930s. Criminal gangs across South America have kidnapped the relatives of many leading South American players, such as Romario, Robinho, Riquelme, Rogerio, and the Milito brothers. In Colombia, reflecting the deep-seated indigenous cultures of violence, 16 players were shot dead in separate incidents between 1994 and 2006. Some clubs such as América of Cali had benefited hugely from close connections to the local *narcos* gangs at the centre of the world's cocaine trade; subsequent prohibitions on relations with drug-related businesses has hit these teams hard.

Football governance has been seriously compromised. Across Latin America, some militant fan formations have forged close ties with club officials, to extort money and to 'assist' candidates during the election of office holders. Football agents have gained particular influence inside

---

[60]For example, in Uruguay, the national championship for early 2004 was delayed by two weeks, as players went on strike to demand better wages. Those in the First Division, many of them on under US$50 per month, demanded a minimum of US$400, with Second Division players seeking US$200. The result led to players over 21 being paid around US$300, rising to US$400 by 2006. A subsequent player strike over unpaid wages lasted two months.

[61]Somewhat ironically, there is one South American football school known as *El Potrero*.

specific national football systems (notably Juan Figer in Brazil, or Paco Casal in Uruguay) and clubs (such as Rosario Central and Talleres Cordoba in Argentina). Attempts to 'clean up' national football systems are often rebuffed by vested interests; in Brazil, for example, the proposed 'Pelé law' to reform the game was diluted down to a mere 11 per cent of its original text (Bellos 2002: 291–2). More successful, however, has been the *Football Fans Act* introduced by President Lula in Brazil in 2003, containing provisions regarding ticketing, safety, financial management, and tournament organization, which initially had been opposed by leading football officials (De Melo 2007: 205–6; *New Statesman*, 3 November 2003).

In line with the expectations of dependency theorists, South American football clubs have tended to look towards European models of economic liberalization and commodification as possible solutions. Brazilian club directors voted in 2003 to double admission prices, to raise supporter socio-economic profiles and to inflate merchandise and catering income. One club president explained, 'Poor people cannot afford to take the bus or pay for food or clothes. They live in misery. We have to work with people who can afford to go to the stadiums' (*Scotland on Sunday*, 28 December 2003).

Leaving aside the issue of the social injustices of such a stance, we may note that these strategies are inherently impractical given the vast economic differences between Europe and Brazil. At the time, half of Brazilian workers earned below $100 per month, hence crowds dropped by around 30 per cent. Leading Brazilian sides like Flamengo and Corinthians might claim to have tens of millions of fans worldwide, but high poverty levels make for low domestic ticket and merchandise revenues. Many South American clubs accrue significant revenues from television – notably in Brazil, at 65 per cent of all turnover in 2002–3 – but the real sum is typically less than one-tenth of the media money gained by Europe's top sides (De Melo 2007: 202).

Admission prices to see Brazil's national team were also hiked, reaching $100 in 2005 for concreted 'stands'. The social consequences were inevitable:

> The hardcore fans, who cannot afford to pay the inflated prices, are reduced to watching the training session on the eve of the game. The predominantly upper middle-class crowd on match day means that, while the likes of Paraguay, Uruguay and Argentina play their home matches in front of intimidating crowds, the atmosphere for a Brazil game is more like a television variety show.

> (*World Soccer*, October 2005)

Hence, despite a carnival reputation, many officials at the 2006 World Cup finals in Germany labelled Brazilians the 'most boring' supporters at the tournament.

Full implementation of the commercialization model would also require South American clubs to change their constitutions. In the UK, individuals or small clusters of shareholders typically own professional clubs. Conversely, South American sides have classically operated as mutual associations that are owned and controlled by members (known in many cases as *socios*) who elect the office-holders. The mutual system can invite indebtedness as presidential candidates who make the most grandiloquent promises on player recruitment are elected but then disappear a few years later, leaving the club's finances in turmoil. Football leaders such as Brazil's notorious *cartolas* often manipulate these 'democratic' mutual systems through corrupt patronage networks while obfuscating club revenue streams.

Thus, it is as an *escape* from the particular culture of patronage and corruption in South American football that the neo-liberal model of club governance has its specific attraction in this region. The privatization model has been introduced in Brazil, Colombia, Venezuela, Chile, and Argentina, enabling some mismanaged sides, such as Colo-Colo in Chile, to escape receivership and obtain profitable valuation. In Mexico, only one of the top 18 teams retains a traditional club structure, while the others are in private hands. In Paraguay, the Libertad club is privately owned and has won several league titles since 2002. In Argentina, the great Racing Club was due to be closed, with debts of around US$60 million, until a special law was passed allowing a private company, Blanquiceleste, to take over and repay debts over a ten-year period. The spread of this free-market model is, in the first instance, an essential indictment of the political–economic strategies of the game's previous controllers. We should note too the disjuncture between football and politics: the neo-liberal model has been rejected by many South American electorates just as it has been embraced within sport.

Overall, South American club football suffers from chronic structural problems that impact upon income, governance, labour migration, facilities, salaries, and general social inclusion. Many of these problems derive from the continent's longstanding structural weaknesses within the global economy. As South American leagues haemorrhage their talents to stave off creditors, European leagues (particularly the Big 5) grow aesthetically and financially stronger by absorbing the world's leading talents. Free-market reforms may improve the commercial practices and financial solvency of South American clubs, while undermining the opportunity for improvements in democratic governance.

It is important also to highlight variations in national experiences and responses in respect of the game's neo-liberal trends. For example, Brazil is evidently plugged into more player export markets than other nations; some of its politicians have tried particularly hard to transform the club game through legislation, yet the nation's stark social inequalities have been more than reflected in football through political chicanery and divisive pricing strategies.

Part 2   Clubs as Transnational Corporations

While Part 1 explored the connections of competitive inequalities and crises to free-market policies, here we examine how leading clubs have been a core constituent of football's liberalized economy. Specifically, we explore the status of the world's leading clubs as transnational corporations (TNCs). We advance a 'global-realist' reading of TNCs in general before moving on to consider four ways in which top football clubs possess transnational characteristics in terms of global reach, corporate structures, labour markets, and branding. Throughout this discussion, we note the important ways in which national or regional variations arise in regard to the particular characteristics of TNC clubs.

By definition, the TNC is a profit-centred business that traverses national borders in trade and investment, and has relatively weaker connections to its 'home' origin compared to prior corporate models. One estimate put the number of TNCs globally as high as 37,000 by the year 2000 (Petras and Veltmeyer 2001: 12). TNCs are sometimes contrasted with MNCs (multi-national corporations), which are understood to have stronger 'home' ties and business links with fewer nations.

TNCs accounted for 95 of the world's largest 150 economic entities in 2005 with Wal-Mart, oil and motor companies heading the corporate list; nation states took the remaining 55 places (*Fortune Magazine*, 25 July 2005). Wal-Mart alone reported annual revenues that were higher than the combined GDP of all sub-Saharan African nations (Stiglitz 2006: 187–8). One recent estimate suggested that 60 per cent of global trade involved listed transactions *within* the world's top 100 TNCs.[62] Football-related TNCs include BSkyB, Nike, and adidas, while leading governing bodies and clubs derive huge revenues from corporate 'partners' in the telecommunications, automobile, finance, and 'fast food' industries.

One early discussion distinguished three kinds of TNC along territorial lines (Perlmutter 1972). First, 'ethnocentric' corporations are controlled by home-based headquarters. Second, 'polycentric' corporations facilitate greater local self-determination within centrally defined margins. Third, 'geocentric' enterprises are controlled by globally mobile managers, who may be interpreted as constituents of a 'transnational capitalist class' (Sklair 1995: 61, 2001).

The extent to which this third variant of TNCs is evident within the world economy is strongly debated. Some 'globalist' perspectives indicate that geocentric TNCs are highly prominent within a 'borderless world' (cf. Ohmae 1990, 1995; Strange 1994; Castells 1997: 261). Conversely, more cautious, global-realist perspectives recognize the continuing 'crucial' national ties of TNCs, notably through jobs and investment (cf. Wilkins 1998: 95; Doremus et al. 1999).

---

[62]The practice of 'transfer pricing' is particularly exploited, to manoeuvre revenues throughout corporations internationally and thereby minimize tax liabilities (Prem Sikka, the *Guardian*, 30 June 2003).

In theory, the 'truly transnational corporation' (or TTNC) would have definitively transnational features such as a global spread of elite employees, shareholders, and directors; worldwide research and development; and acute flexibility in product development and micro-marketing (Bartlett and Ghoshal 1989; Smith 1997; Sklair 2001: 2–3). In reality, there are very few TTNCs. Many TNCs (like Coca-Cola and GM) still recruit senior management from their 'home' nations. Some nations, notably the United States, possess citizenship rules that restrict ownership and/or control of specific TNCs. Typically, less than half of a TNC's operations and employees are based abroad; legal, fiscal, and technological regulations tie businesses to nation states; and corporate brands are still often strongly identified with specific nations (cf. Weiss 1997: 9–10). Indeed, Weiss discerns three other trends in leading corporations: the national bases of production; the escalating importance of North/South divides; and regionalization, notably in Asia. Most foreign direct investment (FDI) involving TNCs is not distributed globally but regionally, especially to developed northern nations.[63] Additionally, the notion of a truly global product, featuring globally sourced components, is more mythical than real (Chang 1998: 227–30). Moreover, despite the exponential growth of transnational capital flows since the early 1980s, states provide strong subsidies to their 'national TNCs' to promote profitability and job creation (Ikeda 1996: 66).

Different kinds of interrelationship arise between TNCs. Many 'national TNCs' enter 'inter-enterprise alliances' while seeking support from 'state machineries'. TNCs have also been at the heart of the growing value of business mergers and acquisitions, which rose from around US$500 billion in 1986 to US$4 trillion in 2006. Alternatively, despite anti-trust or anti-monopoly legislation, concerns remain that the restricted number of TNCs in certain industries precipitates de facto market cartelization. Thus, the real competition between TNCs often arises over advances in research and development.

TNC clubs: a global-realist perspective

Leading European football clubs – notably the regular competitors in the Champions League – share many characteristics of TNCs as understood in a global-realist sense. Certainly, these clubs are significant economic entities. According to *Forbes* magazine in 2008, the top dozen clubs in commercial value were based in the four richest leagues, with Manchester United (US$1.8 billion) well ahead of their nearest competitors, Real Madrid (US$1.285 billion), Arsenal (US$1.2 billion), Liverpool (US$1.05 billion), and Bayern Munich (US$917 million).[64]

---

[63]One-third of all FDI in the developing world is internally sourced (*The Economist*, 8 April 2005).

[64]See www.forbes.com/lists/2008/34/biz_soccer08_Soccer-Team-Valuations_Rank.html

In Perlmutter's terms, elite clubs like Manchester United and Real Madrid remain 'ethnocentric' entities, sustaining vital symbolic and strategic ties to their 'home' cities and regions. For the world's richest 20 clubs, actual match-day visitors can contribute large proportions of total revenues, but it is important to highlight significant national variations. The proportion is highest at Scottish (46 per cent), Portuguese (45 per cent), and English (peaking at 43 per cent, at Manchester United) clubs, and lowest in Italy (7–14 per cent) (Deloitte 2007b). The 'ethnocentric' is also very evident in clubs' commercial branding, which often emphasizes team colours, crests, and links with past playing heroes.

Some TNC clubs have a limited array of 'polycentric' and 'geocentric' characteristics. Some have established firm marketing outlets in Asia and North America, and have recruited 'senior management' (e.g. head coaches, to a lesser extent, chief executives) at an international level. However, reflecting particular national responses to the global labour 'free market', ethno-linguistic or cultural commonalities still influence recruitments: for example, Iberian sides favour South American rather than central European coaches. Geocentricity would be more evident if clubs played 'home' fixtures outside of their city base, or sought to obfuscate their geographical origins, such as when the Italian 'Super Cup' fixture was staged in the United States in 1993 and 2003. However, the world is not sufficiently 'compressed' for geographical distance to be irrelevant in tightly scheduled football seasons; thus, for example, the proposal in 2004 to have Scottish teams play mid-season fixtures in Australia was dismissed as simply impractical.

Geocentrism is more evident in the growing complexity of transnational club ownership and investment. The ENIC organization – with holdings in English, Scottish, Italian, Swiss, Greek, and Czech clubs in the late 1990s – was a forerunner of transnational ownerships. Individual cases of international ownership are more commonplace. In 2008, ten EPL clubs were owned by foreign nationals, most of whom had invested heavily since 2003: these included the top three sides, Manchester United (bought by the American Glazer family in 2005); Chelsea (Jewish-Russian oligarch Roman Abramovich in 2003, who also held strong ties with CSKA Moscow); and Liverpool (two US sports entrepreneurs, in 2007).[65] Other sides with foreign ownership were Aston Villa (American Randy Lerner, in 2006); Derby County (US GSE Group, in 2008); Fulham (Egyptian Muhamed Al Fayed, in 1997); Manchester City (bought by former Thai Prime Minister Thaksin Shinawatra, in 2007 then sold to Shiekh Mansour bin Zayed AL Nahyan of Abu Dhabi in 2008); Portsmouth (French-Israeli, with Russian roots, Alexandre Gaydamak, in 2006); and West Ham United (Icelandic consortium, in 2006).[66] Spotlighting the interpenetration

---

[65]Additionally, by early 2008, the largest shareholder in Arsenal was the Russian oligarch Alisher Usmanov, who was also on the board of the Dinamo Moscow side.

[66]In 2006, Sunderland were bought by an Irish consortium, though we note the long-standing ties between the UK and Ireland in football, and in 2007 a Hong Kong investor became Birmingham City's largest shareholder.

of football by other transnational sporting systems, three of these clubs were purchased by owners of US sports franchises. England is said to have three of the world's richest clubs when calculated according to owner wealth, at Manchester City, Chelsea and Queens Park Rangers; the latter is a London club in the lower divisions (as at 2009), but is jointly owned by Formula One magnates Bernie Ecclestone and Flavio Briatore, with a further 20 per cent held by Indian steel tycoon Pramod Mittal. More widely, some club ownership by non-nationals is structured through parent companies registered in tax havens (the *Guardian*, 14 March 2007). In Scotland, the Irish businessman Dermot Desmond has a controlling stake in Celtic, after the Scots-Canadian Fergus McCann had masterminded the club's privatization, and in 2005, Hearts were bought by the Lithuanian businessman, Vladimir Romanov, whose bank is also heavily involved with the Kaunas club.

Elsewhere, Israeli football has attracted several European tycoons, notably Gaydamak at Beitar Jerusalem; Leviev, another Russian, at Hapoel Tel Aviv; and the German Daniel Jammer at Maccabi Netanya. In Spain, Alavés was acquired by the Ukranian-American Dmitri Piterman; in late 2003, an Argentine businessman bought a controlling stake in the Spanish Second Division club Leganés and hired numerous compatriots in a failed bid to win promotion. In Greece, a Saudi sheikh and Spanish investor took over the Aris Salonika club. In Vienna, the Austria Wien club was acquired by billionaire Frank Stronach, an émigré returned from Canada. In Eastern Europe, the steel magnate Pramod Mittal owns CSKA Sofia and Otelul Galati (of Romania). In Latin America, Mexican businessmen have bought controlling interests in clubs in the United States, Costa Rica, Chile, and Colombia. Among 'near-misses' in international investment, Roma were almost sold to the Russian petrol company Nafta Moskva in early 2004; in 2007, the Dubai-based DIC group narrowly failed to purchase Liverpool, and Olympique Marseille rejected Canadian Jack Kachkar's €115 million takeover bid. As the global status of TNC clubs intensifies, these transnational patterns of ownership and investment will only increase.

Early signs of inter-enterprise alliances are evident between some clubs across continents. Eyeing the enormous Chinese market, Sheffield United bought a controlling stake in second division side, Chengdu Five Bull. Partnership deals have been agreed between Real Madrid and Beijing Guo'an, Bolton Wanderers and Wuhan Guanggu, Rangers (of Scotland) and Shenzhen Jianlibao, and Charlton Athletic and Shanghai United. Everton sought strong inroads through sponsorship deals with mobile phone company Kejian and the recruitment of Chinese internationalist Li Tie, who was released after three years.

Annual reports have still to confirm the transformation of clubs into 'true TNCs'. Most TNC club income is usually derived from participating in national leagues, such as through ticket sales and domestic television. Manchester United officials claimed in 2005 that the club had 75 million fans globally, comprising 23 million in Europe, around five million each in the Americas and South Africa, and 40 million in Asia.[67] Chelsea aim to rival United by targeting the UK, North America, China, and Russia for supporter growth. Yet, converting these followers into club-centred consumers remains problematic. Hence, in 2005, Real Madrid accrued only about 4 per cent of turnover from Asia, with half from China. Manchester United drew only €1 million annually from that region; the targeted figure of €10 million over the next decade would account for well below 5 per cent of club revenues.

The globalist aspirations of TNC clubs are vitiated further by the sensitization of developing markets to rapacious practices. For example, in summer 2005, Real Madrid earned a reported US$4 million from a four-day visit to China, but many local football followers criticized the club's instrumental money-making, poor public relations, and failure to field star players such as David Beckham. Some fans had spent up to US$100 on match tickets, almost half the average monthly salary (*China Daily*, 25 July 2005).

Elite football clubs evidence some business interrelationships that may be found among TNCs more broadly. Unlike the latter, elite clubs do not merge with or acquire each other, while football rules prohibit owners or major shareholders from taking large financial interests in rival teams. Nevertheless, in some nations, certain forms of business reciprocity sometimes arise between individual clubs; for example, in Italy, several Parma–Lazio transfer deals from 1999 to 2001 were driven by ties between the clubs' respective owners, Parmalat and Cirio, with no obvious reasons related to the playing side.

In theory, the unchecked free market is liable to produce individual monopolies within particular fields of enterprise. However, as the 'Louis-Schmelling paradox' in economic theory explains, monopolies in sport are particularly bad for business since athletes or teams that exercise total domination do not attract strong audience interest and so fail to maximize their potential earnings (cf. Neale 1964; Bougheas and Downward 2003). The most profitable arrangement for TNC clubs involves an effective *cartelization* of sporting competition which functions to maintain the 'uncertainty of outcome', to exclude competitive outsiders, and to maximize collective revenues.

In sport, cartels are occasioned when a small cluster of elite teams dominates national and international competitions and works together to advance common political and economic interests. National league systems were introduced to regularize competitive fixtures between clubs and to maximize revenues. However, unlike North American sports, the promotion/relegation principle undermined the cartelized aspects of these football leagues by enabling new clubs to join the leading sides on merit. However, as we noted earlier, given the increasingly uneven distribution of growing revenues within nations, there are reasonable concerns that competitive cartels have effectively formed in the top divisions.

---

[67]See http://news.bbc.co.uk/1/hi/business/3693304.stm

The late G-14 provides the most explicit illustration of cartelization in European football in recent years. Established in 2000 with EEIG (European Economic Interest Grouping) status, the G-14 was effectively the corporate pressure group of 18 of Europe's wealthiest clubs, drawn from seven nations (Millward 2006).[68] The G-14 regularly attracted speculation regarding the possibility of a cartelized, breakaway European league being founded. By acceding to club demands over compensation for players on international duty, the major governing bodies in football successfully persuaded the G-14 to disband in February 2008. Nevertheless, the possibility of a breakaway European league has not disappeared.

TNC clubs and corporate structures

Some economists have indicated that European TNC clubs are moving from a traditional sporting model towards a more capitalistic corporate structure. The first model – dubbed *Spectators–Subsidies–Sponsors–Local* (SSSL) – relies upon the first three kinds of income, at mainly *local* level. Since the 1980s, it is argued, clubs have moved increasingly towards the second model – dubbed *Media–Corporations-Merchandising–Markets–Global* (MCMMG) – which prioritizes revenues from television, merchandise, and stock flotation, with finances now being increasingly 'globalized' (Andreff and Staudohar 2000, 2002). However, while a convergence upon the latter model may be discerned long-term across football, there do remain significant national differences in terms of corporate structure.

In regard to convergence, just as nation states share institutional frameworks, so football clubs are increasingly likely to have similar commercial departments to pursue sponsors and to sell merchandise. Further business homogenization may arise in stadium ownership and control. In the UK, Iberia, and Holland, stadiums have tended to be owned by clubs; elsewhere in Europe, many club grounds are public assets in the control of local authorities. Ownership of stadiums enables clubs to maximize revenues from match-day tickets, and to accelerate income from advertising, corporate hospitality, and non-football activities like concerts and exhibitions. Thus, German and Italian clubs have looked closely at building their own stadiums to match earnings from their TNC rivals.

In terms of divergence, significant variations remain in regard to club governance. The UK has tended to be a leader in the conversion of clubs into businesses, with most sides registered as joint-stock companies by 1923 (Buraimo et al. 2006). Tottenham Hotspur became the first European team to float on stock markets in 1983, followed by 21 other British sides by 2005. In contrast, Italian teams were only converted into 'stock' companies in 1966, while in much of Germany, Spain, Portugal, and

---

[68]The clubs were Internazionale, Juventus, Milan (Italy); Arsenal, Liverpool, Manchester United (England); Barcelona, Real Madrid, Valencia (Spain); Bayer Leverkusen, Bayern Munich, Borussia Dortmund (Germany); Marseille, Lyon, PSG (France); Ajax, PSV (Netherlands); and Porto (Portugal).

Latin America, clubs have been traditionally run as mutual associations that are owned and controlled by individual members.

In Europe, some varied departures from the mutual association model have occurred. In France, different mixes of private investor, supporters' association and local authority have long been controlling forces within clubs. The successes of small-town clubs (notably Auxerre and Lens) are attributable partly to local authority ties and collectivist principles. The French league distributes collective revenues quite evenly among clubs, and opposes large speculative investments in playing squads. However, in a switch towards free-market orthodoxy, the collectivist *exception culturelle* was seriously compromised when new legislation in 2006 permitted Lyon to become the first French team to float on the stock exchange.

In Spain, a 'Sport Law' (*ley del deporte*) was enacted in 1990, requiring indebted clubs to convert into limited joint-stock companies or 'SADs' (*sociedad anonima deportiva*). Only four clubs – Athletic Bilbao, Barcelona, Osasuna, and Real Madrid – remained as membership associations. The SAD system enabled clubs to cancel debts of €192 million (Ascari and Gagnepain 2006: 78). In Germany, clubs were restricted to a mutual association model until 1998, whereupon they were permitted to sell just below 50 per cent of their shares on the open market, with the remaining majority held by members. By the year 2000, three distinctive business models were evident among Bundesliga clubs. First, clubs like Bayern Munich and Cologne upheld the old 'registered society' model, featuring strong 'bottom-up' influences through committee elections. Second, clubs like Werder Bremen and Schalke 04 reflected the 'AG model', with a supervisory board working like that of a public company. Third, clubs like Borussia Dortmund, Bayer Leverkusen and Eintracht Frankfurt were nearer to the 'joint stock' model, with less membership influence and greater degrees of structural organization (Wilkesmann and Blutner 2002). In Portugal, since 1998, several clubs have adopted the SAD commercial model, notably Sporting Lisbon, Porto, and Benfica (with 33 per cent of stock floated), although high debts, poor management of player resources, and allegations of corruption have tended to persist.

In the Far East, the evidence points towards a selective and distinctive adoption of neo-liberal principles, notably through clubs being owned by corporations rather than rich individuals. In Japan, for example, the national football league was founded for company sides in 1965; the new J-League, starting in 1993, saw clubs follow European and South American procedures by naming themselves after locations, but corporate ownership remained crucial. In Korea, the national government pressured companies to create a professional league system. Of the top 14 sides, nine were owned by companies such as Hyundai, POSCO, and Samsung, while the other five were formed and owned by local governments.

In post-communist systems, the old State associations of clubs tended to be replaced quickly by private corporate ties. In Vietnam, economic liberalization during the 1990s saw the privatization of half the top sides;

thus, the Railways team was acquired by the Asia Commercial bank, and Vietnam Airlines built ties with the Hanoi Police side, while the police side in Ho Chi Minh City was bought by East Asia Bank. In Eastern Europe, under the Marxist-Leninist regimes, top clubs had been entwined with specific state institutions, such as sides named Dinamo (security services) and Lokomotiv (railways). The post-Soviet system required most clubs to find new commercial owners, hence in Moscow all sides except Lokomotiv were privatized; in Romania, Dinamo Bucharest remained close to the Ministry of the Interior, but the Steaua team went private.

Major differences exist in the financial shelters afforded to clubs by local authorities and national governments. We noted earlier the connections between Spanish clubs and local authorities. Italy's government has become more interventionist, forwarding in February 2003 the *decreto salva calcio* that would permit clubs to spread their losses over ten years, thereby slicing debts by over 70 per cent from €1.318 billion to €400 million. The decree contravened EU accounting standards, and was challenged by the European courts (Baroncelli and Lago 2006: 14). The recent Petrucci Law allows the football authorities to take control of bankrupt clubs, to find new owners while the club is relegated.

In Belgium, there are differences *between* the different regions in public support for clubs. In Wallonia, more interventionist government ensures that the local authorities assist clubs to modernize stadiums, thereby enabling monies to be transferred into player recruitment and wages. In Flanders, local government avoids clubs in financial disarray (Dejonghe and Vandeweghe 2006: 110).

Overall then, it would be premature to argue that the free-market, corporatization model will be institutionalized by all professional football clubs or national sport systems. While forms of convergence are occurring, the privatization model has hitherto taken different legal and institutional forms according to cultural context. Notably, financial analysts advocate a highly contextual strategy, advising clubs and nations to avoid slavishly imposing textbook business strategies upon their football environment, and to be responsive to the particularities and peculiarities of their specific supporter bases (Deloitte 2004a: 20). Moreover, within the football marketplace, we find that emotional and personal factors are still apparent in financial transactions. Many takeover offers and small investments in club football are motivated, at least in part, by the desire to gain social status, or to derive personal utility from involvement with a nationally or globally prominent side (cf. Harmes 2001: 111).

Player recruitment

A further domain in which the TNC status of top international clubs can be explored relates to labour recruitment. Some evidence suggests that, at the apex of world football, a growing 'A-list' or 'transnational capitalist class' is circulating, comprising players, coaches, and agents (Lanfranchi and Taylor

1999: 225–9; Sklair 2001). Thus, most Western European clubs in the Champions League, especially those entering the later rounds, feature a minority of national-born players. In the UK, top clubs such as Arsenal, Celtic, Chelsea, and Rangers have fielded teams composed entirely of 'non-national' players. Among the top 12 richest clubs in 2005/6, foreign players constituted over 75 per cent of the 'List A' players at Arsenal (87 per cent), Internazionale and Chelsea in the Champions League for the 2006/7 season; the remainder of sides featured squads with over 35 per cent of imported players.[69] In turn, Europe-based players dominate South American and African national sides. At the African Cup of Nations, since the year 2000, at least half of the registered players have been Europe-based, and the most successful teams are far more diffuse.

Despite these processes, we do not advance a globalist argument regarding the complete deterritorialization of players at TNC clubs. Player recruitment may be understood in terms of 'disaggregation', as these team 'parts' are sourced locally, regionally, and globally (cf. Mair 1997). The truly 'global' team (like the 'global car') emerges only rarely. Most European football nations emphasize the 'integration' of foreign recruits within the distinctive occupational subcultures of players, and into the competitive ethics and rule interpretations that prevail at national level. For example, overseas players entering the UK must acclimatize to a fast-paced game involving a relatively high proportion of combative tackles, and are expected to follow particular sporting customs such as *not* asking referees to book or dismiss opponents.

Leading European clubs prefer players from 'homophilous' nations with regional or post-colonial ties (cf. Rogers 1962). In other words, in football's labour markets, TNC clubs still practice particular forms of cultural 'glocalization' in recruiting 'foreign' players from culturally similar nations while also according status to symbolic local or national figures. For example, English and Scottish clubs have long favoured players from across the UK, Ireland, Western Europe, and Scandinavia (Lanfranchi and Taylor 1999; McGovern 2002). Elsewhere, regional patterns remain: Iberian clubs look to South America for cheap, talented players; southern and central African players migrate towards South Africa; North American clubs look south; and Australian clubs look to the UK or the Pacific islands. Elite players prefer to move to a society where the weather, food, and language are relatively familiar, enabling them to train, socialize, and relax according to habit. However, reflecting the tenacious hold of residual value systems in football, even the world's leading clubs often do little to assist their highly expensive imports to acclimatize in socio-cultural terms (Mora y Araujo 2007).

---

[69]Clubs register up to 25 List-A players for each season. The figures for Juventus are derived from the 2005/6 season. For English clubs, British and Irish players are not counted as 'foreign', given the long history of football connections and deeper cultural and structural ties between these nations.

In turn, major differences arise in Europe over the national distributions of non-European players. In the Big 5 leagues, the number of foreign players more than doubled over ten years, after the Bosman case, from around 460 in the mid-1990s to almost 1000 in 2006. England attracted the greatest share (over 280), mostly from Western Europe. Germany and France both drew around 190, the former mainly from mainland Europe, and the latter taking nearly half from Africa, especially Francophone regions. Spain drew around 170, with almost two-thirds coming from Latin America. Italy drew the lowest figure, around 160, of whom half hailed from Latin America (Poli and Ravenel 2006). By 2008, six leagues – led by England (59 per cent), followed by Portugal, Belgium, Germany, Greece, and Russia – were importing more than 50 per cent of their registered players from other nations (Besson et al. 2008). Significant national divergences also arise in coach recruitment: Italian, German, and French clubs favour their own national coaches; top English clubs recruit from Europe, but lower teams are loyal to the UK; and outward-looking Spanish sides tend to favour Latin Americans or former La Liga players from abroad.

TNC clubs still draw a significant minority of players – particularly defensive ones – from home nations. 'Home' players are often accorded a totemic status at clubs and typically claim the captain's armband. For example, for the 2004–5 season, nation-based club captaincies included: AC Milan (Italy's Paolo Maldini), Barcelona (Spain's Carles Puyol), Bayern Munich (Germany's Oliver Kahn), Chelsea (England's John Terry), Juventus (Italy's Alessandro Del Piero), Manchester United (Ireland's Roy Keane), Porto (Portugal's Francisco Costinha), Real Madrid (Spain's Raúl), Roma (Italy's Francesco Totti), and Valencia (Spain's David Albelda). Home players are typically viewed as the 'heart' of the team; renowned worldwide, but personifying the club's local or national identity.

Moreover, in a challenge to the free market in elite labour, UEFA and FIFA have sought to sustain the national identities of teams through limiting the participation of non-national players. Following EU consultation, UEFA introduced the 'homegrown' rule for the 2006/7 season, whereby clubs in European competition were required to list four of their 25 'A-list' players as 'locally trained'; the figure rose to eight over the next two seasons. While the measure sought to protect ties between clubs and local areas, the lack of specific stipulations on player nationality would allow some young, non-national players to be classified as 'homegrown'. Alternatively, a FIFA-proposed '6+5' model, limiting clubs to the fielding of only five foreign players by 2012, would contravene European labour laws.

Labour recruitment and investment is also apparent in the strategic partnerships formed between clubs. Lower-status overseas clubs often act as 'nurseries' (or forms of labour entrepôt) for TNC teams, enabling non-EU players to gain residency and employment permits. Belgium has relatively weaker laws regarding joint citizenship rights, thus several of its clubs fulfil 'feeder' roles for English and Dutch teams: for example, Beveren with Arsenal, SV Brugge with Blackburn Rovers, FC Antwerp with Manchester United, and Westerlo with

Chelsea and Feyenoord (Dejonghe and Vandeweghe 2006: 107–8). These practices also provide one solution for TNC clubs in their intensive struggles over 'research and development', notably in sourcing, recruiting, housing, and honing the best emerging young talents at a worldwide level.

The recruitment of some foreign players by clubs may be viewed as a form of extra-football FDI, in order to maximize particular revenue streams. Exceptionally, Real Madrid claimed that their four-year association with the supreme *galáctico*, David Beckham, had generated €560 million for the club. More generally, buying Asian players can boost the business interests of clubs, owners and leagues in the Far East, although the issue of improved football results is sometimes debated.[70] The Austrian club Red Bull Salzburg signed Japanese internationals Alex and Tsuneyasu Miyamoto in 2007 in part to help their owner, an energy drinks magnate, penetrate the Asian markets.

Some surveys suggest Serie A is the most popular European league in Japan, largely due to the historical recruitment of Japanese players. When Japan's Hidetoshi Nakata played for five Italian sides between 1998 and 2005, the clubs benefited from intensive Japanese media coverage and an average 700,000 daily hits on the player's website (the *Guardian*, 24 July 2001; Moffett 2003: 194–5). Arsenal purchased the Japanese Junichi Inamoto for €3.5 million in July 2001, and were assumed to have earned more from Japanese merchandise sales; Inamoto played in three minor matches and was released within one year. In Germany, Hamburg's signing of the Japanese Naohiro Takahara helped the Bundesliga's 'brand recognition' in Japan, while Shinji Ono enabled Feyenoord of Holland to derive around 15 per cent of turnover from the Japanese marketplace. When Celtic signed Shunsuke Nakamura in 2005, Japanese subscribers to the Scottish Premier League rose from 100,000 to 1.2 million (*FIFA Magazine*, June 2007).

Similarly, Manchester United's recruitment policies are worth consideration, with US players Tim Howard and Jonathan Spector joining as the club sought to bolster its American marketing. In January 2004, United recruited teenage Chinese striker Dong Fangzhou, dispatching him to Royal Antwerp to develop his talents and make him eligible for a Belgian passport (and thus guarantee his future EU-based employment). United's initial payment (€500,000) was worthwhile venture capital on a player who could, with first-team exposure, secure premium symbolic entry for the club within the massive Chinese market.

Branding

The language and logic surrounding market 'branding' is an important dimension of TNC clubs. Reflecting the business origins of the word, glocalization

---

[70]Such transfers tend not to undermine the coaches' powers within clubs. High merchandise sales may increase transfer budgets for new players. If their abilities are unconfirmed, players may be restricted to less important fixtures or performing simpler functions within the team. No director would jeopardize the club's competitive (and thus financial) status by insisting that highly marketable, weak players must feature in the team.

processes are evidenced in the branding strategies of TNC clubs, which involve both homogenizing and heterogenizing dimensions.

At first glance, branding has a homogeneous basis: global brands all have distinctive names, logos, market positions, pricing structures, distribution channels, and assumed 'values' (Mooij 1997). In football, TNC clubs like Real Madrid and Manchester United tell transnational tales about their histories of success, exciting playing styles, recruitment of star players and coaches, and their promises of spectacle (for example, Manchester United's Old Trafford repackaged as the 'Theatre of Dreams'). Additionally, in general, *football* clubs may be viewed as 'product invariant' entities; unlike most other TNCs, they cannot reinvent themselves entirely in different sports or other commercial realms.[71]

Nevertheless, just as soft-drinks manufacturers adapt flavours to suit regional tastes, so TNC clubs may vary their 'message' to particular markets. For example, on international tours, team players from host nations are given greater public relations duties to reach home audiences; in relatively new football nations, such as China or Japan, celebrity players are most prominent, to attract new (especially female) supporters. To resist 'brand ageing' and the end of 'product lifecycles', TNC clubs introduce 'revitalizing' measures such as new kit designs, and recruit new coaches and players to safeguard future successes (Kapferer 1992: 321–7). Yet clubs are also wary of destabilizing brand identity through excessive innovation, such as when players are constantly bought and sold, team shirts are continually redesigned, new coaches employ radically different playing styles, or the team fails to win trophies.

Football clubs thrive on intensive 'market' particularism and partisanship, inculcating the assumption that all football followers construct club or player allegiances (or 'brand loyalties') that can be converted into the purchase of related products. Football bestows strong brand 'equity' on products such as replica shirts that accrue premium added value through club or player association. Such products outstrip other branded items (such as cars or soft drinks) by defining the consumer's identity as a form of cultural partisanship. To extend that identity statement, TNC clubs market a smorgasbord of 'subbrand' products such as leisurewear, foodstuffs (e.g. biscuits, beer), financial services (e.g. car insurance, credit cards), and household items (e.g. bed linen, kitchen clocks) (Hart 1998: 211).

Football branding in part connects the game to global merchandise corporations. In 2006, Nike and adidas reported annual football merchandise sales in the region of US$1.5 billion and €1.2 billion respectively (the *Observer*, 28 May 2006). TNC clubs particularly generate enormous sales for associated merchandise corporations. In 2006–7, the leading six European leagues (the Big Five plus the Netherlands) were estimated to have generated over €360 million in shirt sales; Germany, followed by England and France, were the biggest markets, with around €70 million earned by five clubs (Manchester United, Bayern Munich,

---

[71]However, some TNC clubs have displayed vertical diversification by establishing successful sister clubs in other sports, such as with the basketball wings of Spanish and Greek sides.

Real Madrid, Lyon, and Chelsea).[72] Thus, aggressive merchandise TNCs pay high fees for brand association with leading sides: for example, Nike's €300 million, 13-year contract in 2000 with Manchester United, or its €130 million, 10-year deal with Arsenal in 2004.

In turn, football is presented as a merchandise contest, as sportswear manufacturers vie for association with the most successful and popular teams. In some circumstances, TNC struggles may challenge the close historical and symbolic ties between football and merchandise institutions. For example, the German Football Association (DFB) has been deeply connected to the German merchandise TNC adidas since 1954. These bonds were threatened when Nike offered the DFB a deal worth around €500 million over eight years from 2011 – almost five times the value of the existing adidas offer that was still some €200 million below that of its competitor.

TNC clubs enter inter-enterprise alliances with non-football corporations to aid brand-building synergies. TNC clubs favour global brand status, enabling symbolic association with target markets (e.g. North America, Asia) or with modern products and services; in 2006, most leading European clubs were sponsored by financial, insurance, or tourism corporations, with smaller numbers backed by car manufacturers and gambling organizations. In 2007, the top dozen annual deals were rooted firmly among the Big 5 clubs, with Manchester United (tied to AIG for €14.1 million), Juventus (Tamoil, €12.8 million), Bayern Munich (T-Com, €11.5 million), Chelsea (Samsung, €11 million), Real Madrid (Siemens, €9.7 million), Spurs (Mansion, €8.5 million), Dortmund (E.On, €8.3 million), and Lyon (Renault, €8.3 million) all well ahead of the rest (*Forbes*, 16 May 2006). Further sponsorship presents itself through the sale of ground-naming rights, for example with the Allianz Arena in Munich, the DKB Arena in Rostock, and Arsenal's Emirates Stadium (as part of a €100 million package with the airline).

Selective marketing associations are also promoted by the avoidance of 'sponsor clutter', which arises when team kits are plastered in numerous corporate logos. In exceptional circumstances, the refusal of certain clubs to carry corporate sponsorship may, in a competitive framework, be interpreted as a kind of 'branding' exercise; the appeal to higher values or purposes in turn puts an additional intangible commercial value on the club's global 'brand' identity.[73]

Transnational brands derive significant value from their football partnerships. In the early 2000s, Siemens paid around US$12 million annually for the shirt sponsorship of Real Madrid, during which time the company's world market share rose from 17 per cent to 21 per cent; market share in Brazil rose by 60 per cent, largely helped by association with Real Madrid's Brazilian stars. In 2003, Juventus' sponsors, such as Tamoil and Lotto, reportedly earned over

---

[72]See *FIFA Magazine*, May 2007.

[73]In 2006, Barcelona broke with its long tradition by permitting advertising on team shirts. However, in line with their social and political values, rather than focus on commercial possibilities, Barcelona elected to promote UNICEF without charge, and agreed to donate £1.5 million towards charitable causes during the five-year agreement. Barcelona was listed as the second richest club in the world for the season 2005/6.

€120 million from their football ties. Negative brand equity can arise, for example where clubs forge strong bonds with particular sponsoring TNCs, which in turn encourage rival fans to buy competing products. Yet such oppositions may be viewed as having a broader function in intensifying existing brand identification, and underlining more generally football's global status as a medium for infusing products with emotional energy.

Of course, leading clubs are not alone in forming close bonds with major TNCs. Football's governing bodies, most notably FIFA, have been particularly adept in branding their tournaments through lucrative deals with global corporations. For example, Coca-Cola's extended sponsorship deal with FIFA, from 2007 to 2022, cost the company around US$500 million. For the 2010 World Cup finals in South Africa, FIFA was set to charge its six 'Worldwide Partners' around US$125 million apiece, with up to 14 other sponsors likely to pay around US$40 million each. For the 2002 tournament, FIFA sold licensing rights that enabled more than 280 companies to manufacture and sell over 500 products, which in turn generated worldwide retail sales of approximately US$1.5 billion.[74] To protect copyright, FIFA won 1900 post-tournament cases across 88 countries against those manufacturing or selling around 3.2 million counterfeit goods.[75]

Concluding Comments

Evidently, elite world football, particularly in Western Europe, has undergone profound economic transformation, largely through the exponential growth of its external revenue sources, notably television. Market deregulation and liberalization have underpinned these commercial changes, giving rise to intensified national and international inequalities between clubs, as well as among players, coaches, and officials. The other side of football's gilded coin has witnessed greater levels of club indebtedness, bankruptcy, and dependency, particularly in South America and Africa. In Western Europe, during the early 2000s, the 'millennial' or apocalyptic discourses on economic crisis were justifiable in some instances but premature in many cases, as leading teams and leagues have continued to strike ever-larger television deals. This revenue stream, along with possible intensive investment from billionaire owners, has become even more important amidst the financial crises of the late 2000s.

Despite the emergence of TNC clubs since the late 1980s, we are still some way from the full triumph of naked neo-liberalism within football. Just as the world economy displays different or multiple forms of capitalism, so various political, legal, and cultural forces shape the manifestation of the free market upon football in diverse ways.

First, significantly different systems of corporate governance still arise internationally in club football. To put it another way, some nations adopt

---

[74]See www.fifa.com/en/marketing/licensing/index/0,1315,10,00.html

[75]FIFPro, the players' world union, derives sizeable revenues from the endorsement of electronic games.

more protectionist policies towards the free market than do others. In South America, Iberia, and Germany, the mutual-association model of club governance has not been entirely abandoned. In the developing world, some clubs still rely on public sector assistance to secure success (Amara and Henry 2004). In Nigeria, for example, leading clubs are typically backed by state authorities; thus, top clubs like Enyimba cost local authorities around US$5 million each year. In Angola, despite long-standing military conflicts, the football system has been financially settled through ties between clubs and state organizations, such as oil companies, the military, or the police. Additionally, television deals for UEFA and many national club tournaments are struck not by individual sides, as the free-market system would expect, but collectively by football leagues or governing bodies.

Second, and to the chagrin of some neo-liberalists, football's regulatory bodies still restrict the trading freedom of clubs to a greater degree than one finds in other 'industries'. Dimitry Piterman, owner of Spanish team Alaves, lamented the restrictions within football's labour markets when noting:

> If Nike has to pay 20 bucks an hour in the US, they move to Taiwan and pay one buck. Why can't a football club do the same? The club can't move, but it should be able to use other markets. Why can't I buy 10 Brazilians if it helps my club compete? And how can you limit professional freedom? If you sack a coach here, he can't manage another team that season – why? A player can only play for one team in the Champions League – I don't get the story on that. Often the rules conflict with civil laws.

> (*World Soccer*, February 2006)

Third, we should not forget the social and political criticism that has been directed towards football's 'hypercommodification', the entry of 'market rhetoric' to depict fans as 'consumers', and the intensified surveillance or control of spectators.[76] In Mexico, for example, fans of the Puma club campaigned against the commercialization of team emblems by Nike and refused to accept sponsorship for supporter motifs (Magazine 2007b: 119–22). Various policies have been advocated to challenge the widening inequalities between different football economies. For example, the proposed 'Coubertobin tax'[77] would see levies imposed upon international transfers, notably involving young players, and thereby further compensate clubs for nurturing fledgling talents (Andreff 2004).

Finally, other football institutions typically provide alternative political–economic frameworks to neo-liberalism. In the next two chapters, we examine alternative political standpoints to the neo-liberalist credo.

---

[76]See, for example, Conn (1997); Horton (1997); Armstrong and Giulianotti (1998b); Giulianotti (2005b, 2007); and Walsh and Giulianotti (2006).

[77]The Tobin tax, as recommended by the Nobel Prize-winning economist, seeks to impose a levy on short-term transactions of foreign exchange, with one possible consequence being the raising of tax revenues that might help developing countries. The 'Coubertobin tax' combines this standpoint with some of the internationalist ideals associated with Baron Pierre De Coubertin, founder of the modern Olympics.

4

Politics: Nations, Neo-Mercantilism and International Governance

Introduction

Football's global political field reveals a growing multi-polar complexity, with a broad array of institutional actors, ranging from international governments to local player agents. Particular interest is reserved for the position of national societies, given their historical contribution to the game's political development. While neo-liberalism impacts directly upon football, other political–economic policies and ideologies are evidenced in the practices and strategies of different agents within the global game. Here, we consider the *neo-mercantilist* model of political–economic arrangements that define the interests of national and international institutions such as football's governing bodies and state/supra-state actors.

Our discussion is divided into four main parts. First, we explore the complex interrelationships of nations to globalization processes, paying particular attention to the so-called 'club versus country' struggle. Second, we explain our theorization and application of neo-mercantilism in regard to football, highlighting the 'systemic pressures' contained within this political–economic theme. Third, we consider international governance as a further political–economic force that consistently challenges neo-mercantilism and neo-liberalism, while exploring also its particular pathologies such as corruption. Fourth, we outline and assess some arguments regarding the potential reform of football's governance according to democratic and cosmopolitan principles.

State of the Nation: International Football

The nation state and globalization

As we demonstrated in Chapter 1, national identity and nation states have been crucial, elemental reference points in the history of football's globalization since the late nineteenth century. Here, we argue that football reveals ways in which nation states remain potent and highly adaptive societal units with regard to contemporary globalization.

We should state at the outset that we understand the nation state in conventional analytical terms, as conjoining a *nation* and a *state*. A nation refers to a social collective, a people, which harbours among its constituents particularly strong cultural commonalities and symbolic solidarities, such as in terms of heritage, ethnicity, homeland, and language (cf. Anderson 1983; Smith 1986). A state refers to an apparatus of government that exercises sovereignty over a defined territory and population (cf. Weber 1958). Nation states have been the primary collective units of the modern age, since the principle objective of political nationalism has been either to establish or to extend the sovereignty of these entities. Historically, there have been far more nations than states, while nation states are themselves highly varied and changing entities (Holton 1998: 81; Walby 2003: 531). Some nations lack corresponding states (e.g. Scotland, Catalonia), while some states want for deep national solidarity (e.g. Malta, as well as the British Empire in the Indian sub-continent) (McCrone 1992; Baldacchino 2002).

Nation states advance ideologies of primordiality, 'imagined community', and 'shared fate' to bind their peoples into forms of collective identification, notably through national education systems and mass mediatization, and in ethno-symbolic terms through cultural fields such as sport (cf. Anderson 1983; Gellner 1983). While these processes reify the nation state/nationalism couplet, most nations have long possessed significant degrees of ethnic diversity. Thus, in the New World particularly, the theme of polyethnicity has 'returned' from the 1920s onwards, rather than been a contemporary discovery (McNeill 1986).

Nevertheless, for some analysts, it is recent processes of globalization that have ineluctably undermined national identification and the powers of nation states. Ohmae (1995) asserts that the 'Four Is' of investment, industry, information technology, and individual consumers have become increasingly global in orientation, hence the nation state's intermediary functions are evermore superfluous.[78] Appadurai (1998: 19, 22) avers that 'the nation state, as a complex modern political form, is on its last legs', while diverse 'diasporic public spheres' have become 'the crucibles of a postnational political order'. Beck (2004: 26–7) dismisses the national as a 'zombie-category' inhabited by 'the living dead'; as we have moved into the age of a 'second modernity', our 'political coordinates' have shifted into the transnational and cosmopolitan. More generally, the 'new medievalism' thesis contends that numerous pressures, including internal ethno-regional conflicts and powerful transnational institutions, are fragmenting Westphalian national sovereignty (Gilpin 2001: 391; cf. Walby 1999: 124). In turn, some have argued that transnational issues and problems – notably 'terrorism' networks, organized crime, universalistic human rights, and ecological degradation – all endanger and outmode the nation state (cf. Krasner 1993; Strange 1994; Beck 1999).

Alternatively, sceptical and circumspect analyses insist that nation states remain significant international forces (cf. Hirst and Thompson 1999). Robertson's (1992: 184) earlier judgement that 'there is nothing to suggest

---

[78]According to Ohmae (1993: 78), 'the nation state has become an unnatural, even dysfunctional, unit for organising human activity and managing economic endeavour in a borderless world'.

that the nationally organized society, more specifically the state, is about to wither away', remains highly pertinent. Indeed, Robertson and other analysts (e.g. Meyer et al. 1997) consider that the very *emergence* of nation states has been a long-term aspect of globalization. Elsewhere, Castells (1997: 306) indicates that nation states have maintained their cohesion through resurgences in communalism and nationalism. Notably, nation states still move to protect their political–economic interests, to the extent that variants of 'global fascism' have appeared, most obviously through US military expansion abroad (Robinson 2004: 150; Falk 2005: 223).

Let us consider too the common argument that new institutional forces erode nation state powers. As Rosenau (1997: 43–4) puts it, influence has moved 'outwards to transnational and supranational organizations, sidewards to social movements and NGOs, and inwards to subnational groups'. To begin, we should appreciate that the nation state retains powers denied to its apparent 'competitor' institutions. Indeed, TNCs are *attracted* to strong market-orientated states that can secure political–economic stability and pliant workforces. Supra-state formations like the EU still lack crucial state-defining powers, such as exercising military violence, raising taxes directly from citizens, and tackling hitherto 'private' social practices such as smoking (cf. Walby 1999).

Some analysts have argued plausibly that nation states have adapted and revitalized within these new circumstances.[79] The interdisciplinary realm of urban studies has employed the keyword *glocalisation* in an innovative way, and in some differentiation to its usage elsewhere in this book (note too the different spelling here – with an 's', not 'z'). Glocalisation serves to explain the 'rescaling'of nation state powers, upwards to supra-state entities (like the EU and WTO) and downwards to local and regional authorities (cf. Swyngedouw 1992, 1997: 158, 2004; Brenner 1999). Glocalisation processes actively engage nation states in major political–economic transformations such as the strengthening of regional entities and the expansion of city infrastructures and 'inter-urban networks' (Brenner 1998: 5).

The pressing nature of some issues promotes these glocal shifts – for instance, environmental policies are most effective when implemented via supra-state agencies and strong assistance from local or regional institutions (Blatter 2004). In turn, the nation state itself is transmogrified into a 'glocal state' or a 'glocal competition state regime', in Brenner's terms (1998, 2004), positioning itself strategically between transnational and local political processes. In recent decades, glocal states in Europe and North America have accelerated transnational interdependencies through free-market economic strategies, followed by policies of 'glocal developmentalism', for example by part-funding local regeneration projects to rejuvenate post-industrial wastelands.

---

[79]'Catalytic' nation states have been identified in particular in Asia, for long-standing work in attracting TNC investment and exporting governmental practices (cf. Weiss 1997).

Crucial questions arise over the making of nation states in the context of complex transnational migration patterns and the construction of polyethnic identities. Some of the largest contemporary nation states are increasingly characterized by their ethnic diversity. In nations like Australia and Canada, inter-ethnic differences and conflicts do not, in themselves, always invalidate the nation state per se. Further complexity is added by the social construction of indigeneity in recent years through First Nations discourses regarding primordial ethnicity (Niezen 2003). In response, the nation state may move towards an official, prima facie, oxymoronic ideology which celebrates the multiplicity of nationalities as a defining feature of its collective nationhood (Robertson 1998b).

On the other hand, questions arise over whether the ethno-symbolic solidarity of nation states may be extended beyond national borders, to engender deep continental bonds or indeed to build a common continental or global indigenism. Habermas (2001: 58), for example, considers that a 'solidarity among strangers' may in theory extend across Europe to produce a vibrant public sphere and inclusive political culture. It would appear, nevertheless, that we are some distance from this eventuality. For some, the current European Union retains a 'simulacrum of national traditions' that is lacking in the 'crafted authenticity of the nation state and the assumed "naturalness" of national identity' (Axford 1995). Even if a popular, democratic, continental compact were to be conceived, *realpolitik* would almost certainly intrude, as more populous or wealthier ethnic groups position themselves to dominate government and civil society (Žižek 2002: 124).

Football and the nation

When we turn to elaborate these observations in regard to football, we may begin by noting that the game harbours two relevant 'national' institutions: first, the national associations, which most closely resemble nation states within the game; and second, to a lesser extent, the nation states themselves, with particular reference to their sport-related policies. In the following, we focus particularly upon the national associations.

As a nation *state*, the national football association comprises an internationally recognized apparatus of government over the game within specific national territorial boundaries. As a *nation* state, the national football association controls the national football team, which embodies the nation in strong ethno-symbolic ways.

Historically, national associations have been the key political units across football's international relations, and are permitted to apply for full FIFA membership if they represent 'an independent state recognized by the international community'. The nation state principle extends back to the first years of FIFA's existence, when for example Bohemia was denied entry as it was an Austrian territory, while the independence of Finland and Norway saw both nations granted full membership in 1908 (Goldblatt 2006: 233–4). The four British football associations have always received special treatment, given that they long predate the 1904 foundation of FIFA; moreover, as the 'cradles of football', their participation bestowed particular legitimacy upon the fledgling global body.[80] In turn, football participation has played a crucial role for nation states in the international politics of recognition. By 2008, FIFA had more national members (208) than the United Nations (192). The integrity of nation states within football's system of governance is confirmed by the game's governing bodies, which prohibit the movement of clubs across national boundaries into 'foreign' league systems.[81]

FIFA's statutes strengthen the ideological hand of 'nationless states', while placing 'stateless nations' in problematic positions. FIFA membership provides new nation states with a potent cultural sphere within which strong nationalistic rituals may be developed and extended. Conversely, most 'stateless nations' are denied FIFA membership, including semi-autonomous regions (e.g. Greenland, South Lower Saxony, Zanzibar), unrecognized separatist states (e.g. North Cyprus), or peoples without settled territorial powers (e.g. the Roma, the Sami). The 'New Federation Board', formed in December 2003, represents many of these 'outsider' nations, and staged its inaugural tournament, the Viva World Cup, in 2006 (Menary 2007).

Football's governing bodies argue that they remain consistent in applying FIFA statutes to determine official membership. Outsider nations, however, complain that *realpolitik* is most prominent, as powerful FIFA members have tightened admission criteria effectively to exclude small football federations that offer little in financial rewards; the case of the Pacific island nation of Kiribati is illustrative, in being a FIFA outsider, yet a UN and IOC member.[82] In Europe, small principalities such as Andorra, San Marino, and Monaco are UN and IOC members. Andorra and San Marino have been FIFA members since 1996 and 1988 respectively; Monaco, however, has avoided pressing hard for FIFA membership for fear of its leading club, AS Monaco, being evicted from the French football league. However, the fact that Greenland and the Faroe Islands are both similarly sized autonomous provinces of Denmark, yet only the latter has been admitted to FIFA, points to the somewhat arbitrary basis upon which the game's governing body decides 'national' status and thus grants membership.

---

[80]The four British associations were England, Scotland, Wales, and Ireland. In Ireland, two rival associations emerged: the Irish Football Association (or IFA, based in Belfast), and the breakaway Football Association of the Irish Free State (FAIFS), founded in Dublin in 1921, a year before the creation of the Irish Free State. While the four British associations were in self-imposed exile from FIFA, the FAIFS was soon accepted into football's international community in 1923.

[81]Occasional exceptions do arise, for highly specific reasons. For example, in the UK, Berwick Rangers, based in the English border town, joined a local Scottish league in 1905, and have since remained in that national football system. Welsh teams such as Cardiff City and Swansea City joined the expanding English league prior to 1914. Ethno-nationalist conflict in Northern Ireland saw Derry City permitted to join the Republic of Ireland's football league in 1985.

[82]See http://news.bbc.co.uk/sport1/hi/football/6107012.stm

Some popular but somewhat limited arguments contend that, unlike global politics, football affords a 'small nation' view of the world, wherein 'all members are equal, each with its particular place in the bright and vibrant palette of nations' (*FIFA News*, December 1999). In turn, some small nations interpret the game as a positive metaphor for the free-market's potentialities: as Tanzanian President Benjamin Mkapa proclaimed at the World Economic Forum, 'globalization can deliver, just as Tanzania can play in the World Cup and win it' (Gibney 2003: 7). The problem with these arguments is that *realpolitik* is harder to dislodge: Tanzania, which ranks near the foot of the UN's Human Development Index, lacks influence inside FIFA's corridors of power and has never qualified for the World Cup finals.

In general, football tends to confirm the continuing significance of the modern nation state model. Football tournaments involving national teams draw the largest television audiences and, to appease popular demands, have been extended in recent years to accommodate more competitors. Fixtures involving the national team still encapsulate and dramatize senses of 'shared fate' across the imagined communities that comprise the nation, increasingly beyond territorial boundaries and among large diasporic groups. At elite club level, there are some signs of 'solidarity among strangers' at continental levels, notably in pan-African backing for African national sides at the World Cup. However, only golf's Ryder Cup features strong rituals of popular, sport-focused, European identification among players and spectators.

Some aspects of intensified economic globalization may strengthen the nation's status in football. Many leading South American and African play-ers are employed in Europe, and are only seen by local fans when playing for the national side. Moreover, as many nations have lost particular national symbols and political–economic autonomy – for example, in South America, with the demise of national airlines, currencies, public utilities, or the freedom to choose welfare policies – so the national football team and its colours acquire additional symbolic importance to the people (the *Observer*, 10 February 2002).

In turn, national elites endeavour to tap into football's popular appeal. The game provides an important organizational framework for enhancing national connectivity alongside state-sanctioned strategies of integration and legitimation. At club level, the participation of 'provincial' teams in the national league system helps to integrate peripheral communities within the nation state.[83] Official discourses often present national football suc-cesses as a legitimization of state strategies; for example, some Iranian politicians argued that national qualification for the 1998 World Cup finals

---

[83]Hosting the 1999 Copa America enabled Paraguay to build new stadiums outside of Asuncion, notably in Pedro Juan Caballero and Ciudad del Este, from where representative teams were admitted to the national league. Uruguay and Brazil have also engaged more peripheral football settings in recent years.

was 'a political victory' for the Islamic state (the *Independent*, 12 June 1998). In the West, political leaders routinely seek some reflective popular benefit from association with successful sides, particularly national teams. At the very least, football may serve state interests by constituting an 'integrative enclave', whereby ruling elites and dominant institutions seek to secure greater legitimacy among marginalized or oppressed minorities. This particular role of football has been identified in Israel among Arab-Palestinian peoples (Sorek 2007).

In Latin America, populist leaders and military *juntas* were particularly keen to associate their regimes with successful teams, though with questionable political consequences (Miller 2007). In Africa in recent years, football has been manipulated by incumbent elites. Zimbabwe's long-time leader, Robert Mugabe, introduced the highly expensive Unity Cup for domestic clubs, while his propaganda chief, Jonathan Moyo, sought to exploit the national side's qualification for the 2004 African Nations' Cup finals. Eight years earlier, Nigeria's military dictator Sani Abacha insisted that the national side should not fly to the African Cup of Nations in South Africa, as the hosts had criticized his execution of the human rights campaigner, Ken Saro-Wiwa.

New political regimes seek to establish themselves through symbolic transformations within and through football. For example, in the former Zaire, under President Mobutu, the national team was nicknamed 'The Leopards' and wore the animal's face on its shirts, in deference to the leader's favoured fur and his stated policy of 'Zaireanization'. After seizing power in 1997, Laurent Kabila changed the nation's name, flag, currency, and football team symbols: the new side was rechristened 'The Lions', playing in yellow shirts with blue shorts and sleeves. Elsewhere, following periods of civil war or during military occupation, football matches have been staged to symbolize the normalization of everyday life, such as in Afghanistan and Iraq after US-led invasions (cf. the *Guardian*, 16 February 2002). In Northern Ireland, after paramilitary movements had agreed an end to violence, the government mooted the erection of a new national sports stadium on the site of the old Maze prison where convicted terrorists had been jailed.

A further issue here concerns the construction and protection of the nation's 'brand' identity within and beyond football. In concert with export and tourist marketing, all nations 'brand' themselves through association with particular national products or commodities, and by elaborating specific invented traditions – consider, for instance, Scotland, with its mythical mix of tartanry, Highland pageants, the saltire flag, whisky, shortbread, and other goods (cf. Nairn 1977; McCrone et al. 1995). Yet there are rather limited legal safeguards for nation states to control or profit directly from the marketing of their brand derivatives. Disney and Microsoft may act swiftly to prosecute traders who pirate logos, but the United States and the UK are unable to remove national titles or flags from garments made and sold across Asia or Latin America. In football, we find similarly that clubs, national leagues, governing bodies, and leading competitions carry registered trademarks, but national titles and flags are freely stitched into sporting and leisure garments without fear of infringing copyright.

In theory, national societies and their associated institutions (including football associations) are losing financial returns and political control through this siphoning of their brand identities. In turn, some supporter movements have acted to prevent commercial forces from hijacking specific national brand identities. For example, one group of Scotland football supporters elected to trademark their popular nickname ('The Tartan Army'), to avoid its capture by market-centred interests.

Turning to glocalisation processes, football does contribute significantly to the rescaling or transformation of nation states vis-à-vis other institutions and organizations. In the 'upwards sense', national associations have collaborated with continental and global bodies to create more expansive and lucrative tournaments, such as UEFA's Champions League. Stronger regional and continental relationships are evidenced in new football tournaments and organizations; in 2004, for example, the Arab Football Union hosted a 32-team competition, and a winter 'Royal League' was founded with four clubs apiece from Denmark, Norway, and Sweden. In 2005, five North African football associations formed their own regional federation, and in 2007 the 12-team Baltic League was founded by three ex-USSR states.

National identity has been explored more fully in an 'upward' sense, as an increasing number of 'foreign' players with parental or grandparental ties are able to switch from their nation of birth. The so-called 'granny rule' was assiduously exploited by Jack Charlton's Ireland team during the 1980s and 1990s. In other circumstances, citizenship laws have been manipulated to enable foreign-born players to compete for the national side, such as in Japan where Brazilian Wagner Augusto Lopes was 'naturalized' in time for the 1998 World Cup finals (Chiba et al. 2001: 215). By 2007, five Brazilian-born players had been recruited to represent Japan. In African football, for the 2004 Nations Cup finals, Rwanda featured nine 'foreign' players, Tunisia had two Brazilians, while in qualifying fixtures, Mauritania fielded four Frenchmen and Togo five Brazilians. FIFA later moved to block the immediate naturalization policies of Qatar, whose national football squads had featured over 80 per cent of players born abroad. Nevertheless, as transnational migration processes intensify, and as players explore their complex genealogies, so greater numbers of 'dual citizenship' or 'multinational' elite players will emerge, and football will reflect the ethnonational heterogeneity of nations.[84]

---

[84]Dual citizenship status can have highly ambiguous consequences for players, notably those in developing nations. Some, such as Algeria's Rachid Mekloufi during the 1950s, have been viewed with ambivalence by both nations (Lanfranchi and Wahl 1996). In more recent times, players like Chile's Iván Zamorano have accessed dual citizenships, attracting great national pride for their European exploits while being personally divorced from the life experiences of their compatriots (Wong and Trumper 2002).

In terms of glocal 'rescaling' in the 'downward sense', football does allow for the stronger representation of regional, 'sub-national', or polyethnic identities, though not necessarily to the long-term detriment of the nation state. For example, in Spain, unofficial Basque and Catalan national teams have contested regular fixtures in recent years, yet players from both regions still represent the Spanish national team.[85] More generally, the 'glocal developmental state' is evident in the role played by football and other sports in urban regeneration policies, notably in building new stadiums, attracting tourism revenues, and piggy-backing on sporting successes to 'sell' cities to international investors.

In nations like Australia, Ireland, and the United States, football holds a glocal 'post-national' status. The professional game remains most popular among ethnic communities and a niche enterprise relative to established 'national' sports (Giulianotti 1999a). In Australia, football's post-war domination by southern European immigrants led some in the dominant Anglo-Irish communities to stereotype racially the sport as 'wogball'. Subsequently, the Australian football authorities sought to 'de-ethnicize' or 'Aussify' these ethnic clubs, despite the policies of 'forced assimilation' and 'ethnic cleansing' being contrary to the ethos of multiculturalism (Mosely 1994; Danforth 2001).

On Ireland, we noted earlier that the national football team served to represent the Irish diaspora. Additionally, support for the team has symbolized a form of backing for the existing Irish nation state, as a legitimate entity *in itself* that makes no territorial claim upon Northern Ireland. In this sense, the football team's symbolism has stood in some contrast to the Gaelic Games, such as hurling and Gaelic football, whose political histories long promoted unification of north and south (Holmes 1994; Giulianotti 1996).

In nation states where football is the dominant sporting code, the national team may be a focus for more intensive ethno-national differentiation and division. In African states like Egypt, Nigeria, Ghana, and Cameroon, many football followers complain that coaches select players along tribal lines, hence the recruitment of ethnically neutral, foreign coaches can promote a sporting meritocracy. In Northern Ireland, the national team is a focus of politico-cultural divisions, with the majority Protestant–Unionist community dominating the supporter culture and often directing sectarian abuse towards their team's Irish-Catholic players. In turn, many Irish Catholics adopt ambivalent or oppositional standpoints towards the national team's dominant culture or raison d'être.

Reflecting the growing cosmopolitanization of football, it appears that in Western Europe at least, followers of the game are increasingly favourable towards the diverse ethnic composition of club teams. This

[85]Further back, in 1958, Algerian players participated in a world tour to represent the nationalist FLN (Algerian Front de Libération Nationale) – an act viewed by one commentator as 'a harbinger of the birth of a nation' (Bromberger 1995: 295). In Turkey, some analysts considered the successes of the Kurdish team, Diyarbakir, to have been encouraged in part by the state's assimilative and internationalist strategies (*The Economist*, 4 August 2001).

process may disclose a more complex move in northern Europe from a *jus sanguinis* form of solidarity, founded on the community of blood, towards the *jus solis* principle, centred on a 'right to the soil' that is otherwise associated with some southern European or South American nations (cf. Bromberger 1994: 173). This embracing of ethnic diversity, wherein the club becomes a distinctive 'world space', has significant parallels with the development of national museums through the early twentieth century. The latter were intended not simply to showcase national art, but more importantly to advance the nation's claims to being the greatest (yet distinctive) custodian of world artistic achievement.

Nevertheless, it is also clear that ethnic minorities and diasporic communities do not have simply predictable or fixed national identities, and so rework their relationships to the host society in complex, uncertain, and sometimes reversible ways. In 1998, for example, the World Cup-winning French team was multi-ethnic and portrayed by many as embodying a forward-looking, integrated nation comprised of 'Blacks, Blancs et Beurs'. The 2001 fixture between France and Algeria in Paris, by contrast, saw the 'visiting team' field many French-born players, while French-Algerian spectators from the suburban *banlieues* conveyed strong messages of ethnic alienation: many booed the Marseillaise, some chanted for Osama Bin Laden, and younger fans invaded the pitch (Dine 2002; Beyria 2005).

Forced migration – through war, famine, or political persecution – constitutes the most disempowering type of population movement. Forced migration undermines the national football infrastructure by destabilizing competitions and evacuating potential players and spectators. War-torn Liberia has been forced to play 'home' international matches in neighbouring Ghana with teams comprised largely of refugees. Perhaps the most famous football refugees were the Hungarian trio, Puskás, Kocsis, and Czibor, who landed in Spain after the 1956 Budapest uprising had been crushed by the Soviet Union; Puskás went on to play for Spain a year later (Goldblatt 2006: 410). Longer term, however, refugee communities may function as a significant national resource and symbol. In the mid-1990s, Angola's national team was largely hewn from the four million refugees in Portugal who had fled the civil war. The Al-Wihdat football team, based in Jordan, has been a potent ethno-national symbol for Palestinian refugees (Tuastad 1997).

The apparently 'dysfunctional' aspects of football also confirm the continuing significance of national identities. Football hooliganism among European fans is typically informed by strong nationalistic sentiments, as well as being a violent competition between rival groups for nationally defined subcultural status. At a global level, noteworthy incidents of football violence in recent years have included the Turkey–Switzerland World Cup play-off fixture in 2006 when a post-match brawl erupted among rival players and officials. Afterwards, FIFA President Sepp Blatter considered whether national anthems should be removed from some fixtures as a way of smothering excessive nationalist sentiments.

Histories of national military conflict and oppression continue to impact upon international football. After the 1990 Gulf War, football tournament organizers were required to separate Kuwait and Iraq in all draws. In Palestine in the late 1990s, the national league could not function while the national team struggled to meet its fixture commitments due to Israeli occupation and restrictions on movements. Fixtures between Balkan teams frequently generate fan violence, while the China–Japan rivalry has spilled over into rioting, notably after one fixture in August 2004.

Of course, football has long mirrored, and at times has intensified, specific ethno national rivalries and antagonisms, particularly between bordering societies, as illustrated by fixtures between Germany and Holland, Argentina and Brazil, Turkey and Greece, Scotland and England (Kuper 1994). In recent years, transnational flows in football's labour and financial markets have opened up new possibilities for the expression of international animosities. In England, we noted earlier the popular anti-American discourses generated by Liverpool supporters towards their club's US owners. The extent to which Eastern European or Jewish club owners, players, and coaches will encounter chauvinistic or xenophobic discourses is worthy of close monitoring.

Football nation contests: club versus country

The 'club versus country' issue is one of the longest-running and multifaceted political disputes in football, and crystallizes some of the fundamental debates regarding the nation and nation state vis à vis globalization.

Among football's supporters and players, the question centres upon perceived differences of interest and status between certain club and national team cultures, for example in recent years involving England and Manchester United, Scotland and Rangers or Celtic, or Germany and Bayern Munich. More established concerns have centred on 'home' players over possible loyalty splits regarding club and nation. However, as labour markets have globalized, more complex differences arise in relation to the imported player, his club, its supporters, its home nation, and his national team. For instance, before the 1990 World Cup semi-final between Argentina and Italy in Naples, Maradona (then playing for the local Napoli club) argued that Neapolitans should support his Argentinian team, in part because of the *mezzogiorno* divide in Italy. Maradona's request generated widespread public comment and was largely unsuccessful, but did spotlight the underlying divisions and tensions in Italian society before international audiences.

Nevertheless, some supporters do remain sympathetic to their club-team players, even when the latter are playing for opposing national sides. For example, during a Turkey–Georgia fixture in the Turkish city of Trabzon in 2004, many local fans showed strong support for the Georgian player, Shota Arveladze, who at the time was also playing for the local club team,

Trabzonspor. These and other incidents give credence to the argument that certain forms of club or regional solidarity can supersede allegiance to the national side.

While most supporters recognize that non-national club players should compete intensively in all international fixtures, controversial incidents can intensify nationalistic standpoints and transform these imported stars into football 'folk devils'. For example, at the 2006 World Cup finals, during the Portugal–England fixture, the Portuguese winger Cristiano Ronaldo was instrumental in having his Manchester United team-mate, Wayne Rooney, sent off; Portugal went on to win on penalties. Ronaldo's actions, and his celebratory 'wink' upon Rooney's dismissal, were captured fully on television, and attracted widespread criticism and condemnation from English players, media, and supporters. Ronaldo was jeered intensely by opposing club fans when the English football season started, but the power of his club team and manager helped strongly to smooth over the conflict; coach Sir Alex Ferguson insisted Rooney and Ronaldo were 'the best of pals'.[86]

Clubs are increasingly tied into transnational business and competitive configurations that extend beyond the nation state. Inter-club frameworks – including the Champions League and G-14 – appear as inter-city and inter-urban matrices that enhance the market repositioning of regions and which connect favourably with transnational forms of post-industrial capitalism (Brenner 1998: 5). However, as yet, the European sport/city matrix is some way short of the American sporting model, wherein civic authorities are pressurized into financially assisting the sporting 'franchise' in order to protect their 'major league' status (cf. Euchner 1993).[87]

In recent years, the club versus country conflict centred particularly upon the industrial control of players. First, as we noted in Chapter 2, the G-14 had been particularly concerned that clubs were not being compensated for allowing their players to compete in international fixtures or tournaments. The G-14 argued that the 2002 World Cup finals necessitated 24,000 hours of work by players with the subsequent costs (in pay, injuries, and general exhaustion of human assets) being shouldered by clubs.

Backed by the G-14, Belgian club Charleroi took FIFA to the European Court of Justice to win compensation for an eight-month injury suffered by their player, Abdelmajid Oulmers, while playing for Morocco in 2004. Football's governing bodies and various sports ministers contested the claim, arguing that compensation payments would destroy highly popular international football and was against the public interest. Such payments could potentially bankrupt many national associations in developing football nations. However, this dispute was effectively resolved in February 2008 when the clubs and governing bodies agreed to compensation packages for international players.

---

[86]See http://news.bbc.co.uk/sport1/hi/football/teams/m/man_utd/5268768.stm

[87]Many critics attack the 'corporate welfarism' afforded by local authorities to US sport franchises.

Second, some governing bodies have become concerned by the practice of TNC clubs in 'hoarding' or rarely playing leading players who would otherwise be selected by other teams. Hoarded players are often recruited directly from rival sides with the partial aim of weakening these competitors.

Third, many national team officials and coaches argue that the tendency of elite clubs to feature a multinational playing staff serves to retard the competitive and technical development of home-grown players. For example, Ukraine's national team coach, Oleg Blokhin, complained in 2006 that the registration of over 140 imported players in the national league was greatly undermining the standard of national players at his disposal. When England failed to qualify for the 2008 European Championships, critics (including UEFA President, Michel Platini) directed at least part of the blame towards the EPL, where most players are imported. Moreover, some football officials, supporters, and player union representatives argue that the influx of 'foreign mercenaries' into national leagues can sever the crucial emotional bonds between teams and fans.

To challenge these trends, and to protect the 'special public status' of football, UEFA introduced measures to cut playing squad sizes to a maximum of 25 for the 2006/7 season; all sides were to have at least eight 'home-grown' players by 2008, of whom four must have spent three seasons at the club while aged 15–21. FIFA regulations also prohibit the transfer of under-18s across continents, to safeguard against the traffic in minors, and as a response to media exposures of European clubs' maltreatment of young Africans.

In return, many elite clubs argue that UEFA's measures constitute a 'restraint of trade', contrary to European law, and work to get round these regulations. Some clubs have relocated entire families to Europe: Arsenal's recruitment of the Mexican Carlos Vela, and the switching of his family to Spain (where, after two years, he gained an EU work permit), is illustrative. In Europe, leading English sides have been particularly prominent in raiding smaller sides to recruit teenage players who are set to turn professional – a practice likened to piracy by one Italian coach.[88] In turn, the youth academies at English clubs become filled with more imported players, thus further undermining the development of young national talents.

Thinking further ahead, it is likely that more polarized approaches towards clubs and categories of national citizenship will become apparent. On the one hand, as dual citizenship or naturalization is more freely secured, and as free-market regulations have impacted upon sport, so we move nearer to the far extreme, which already occurs in many other labour markets, wherein elite players might be freed legally to switch their representative nation. On the other hand, leading football officials such as Blatter and Platini have sought to reaffirm national identity and status by advocating strict limits on the number of non-nationals at clubs. Blatter in particular has championed a '6+5' rule that would see

---

[88]See http://news.bbc.co.uk/sport1/hi/football/7324517.stm

only five non-national players starting fixtures.[89] Football officials have claimed significant encouragement from European political agreements, notably the Nice Declaration (2000) and the Lisbon Reform Treaty (2007), which recognize sport's 'special status' as a social sphere that is potentially exempt from free-market regulations (*International Herald Tribune*, 19 October 2007). Yet, some European politicians have registered their disquiet about football's financial practices and commercialization, which would suggest that this 'special status' is potentially questionable. Moreover, in a reassertion of EU labour laws, the '6+5' proposal was considered and flatly rejected by the European Parliament in May 2008.

Interim Conclusions

Overall, these observations on the football–nation relationship point towards three interim conclusions. First, in analytical terms, nation-focused football continues to have a double-edged relationship to the nation state and national identity. Football both reflects and contributes to the changes and continuities in the powers, status, and functions of the nation state, and in shaping the meaning of national identity. More specifically, and second, football illuminates the continuing importance of the nation state and national identity. Third, football spotlights the strong reflexivity of social actors and groups in protecting or adapting state forms in relation to changing circumstances. For example, the nation state and nationality undergo 'glocal' adaptations such as in the strengthening of regional and 'sub-national' identities, the utilization of football within cultural regeneration strategies, and the construction of fresh forms of national identity in polyethnic contexts. Recent eruptions from the 'club versus country' tension confirmed the strong political–economic and legal pressures that confront national associations in football, particularly concerning labour power.

The relationships of football, the nation, and national identity come into sharper focus when we consider the 'neo-mercantilist' model of political relations within the game.

Neo-Mercantilism

Theoretical framework and football context

Our theorization of 'neo-mercantilism' provides an updating and modification of the term 'mercantilism'. Prominent in Europe during the seventeenth and eighteenth centuries, mercantilist policies were characterized by the attempts of nations (notably Britain, Spain, and the Netherlands)

---

[89]FIFA's rules had allowed uncapped players to 'switch' their national allegiance after living in the new nation for two years. To tighten the regulations, the FIFA Congress in 2008 voted to raise that term to five years.

to establish economic self-sufficiency, strong agricultural and industrial bases, a growing population, and potent sea power to secure international trading posts, all under the aegis of a powerful regulatory state. International struggles between mercantilist powers were understood essentially as zero-sum games, wherein one nation's expansion inevitably occurred at the expense of rivals.

In partial differentiation from alternative definitions (e.g. Hettne 2005), we update this definition so that *neo*-mercantilism refers to the self-protecting and self-aggrandizing policies initiated since 1945, principally by national societies but also by supra-state institutions and international governmental organizations (IGOs). Neo-mercantilism may feature partnerships between particular nation states, or nations and international organizations, where collaboration yields collective benefits or achieves common policy goals.

In being more 'state-centric', neo-mercantilism stands in some analytical contrast to neo-liberalism. Neo-mercantilist policies are intended partly to satisfy the transnational aspirations, and to contain the separatist impulses, of corporations and peoples that are largely under the jurisdiction of state-centric apparatuses. Since 9/11, militarized variants of neo-mercantilism have been evidenced by the reassertion of the Western military–industrial complex, notably through the US-led invasion of Iraq, and an emergent governmental 'totalitarianism' that intensifies 'homeland' securitization and surveillance (cf. Pieterse 2004; Robinson 2004: 150; Falk 2005: 223; Robertson 2007a).

We identify neo-mercantilism within football as operating principally among national football associations and national league systems, frequently in conjunction with the nation state itself. The relevant authorities engage in close and often conflicting relationships with TNC clubs and other large corporations whose interests would be more obviously served by neo-liberal policies. The deep historical roots of football's neo-mercantilism may be traced back to European mercantilism and colonialism. However, contemporary neo-mercantilist strategies are no longer buttressed by militarized coercion, but are realized more effectively in consensual terms through capturing the industries, incomes, and imaginations of foreign markets.

Basic forms of neo-mercantilist struggle arise between sport governing bodies over domestic and international markets. For example, in England, the regular extension of football's season into the summer months has encroached greatly upon cricket's established terrain. In North America, less successfully, the MLS has struggled to establish itself within a sporting calendar dominated by the 'big four' sports (American football, baseball, basketball, ice hockey).

In Europe, national football associations and league systems must perform effectively in order to meet the business ambitions of their member teams, especially TNC clubs in the Big 5 nations. For example, the German or English leagues emphasize the 'added value' that is gained by all clubs from participating in national tournaments, and from the sale of television rights to these competitions on a *collective* basis, rather than club by club, to media corporations at home and abroad. National bodies argue that strong competition branding provides member clubs (including TNC ones) with the ideal platform for building and sustaining transnational markets. Revenues raised from these competitions are distributed among member clubs with the remainder deployed to pursue aggressive marketing in fresh locations. Long-term neo-mercantilist strategies are most beneficial: thus, Italian and German league football attracts good audiences in China, in part because television coverage extends back to 1991 and 1995 respectively.[90]

Interlocking deals with TNCs assist neo-mercantilist league strategies. For example, deals with telecommunications companies enable league systems to establish new market presences. Meanwhile, images of star players in the national league are emblazoned across TNC products, thereby providing league systems with additional market entry points.

Nation states play significant neo-mercantile roles in establishing receptive conditions for expanding the football 'industry', such as by securing public order (notably in tackling fan violence), settling contractual disputes, and often providing tax breaks that safeguard businesses and profitability. National football associations and the nation state also cooperate to attract and to host sporting mega-events. Large state investment in sporting infrastructure can directly benefit domestic and international businesses, and augment tourism revenues. For example, the governments of South Korea and Japan spent around US$8 billion combined on preparations for co-hosting the 2002 World Cup finals. Optimistic projections claimed that the tournament generated an estimated US$78 billion in direct and indirect financial benefits for South Korea, increasing national export values by around US$150 billion (*Asia Times*, 27 June 2002). For the 2006 World Cup, despite economic stagnation and spending restraints, the German government invested an initial €430 million, an additional €1.5 billion on stadiums, and €4.4 billion on further infrastructure improvements (*World Soccer*, September 2005). Germany expected to attract around five million visitors for the 2006 World Cup finals, netting €3 billion in fresh tourism revenues. South Africa's hopes are somewhat more modest for 2010, expecting around 400,000 visitors to generate 160,000 jobs, although by 2007, FIFA had claimed to have generated around US$3.2 billion for the tournament.

Russia provides a potent and distinctive illustration of state-influenced neo-mercantilism in regard to football and sport more generally. Since 2000, the Putin-led Russian state has utilized sport to promote national pride within an international context. The state has encouraged and cajoled oligarchs and nationally owned industries to contribute heavily towards major sport projects, such as the US$12 billion development of Sochi, a Black Sea resort, for the 2014 Winter Olympics (the *Observer*, 25 May 2008). In football, the oligarch Roman Abramovich finances a national academy, while the

---

[90]See http://footballdynamicsasia.blogspot.com/2006/04/epl-low-14th-in-chinas-most-watched-tv.html

rise of major clubs has been largely backed by Russian companies, for instance Zenit St Petersburg (sponsored by Gazprom), CSKA Moscow (VTB Bank), and Spartak Moscow (Lukoil). By the late 2000s, Russian clubs paid wages that were directly comparable with leading sides in England and Spain, encouraging the best talents to continue in domestic football.

Neo-mercantilism: systemic pressures

By definition, neo-mercantilism describes a highly competitive economic system. It thus gives rise to several kinds of systemic pressure and fissure between competing economic formations.

First, rival football states battle with each other to secure new overseas markets. Since the late 1990s, the EPL has been the most effective strategist: for the 2003/4 season, it generated around €150 million in overseas earnings, with its main rivals (Italy, Spain, and Germany) trailing with €65 million, €35 million, and €12 million respectively (*DW-World.De*, 2 April 2005). In turn, the EPL insists that it provides a globally recognized platform for individual clubs to build new supporter bases, while rival leagues (notably the German Bundesliga) have looked to mimic English practices, such as by introducing earlier kick-off times that also suit East Asian markets.

Second, neo-mercantile arrangements must counteract the possibility of businesses or institutions seeking to switch their juridical allegiances or to form their own state systems. As we have noted, the most persistent threat in recent years has emanated from Europe's elite clubs – notably the G-14 – over the possible foundation of a breakaway European league. Further pressures centre upon the positions of leading clubs in relatively small European leagues. Teams in Austria, Belgium, Holland, Portugal, Scandinavia, and Scotland harbour strong international ambitions, but may feel trapped in league systems with comparatively low prestige, small domestic television audiences, and equally weak media revenues. Some of these clubs have considered either 'switching state', to join bigger leagues, such as with the Old Firm seeking entry to England; or forming 'convenience transnational states', such as competitions among themselves (e.g. the mooted 'Atlantic League'), to appeal to domestic and international markets (Giulianotti 2003; see also Boyle and Haynes 2004). The 'switching state' option has been curtailed by both the international governing bodies, and by those clubs in the strongest leagues which would otherwise be threatened by the arrival of serious domestic competitors.

A third systemic pressure arises over the conflicting interests of national and international formations. For example, international governing bodies (notably FIFA) provide significant political and resource backing for emerging football nations that seek to nurture their own league systems and national teams. European national league systems and TNC clubs target these emerging football nations for new football consumers and elite players. African and Asian football authorities criticize the intensive local television coverage of European football for diverting supporters away from impoverished domestic clubs.[91] To limit the potential damage, Asian football leagues schedule fixtures to avoid clashing with televised European matches. In 2007, the AFC lobbied intensively and, in the end, successfully, to prevent its showpiece tournament, the Asian Cup, from being upstaged by a Manchester United fixture in one of the host nations (Malaysia), despite backing for the English club's visit from the Malaysian Prime Minister and the Tourist Board.

A fourth systemic pressure concerns the possible morphing of neo-mercantilist frameworks into de facto neo-liberal kinds of cartelization or monopolization. For example, as noted in Chapter 3, most European leagues display a widening competitive gulf between the top few teams and the remainder, while newly promoted sides struggle to survive in the highest division. However, we are still some way from full cartelization or monopolization, wherein the top divisions would formally prohibit promotion or relegation on merit, as occurs in North American sports.

International Governing Bodies: Neo-Mercantilism and International Governance

The position of international governing bodies such as UEFA and FIFA in this context is rather more complex. These federations have a dichotomous political function, relating on one hand to neo-mercantilism and on the other hand to international governance.

First, in neo-mercantile terms, international governing body membership is comprised wholly of national football associations. International governing bodies mirror national league systems in pursuing new spheres of economic influence, for example with UEFA's assiduous promotion of the Champions League, or FIFA's concerted globalizing of football largely through the World Cup. For example, one hagiographic tribute to FIFA's President Sepp Blatter, to celebrate his seventieth birthday, stoked the cult of personality by comparing football's rapid colonization of the world to the more protracted diffusion of Christianity:

> They [Christians] took centuries to accomplish their mission whereas FIFA has achieved a similar goal with football in only decades. It has 'colonised' the earth by planting football in foreign soil and watching it grow. Seen from this vantage point, the FIFA President commands respect over a realm in which the sun never sets but rather is much greater than the largest kingdom ever conquered by a military leader.
>
> (*FIFA Magazine*, March 2006)

International governing bodies or their tournaments also expand to absorb relatively powerful entities to increase their rewards to members. For example,

---

[91]See http://news.bbc.co.uk/1/hi/world/africa/4265291.stm

the Copa Libertadores – the flagship club tournament of South America's associations and CONMEBOL – expanded in 2003 and again in 2005 to include more Mexican clubs, primarily to yield income from this large television and consumer market.

International governing bodies function as crucial cultural intermediaries by promoting the game and educating local publics, thereby preparing the ground for leading European clubs and transnational media corporations to engage these new markets. In such instances, football governing bodies struggle to dislodge or out-manoeuvre rival sporting codes that are established in particular settings, such as cricket in the Asian sub-continent, rugby in New Zealand, other football codes in Australia, and 'American' sports in the United States. In turn, football must face challenges to its national or regional hegemonies from rival sporting codes and leagues, particularly American ones. For example, the NBA has looked closely at expanding into Europe, while some leading US sport marketing groups argue that European cities such as London could host team franchises that are affiliated to the major American sports leagues (the *Observer*, 7, 14 December 2008). Football is also engaged in major transnational struggles with these rival sports leagues over entry to new markets, particularly in Asia. For example, the NBA has gained a strong foothold by cultivating basketball interest among a reputed 300 million Chinese, notably through glamour tours and the feting of imported stars, such as the 2002 'rookie of the year', China's Yao Ming. In future years, India and the Middle East will be further sites of contestation between expansionist sports leagues and federations.

Second, football's international governing bodies differentiate themselves politically and ideologically by emphasizing their governmental functions. Governing bodies are empowered to administer and develop football within their territorial boundaries, and to discipline and even to expel individuals or institutions whose actions are considered injurious to the game's stability and well-being. Thus, any proposed 'breakaway' European club system would risk the effective excommunication of all participants from the established game, including the World Cup finals.

Governing bodies usually claim a moral custodianship of football, in part through such legends as 'For the Good of the Game' at FIFA, and via public association with humanitarian NGOs. In contradistinction to elite club commercialism, governing bodies profess a higher purpose for their existence. For example, Sepp Blatter has observed that 'FIFA is a non-profit association under Swiss law and not a multinational corporation' (*Financial Times*, 17 December 2003). Blatter has also lambasted the game's neo-liberal elements, criticizing the 'pornographic amounts of money' and 'Wild West style of capitalism' that is stoked by TNC club owners, and which has served to enrich 'semi-educated, sometimes foul-mouthed, players' (*Financial Times*, 12 October 2005). Vowing that FIFA would not 'sit by and see greed rule the football world', Blatter accused European clubs of acting as 'neo-colonialists' through the 'social and economic rape' of developing nations, wherein talented young players become trapped in 'a glorified body market'. In 2005, a 'FIFA Taskforce' was launched to investigate football's problems, notably the economic excesses of leading players and clubs, and the loss of competition and national identity in league systems.

These public statements and political actions all tap into the 'higher purpose' claims of governing bodies, but they are, of course, underpinned by *realpolitik*. For example, Blatter's 'anti-colonialist' comments might be read critically in several ways. Politically, they function to shore up backing among elite football officials from developing nations for the FIFA leadership. In historical terms, they are countermanded by FIFA's transformation into a major commercial enterprise from the early 1970s onwards. In socio-cultural terms, the structure of football's governing bodies, and the habitus (and salaries) of their leading officials, compare rather closely to what is found in international business.

To follow on from these observations, we may ask whether it is possible to argue that international governing bodies are essentially *defined* by commercial functions. One way in which this argument may be advanced derives from claims over transformations in the wider state–corporation relationship. For example, Robinson (2002: 215) argues that, within political globalization, a 'transnational state' (TNS) is coming to prominence. Advancing an updated Marxist analysis, Robinson argues that the state has two defining features: 'a historically determined constellation of class forces and relations' and 'sets of political institutions'. For Robinson, a TNS has crystallized in recent decades, since the globalization of capital has enabled class fractions to 'fuse together' to produce 'new capitalist groups within transnational space'. The TNS also features the reorganization of national state institutions, and the creation and consolidation of supranational organizations such as the IMF, the World Bank, the WTO, the EU, ASEAN, and NAFTA.

Robinson's model might be extended to football so that bodies like FIFA and UEFA come to be understood principally as institutional fronts and meeting places for transnational class interests. In other words, these governing bodies are merely mediation points for the common class interests and aspirations of TNC clubs, merchandise and media corporations, sponsors, elite players, and agents.

However, we argue that the TNS model, if applied to football, would lead us to ignore some crucial features of international governing bodies. It would render redundant any serious debate about the meaningful democratic reform of football's international governance. It would certainly exaggerate the unity of football's various 'class factions', and seriously underplay the multipolar and contested politics surrounding the game. To highlight how these different kinds of political force – focused on neo-mercantilism, neo-liberalism, and international governance – play out with each other, we consider briefly the making of Europe's Champions League.

Neo-mercantilism, international governance and neo-liberalism: making the Champions League

The Champions League is at the epicentre of political struggles between neo-mercantile, neo-liberal and international governmental forces. The tournament's contemporary format may be viewed as a compromise wherein the threat of a neo-liberal breakaway league by TNC clubs has been rebuffed (perhaps temporarily) through fresh mixtures of neo-mercantilism and effective international governance by European football's governing bodies. To explain this point, it is worth considering the tournament's recent history in some detail.

The European Cup was established in 1955, and quickly established itself as the continent's premier club tournament. By the late 1980s, the wealthiest European clubs and some top national leagues had become increasingly dissatisfied with the tournament's format: only one side from each of Europe's national leagues was entered, the knock-out system threatened long-term participation, and the growing football interest of pay-TV stations suggested that a league system could generate far greater revenues. Pressures from these clubs and leagues saw the tournament extended, first through mini-league stages in 1992, then by rebranding as the 'Champions League' in 1993, and subsequently in 1997 by allowing second teams to enter from Europe's top eight leagues.

Still dissatisfied, in September 1998, leading European clubs acted independently of football's governing bodies to prepare, with support from top media moguls (Kirch, Berlusconi and Murdoch) and financiers JP Morgan, a cartelized tournament that would accrue over €1.5 billion annually, involve up to 36 teams, and advantage particularly the richest sides. To head off this autonomist threat, UEFA modified further the Champions League to aid the biggest clubs: three and four clubs (and an exceptional five in 2005) were admitted to the competition from the wealthiest football nations, while champion sides from smaller nations were forced to play qualifying fixtures which restricted entry to the lucrative group stages.

The Champions League seemed to deliver in two neo-mercantile senses. First, UEFA reaffirmed its claim as the governing apparatus to meet the commercial aspirations of leading clubs, notably in reaching new markets, such that by the mid-2000s a breakaway tournament appeared to afford fewer benefits to TNC clubs from the largest leagues. Indeed, the greatest gain from such a transformation would fall to big clubs in small leagues rather than teams from the Big 5 (Solberg and Gratton 2004).

Second, the Champions League advantaged the strongest neo-mercantile forces in European football, notably the Big 5 league systems. The Big 5 lobbied most effectively for increased participation by their member clubs, and thus drew additional revenues into the national league. The chief executive of the EPL, Peter Leaver, noted that the threatened breakaway had been a 'very useful stick with which to beat UEFA'.[92] The thwarting of the purported breakaway certainly enabled these league systems to retain the leading clubs. Meanwhile, the Champions League has also strengthened the financial bonds between national broadcasters and leagues. The former are willing to pay higher sums to UEFA for the national rights to the Champions League if a significant domestic audience can be guaranteed – and this is best achieved when more national sides are competing.

By 2008, Champions League revenue stood at around €825 million. In recent seasons, income distribution has been skewed heavily in favour of the Big 5 clubs. Most money is divided among the tournament's final 32 clubs: half is distributed according to tournament performance, the other half according to the *national* broadcasting 'market pool' of each team.[93] Much of the remaining money goes into a 'solidarity' fund for all UEFA member nations. The same distributive model was later applied to the lower-status UEFA Cup, beginning in 2006–7.[94]

Two general observations follow regarding the Champions League. First, the competitive framework favours the Big 5 clubs. In 2004, 16 of the 32 clubs were from the Big 5 leagues; 12 were seeded, thus greatly improving their chances of long progress in the tournament (and status as seeds in the future). Second, a basic participant audit confirms the Big 5's advantages. Whereas in the 1980s, Eastern bloc nations were prominent in the European Cup, the Champions League typically features only three or four of these teams among the starting 32 sides. In the 2002/3 season, around 80 per cent of Champions League income went to clubs from the Big 5 leagues; the three Eastern teams accrued around 3.5 per cent (*World Soccer*, October 2003). Earnings can also differ massively between tournament winners. Bayern Munich earned £31 million in 2001 for winning the tournament, but Porto gained only £17.5 million in 2004 due to Portugal's far smaller television market. In 2004–5, when Chelsea and PSV Eindhoven reached the semi-finals, the clubs earned €16.8 million and €4.8 million respectively, due to weighting for the domestic television markets.

Second, despite its egalitarian title, the 'solidarity fund' has favoured the Big 5 leagues. For example, in 2003–4, around 75 per cent of solidarity payments went to the 15 leagues with Champions League participants; and the Big 5 leagues took more than two-thirds of that money.

Overall, the Champions League's competitive and economic structures represent a compromise between opposing political–economic models. Governing bodies have maintained their international governance of football by

---

[92]See http://archives.tcm.ie/irishexaminer/1998/09/04/phead.htm

[93]'Market pool' national revenues are divided according to the number of national teams in the competition; hence, individual clubs profit from the elimination of their compatriots.

[94]This is not to say that the UEFA Cup had previously guaranteed equal television money among competing sides. For example, Barcelona earned around £5.8 million from their rise to the 2000/1 UEFA Cup quarter-finals, but their compatriots Rayo Vallecano earned only £75,000 from a similar run (*World Soccer*, May 2001).

expanding their neo-mercantile capacities while accommodating the neo-liberal, revenue-maximizing thrust of the game's largest businesses. Meanwhile, the rival forces continue to pursue their arguments. On one side, elite clubs demand further fixing of competitive structures to suit their interests. After being knocked out of the first round of the Champions League in March 2005, the Manchester United chief executive, David Gill, argued that an amended seeding system should protect big teams to satisfy television stations and tournament sponsors. In response, UEFA's director of communications, William Gaillard, observed that such amendments would undermine the tournament's unpredictability and sporting principles. Meanwhile, in November 2007, Europe's leading clubs effectively thwarted the plans of new UEFA President Michel Platini to redistribute many Champions League places from the richest and largest nations to smaller and weaker ones. Longer term, many sports economists consider a full-blown European Superleague will be inevitable at some point in the future (Szymanski and Kuypers 2000; Baroncelli and Lago 2006). The major questions remain as to how it will emerge, and under which political–economic frameworks: as a tournament that is UEFA-endorsed (international governance) and/or UEFA-led (neo-mercantilist), or separatist (neo-liberal).

Global Football Politics: Multipolar Complexity

The political relationships and competing interests between football's governing bodies and TNC clubs are symptomatic of the complex, multipolar power balances within the game's international system. The most significant participants here are FIFA, the various continental and national governing bodies, elite clubs (notably, in Europe as represented in recent years by the G-14), supra-state and nation state forms of government, sport-related TNCs (such as media and merchandise corporations), and elite players (typically, as represented by personal agents or their unions, such as the PFA or FiFPro). The complexity of the international football system has significant scope for future expansion, in part through the greater involvement of additional representative institutions, such as the Association of European Professional Leagues (AELFP, in existence since 1998, formally reconstituted in 2005), the International Association of Football Agents, various NGOs and new social movements connected to football, such as FARE (Football Against Racism in Europe) or Play Soccer Make Peace!

Many conflicts of interest arise both *between* and *within* football's most established parties. FIFA has housed long-standing struggles for hegemony between various national and continental associations, with UEFA's members losing significant ground to the developing world since the early 1970s. The World Cup finals provide the most intensive zone of conflict between the continental associations. Asian and African nations have worked assiduously to increase their allocation of places for the finals. The Asian associations walked out of FIFA's 1999 Extraordinary Congress in Los Angeles, in protest at their low allocation of World Cup berths for

2002. The Oceania federation was similarly infuriated in 2003 when FIFA reversed its earlier undertaking to award the region one World Cup finals berth. A further political flashpoint has been the right to host the World Cup finals. After South Africa controversially failed to win the 2006 event, FIFA introduced a 'rotation policy' that would see the finals move around the continents. The policy is to be dropped after the 2014 tournament, enabling nations in UEFA, AFC and CONCACAF in particular to develop bids for the 2018 event.

Similarly, strong conflicts regularly arise within both neo-mercantile and neo-liberal football institutions. One rather extreme illustration is provided by the corruption in the Italian league system in the early 2000s, as elite clubs sought to fix refereeing appointments and influence results. More generally, recurring battles occur between clubs for greater shares of league broadcasting revenues. Conflicts also arise among cartels of elite TNC clubs. Many TNC clubs complain that Chelsea's high expenditure on players, and willingness to accumulate massive annual losses, distorts competitive 'balances'.

Tense relations may arise between different institutional actors due to competing interests. We have noted the struggles between governing bodies and TNC clubs. At times, these conflicts centre on fundamental, 'politics of recognition' principles. For example, the G-14 were dismissed by the game's governing bodies as a 'pseudo-political' entity, a mere 'lobby group' or 'economic interest group' that they would never formally recognize (*Financial Times*, 17 December 2003). UEFA's foundation in 2002 of the 102-member European Club Forum effectively established an institutional rival to the G-14, while the small but influential body, the European Professional Football Strategy Board, did accord an additional political status to top TNC clubs. In return, the G-14 had threatened to deny recognition of new football tournaments, such as FIFA's 'World Club Championship'.[95]

The increasingly congested football calendar provides a major domain of conflict involving elite clubs and governing bodies. We have noted already the general 'club versus country' dispute. Additionally, governing bodies recommend the reduction of national league sizes and fixture lists to accommodate more international matches, with FIFA occasionally mooting the prospect of hosting the World Cup biennially. Leading European clubs, by contrast, oppose the inauguration of yet more international tournaments, such as FIFA's 'Confederations Cup', and insist that fixtures for established tournaments should be played during particular slots in the football calendar. Struggles over football's global season more generally highlight the limitations of globalization's much-trumpeted time–space compression: all interested parties appreciate that, even at physical peak, athletes can withstand only limited amounts of international travel and repetitive exercise.

While we noted that national football associations and nation states are both relevant to discussion of neo-mercantilism, we should recognize

---

[95]That tough stance was later softened following rule changes to suit European clubs.

that disputes between these two kinds of institutional actor are relatively common. FIFA statutes prohibit national governments from intervening in the affairs of its members. When intervention occurs, FIFA typically suspends the association's membership, notably in developing nations, such as Guinea, Kenya, Macau, Yemen, and Iran, though also in established football nations such as Greece and Poland. While FIFA may complain about 'meddling' politicians, national governments often argue that the domestic football system is chaotic and staffed by incompetent or corrupt officials. We also find that the greater empathy of national governments towards free-market economics can jar with the regulatory and governmental interests of international football bodies. For example, in 2007, UEFA President Michel Platini publicly sought to engage national governments in controlling the 'malign' influence of money within the game, but his approaches were rebuffed by the UK's Labour government on the stated grounds that these were matters solely for football's authorities.

Football's governing bodies have come into conflict with other transnational sporting authorities. Relations with the IOC have not always been smooth; most recently, in regard to anti-doping strategies, FIFA did reach belated agreement with the IOC and WADA in 2003, yet subsequently questioned the standard two-year ban on miscreants. Additionally, the Court of Arbitration for Sport (CAS), based in Lausanne and founded in 1984, was instituted in part to facilitate arbitration in sporting disputes, to prevent the involvement of ordinary courts of law. Football's governing bodies, however, can be reluctant to implement its rulings; for example, despite CAS's ruling that Gibraltar should be admitted to FIFA and UEFA, Spain has lobbied intensively and successfully to block this membership bid.

Complex and often conflict-centred relationships have also arisen between international football governing bodies and supra-state institutions, notably in Europe. Certainly, we should recognize that the European Union and European football's governing institutions have engaged in rituals of co-recognition, and have experienced similar forms of development and expansion since the 1950s. In January 1973, a fixture between teams comprising players from the old and new European Community Members was staged, to celebrate the admission of the UK, Denmark, and the Republic of Ireland. To show symbolic support for each other, UEFA and the EU staged a Manchester United–European All-Stars friendly in Manchester in March 2007 to mark the 50th anniversary of the Treaty of Rome.

Through its Nice Declaration of 2000, the European Council accepted that sports have special social functions that are most effectively guaranteed by sporting federations rather than by other bodies.[96] The European Commission generally views itself as a regulator not a legislator for sport,

---

[96]See www.consilium.europa.eu/ueDocs/cms_Data/docs/pressData/en/ec/00400-r1.%20ann.en0.htm

so that football's governance remains largely with national and continental associations (Weatherhill 2000).[97] However, European governmental institutions have displayed an increasing willingness to challenge perceived pathologies or problems within the football system. Most famously, as outlined in earlier chapters, the *Bosman* case, which had been widely criticized by football authorities as it progressed through the European courts, revolutionized football's employment and transfer system and accelerated players' salary inflation. The European Commission has also challenged the cosy business relationships that develop between leading league systems and small groups of media TNCs. In the early 2000s, the European Commissioner for Competition, Mario Monti, regularly criticized the resulting monopolies, arguing for stronger competitive tendering and the fragmentation of television rights, to safeguard competition and consumer interests. In response, in England, the EPL enabled the Setanta network to compete with BSkyB and to claim two of the six packages of live television fixtures for the period 2007–2010. The EC also probed anti-competitive practices in regard to Spanish league football.

European governmental institutions have also explored the contradictions within sport concerning its special 'social status' and the competing effects of neo-liberal influences. In 2006, European Sports Ministers and MEPs produced separate reviews and reports that advocated major economic and political reforms in football.[98] Some recommendations focused on the negative impact of commercialization, and advocated the introduction of salary caps for players, collective selling of television rights, and further steps to challenge the increasing powers of the richest clubs. A year later, the European Commission produced a white paper on sport which advocated in part far more structured dialogue with sport-related institutions.[99] In 2008, UEFA and several national associations announced their strong opposition towards an EU plan, inspired under the French Presidency, to introduce an EU-appointed 'super-regulator' of European sport who would take control over financial regulations, player development, and transfers in football.

The relationships between professional players and football's major institutions (notably clubs and associations) have become more complex. Historically, as we noted in Chapter 1, football players in most nations had endured particularly weak industrial positions that, while supported by national and international governing bodies, were often contrary to modern labour laws. The struggle for greater industrial freedom has been waged by national player unions and FIFPro (the international player federation), which by 2007 represented around 67,000 registered players in 44 nations; it has also been advanced by the intervention of non-football bodies,

---

[97]An additional conflict arose in Italy: in 2006 the anti-monopoly regulator recommended the collective selling of television rights to Serie A fixtures.

[98]See www.independentfootballreview.com/and www.europarl.europa.eu/meetdocs/2004_2009/documents/pr/631/631110/631110en.pdf

[99]See http://ec.europa.eu/sport/whitepaper/wp_on_sport_en.pdf

notably national governments, European Commission, and national and international legal systems. In turn, football's governing bodies and player unions have engaged in greater football-related diplomacy and subsequent agreements, such as the FIFA–FIFPro deal in 2006.

Commercial influences within football often underpin conflicts between players, clubs, and national associations, notably over rival sponsorship and endorsement deals. David Beckham's move from Manchester United to Real Madrid in 2003 resolved an impending business conflict between the player (backed by adidas) and the English club (backed by Nike) (Veseth 2005). The French star Robert Pires was fined in November 2004 by his football federation (sponsored by adidas) for wearing a Puma t-shirt on television while on national team duty. The German stars Miroslav Klose and Jens Lehmann were reported to have lost several million Euros after being required to drop their Nike endorsements to protect the DFB's sponsor, adidas, during the 2006 World Cup. Advertising 'clutter' and endorsement confusion occur when players, clubs, and national associations sign deals with rival TNCs in diverse industries, notably telecommunications, financial services, and soft drinks. Again, Beckham has long endorsed Vodafone, but his Real Madrid shirt carried the Siemens logo.

The industrial emancipation of players has enabled a new array of social actors to enter the game, particularly player agents and assorted representatives. Agents have been major catalysts in the inflation of player wages and in expanding football's transnational labour markets. In developing nations – notably Latin America – player 'registrations' are often at least partly owned by different agents. While there are external conflicts of interest, agents build personal reputations and wealth on their strength of contacts with managers, coaches, and directors across the world. The general practices of agents provide one significant focus for concerns about institutional problems and corruption within football.

Overall, football's contemporary global political framework features an increasing array of institutional actors, many of whom have diverging, conflicting, or irreconcilable interests. At the very least, the multipolar complexity of football's politics is underlined by the growth of relationships that must be established between these actors, and the intricate balances of power that must be worked through if complex hegemonies are to be negotiated. Significant challenges and contests are identifiable in the relationships between key figures, notably elite players, major league systems, leading national associations, TNC clubs, and international governing bodies, while not discounting the regulatory functions of national and international governmental institutions.

Pathologies in international governance

Evidently, the greater proliferation of institutional actors within football has engendered more complex and uncertain forms of global governance. These processes can in turn precipitate two kinds of problem – *governmental probity* and *socio-political representation* – which we consider in turn.

First, problems of *governmental probity* are associated particularly with the innate abuse of personal status, and corrupt relations between key stakeholders. Leading FIFA officials have been the subject of major corruption inquiries and allegations. For example, Jack Warner of Trinidad and Tobago – a FIFA Vice-President, President of CONCACAF, and close associate of President Blatter – was embroiled in a tickets scandal for the 2006 World Cup finals. Warner had ensured that his family's travel company would obtain special access to tickets for matches involving Trinidad and Tobago, enabling the firm to earn up to US$8 million from the sale of holiday packages to supporters. When local journalists exposed the scam, Warner apologized and announced that his company shares had been sold; he was then reprimanded but not disciplined by FIFA. Warner's son, who continued to profit from ticket-dealing, was later secretly fined US$1 million by FIFA. Corruption charges have been levelled at other senior figures within FIFA, notably those in different confederations across the Americas.

Corrupt relations between key stakeholders are more varied and given closer public attention. Again, FIFA has been subjected to public scrutiny and some legal investigation. In 2002, FIFA's then General Secretary, Michel Zen-Ruffinen, reported that mismanagement, false accounting, and criminal practices were evident in the organization. FIFA President Sepp Blatter abruptly terminated an internal inquiry and Zen-Ruffinen was fired, but a later investigation revealed that ISL/ISMM, FIFA's marketing partner, had established a secret 'slush fund' to bribe elite football officials (Jennings 2007). In another episode, in December 2006, FIFA sacked four marketing executives after a US court ruled that they had lied during negotiations with major sponsors; the dispute cost FIFA US$90 million to end its deal with Mastercard. Six months later, FIFA appointed one of the sacked executives, Jerome Valcke, as its new General Secretary.

FIFA's committees have attracted public attention, notably through a tendency to recruit large memberships from relatively small nations with little domestic development or competitive record in football. There are other concerns that international governing bodies have exacerbated cultures of corruption in some developing nations by bribing football delegates in return for compliant voting.

At the everyday level, match-fixing allegations are widely directed at fixtures, reflecting perceived alliances between referees, club officials, players, and bookmakers. Between 2004 and 2006, these allegations arose in Brazil, Germany, Italy, the Czech Republic, Poland, Turkey, Finland, Romania, Greece, China, and Thailand. In Ukraine, widespread bribing of match officials led the football authorities to allow clubs to import foreign referees to ensure fairer games. The *calciopoli* scandal in Italy in 2005–6 exposed widespread corruption among leading club officials and the football federation; the main offenders, Juventus, were relegated and stripped of their previous two league championships, while Lazio, Fiorentina, and Milan were also punished. In an interesting illustration of the politics surrounding such investigations, the Mediaset company, which was paying over €60 million for television rights to fixtures, pressured the Italian sport system not to relegate the implicated clubs. Mediaset and Milan are owned by Silvio Berlusconi. A sports tribunal initially handed Milan a huge points penalty and ban from the 2006–7 Champions League; on appeal, the sentence was reduced, the ban lifted, and Milan went on to win the tournament in that same season.

Corrupt and illegal practices surrounding player transfers have been revealed across several continents. We noted earlier the pilfering of transfer revenues by Latin American club officials and player agents. In the UK, the 'bung culture', whereby managers are paid large and corrupt fees to facilitate transfers, has been revealed by several investigative journalists and football coaches (Bower 2003). Agents and club officials are often accused of engineering transfers through illegal practices, for example where clubs contact transfer targets who are under contract to other sides (known in the UK as 'tapping up'). International transfers appear particularly problematic to police in terms of documenting payments and concluding negotiations in legal ways.

At club level, notably in Latin America, football politics can be underpinned by corrupt interdependencies. When club officials are elected by members, some candidates pay off militant or 'hooligan' supporter groups in order to guarantee blocks of votes and to intimidate rivals (Duke and Crolley 1996; Giulianotti 1999a). Globally, football officials engage in the corrupt appropriation and distribution of monies, but the problem is particularly evident in Latin America due to financial constraints on many clubs. In Brazil, a congressional inquiry found that the domestic game was rife with corruption and mismanagement. Seventeen officials were targeted for prosecution but the principle offenders remained beyond judicial reach. Other forms of corrupt relationship are fostered among football officials, players, and the media. Some governing bodies or clubs will deny accreditation or interviews to journalists who breach these informal arrangements through critical reporting.

In response to these nefarious practices, it is eminently reasonable to argue for more transparent and closely regulated governance in football. In considering how policies of transparency are to be implemented, it is important to reflect on two crucial issues. First, as Robertson (2007a) has argued elsewhere, political cultures of declared transparency also have their dark and rather undemocratic sides, notably in terms of extending systems of surveillance and social control. Illustrative cases include the enforced ownership or carrying of identity cards (which the Thatcher government had planned to introduce at English stadiums in the late 1980s), and in most nations the insistence upon strict segregation of football supporters at stadiums according to team allegiances. In such circumstances, the wider civil society typically experiences greater regulation than protection.

Second, transparency policies might also impact directly and rather artificially upon the popular cultural logics of football. Indeed, it could be argued that, in anthropological terms, much of football culture plays strongly upon the impossibility of achieving ultimate transparency in thought and deed.

Instead, artifice, suspicion, deception, and the uncertainties of subjective judgement are all crucial themes in the game's popular culture, as illustrated when referees make crucial split-second decisions over highly ambiguous incidents, when players, coaches, and teams, seek to deceive their opponents to gain advantages, and when suspicions of incompetence, bias, or corruption surround the game's officials and analysts.

Attempts by cultures of transparency to 'fix' these problems will encounter significant problems and generate some negative side-effects. Most football cultures already have strong discourses that lament the decline of 'enchantment' and the rise of rationalism, for example in relation to the perceived substitution of tricky, 'deceptive', dribbling players by efficient, measurable performers. Moreover, attempts to resolve more 'technical' judgements in football – notably key refereeing decisions – are not certain to be fully successful. For example, aided by video technology, officials may seek to eradicate 'violent play' or 'injury simulation', yet in numerous instances, referees and even post-match video-analysts may struggle to reach confident subjective decisions on culpability, such as the actual intention of specific players to injure others or to mimic pain. In such an environment, football tactics may be deflected further towards those in other sports, notably basketball, wherein players exploit transparency pressures, to 'draw' apparent 'fouls' and 'injuries' from opponents, and to have heavy sanctions imposed upon 'offenders'.

Thus, overall, while strategies of transparency and regulation serve to combat corruption, we should look very carefully and critically at their unintended, transformative side-effects.

Our second type of problem in football governance concerns *socio-political representation*, which centres on social participation and exclusion. Strong dynamics of social closure within the game's political system can serve to exclude or to deny representative status to significant figures within the game's history and culture. Thus, at national and international levels, governing bodies recognize and regularly consult professional and business figures, notably elite club officials, player unions, match officials, sponsors, and corporate leaders. Far more poorly represented are the grassroots or general 'civil society' of football, such as youth, amateur, semi-professional and women's associations, supporter groups, voluntary officials, and consumers such as television viewers and purchasers of merchandise.

Strong political critiques are directed at the 'hypercommodification' processes that have exacerbated inequalities and disenfranchisements in contemporary football. Various symptoms of this hypercommodification are often said to include the 'mercenary' relationships of globally mobile stars with their clubs; the dubious motives and legal backgrounds of new investors at leading sides; the growing chasm between a handful of TNC clubs and their rivals at national and continental levels; the vast rises in ticket prices at well beyond price or wage inflation levels over the past two decades; profiteering and price fixing regarding club merchandise and television subscription fees; and the intrusion of 'market rhetoric' within the game, wherein 'supporters' and 'clubs' are redefined as 'consumers' and 'brands' respectively (cf. Walsh and Giulianotti 2006).

Many fans flatly reject their description as 'consumers' since they could never consider switching 'brand allegiance' to another team (cf. Giulianotti 2005b). For example, while the EPL has become highly lucrative,[100] public and academic anxieties linger over the weakened status of established, less wealthy supporters (Conn 1997; Walsh and Giulianotti 2001, 2006; Wagg 2004). Many EPL grounds raised admission prices by over 700 per cent between the early 1990s and mid-2000s; in turn, average fan ages rose to the early 40s, as younger supporters in particular were squeezed. Drops in EPL attendances during 2005 and 2006 were attributed by some to exorbitant admission prices.

At major tournaments, supporter groups advance analogous concerns regarding ticket allocation systems, including the large blocks of seats claimed by corporate groups or wealthy spectators rather than long-standing supporters; the small size of many stadiums relative to market demand; the gross inflation of admission prices by event organizers; and the abject failure of football's authorities to prevent 'scalpers' and 'touts' from accessing and reselling tickets.[101]

At the 2006 World Cup finals, 14 per cent of tickets were allocated to tournament sponsors and only 8 per cent to national football associations. Some fans entering the stadium were subjected to possible infringements of their personal liberties and human rights as part of the commercialization process. In one instance, over 1000 Dutch fans at the 2006 World Cup finals were required to remove their orange trousers before entering the stadium, because the offending garments contained the logo of a beer company which was not a tournament sponsor (Eick and Töpfer 2008).

For the majority of football supporters at these tournaments, the dearth of tickets may be partially offset by the opportunity to participate in 'fan parties', where tens of thousands may congregate to watch live fixtures on giant screens. The 2006 World Cup finals in Germany saw these fan parties established successfully in most major cities. However, even these occasions have become subject to commodification, and come to mirror the hierarchical social geographies inside stadiums. At the 2008 European Championships, some 'Fan Zones' were sponsored by major TNCs, and contained corporate VIP areas as well as 'public viewing' stands which charged admission prices (Hagemann 2008).

---

[100]Between 1995–6 and 2002–3, the English Premier League clubs' total turnover quadrupled from £346 million to £1.33 billion. Average club turnover, at £66 million, was eight times greater than in 1991–2 (Deloitte 2004b).

[101]For example, tickets for the 1970 World Cup final in Mexico City sold for between 5 pesos (US$0.40) and 160 pesos (US$12.80). The official admission prices for the 2006 final in Berlin were listed at between €120 and €600, although high social and/or economic capital were also required to access many tickets. Thus, the biggest football festival was to be found in the centre of Berlin, at the 'Fan Fest', where hundreds of thousands of ticketless fans congregated.

Despite their intermittent populism, football's governing institutions have avoided tackling social issues relating to commodification, thereby reflecting the growing gulf between the game's elite stakeholders and grassroots followers. This inertia has legitimized the intervention of some national and supra-national organizations (such as the UK's Office of Fair Trading or the European Commission), to act on behalf of consumers or to preserve the game's special status.

Overall, football's international governance harbours significant problems associated with intensified multipolar complexity, governmental probity, political representation, and social exclusion. These problems tend to possess different emphases and manifestations in accordance with the changing roles and influences of neo-liberalism and neo-mercantilism. For example, neo-liberalism spotlights the greater social exclusion of poorer supporters from attending prestige fixtures. Neo-mercantilism highlights the increasingly marginal role of spectators, compared to the major clubs and league marketing people, in shaping future policies in the game. The next stage is to consider in what ways the political system within football may be modified or transformed.

Democracy and Cosmopolitanism

Thus far we have explored three models of political–economic governance within football: neo-liberalism (notably in Chapter 3), neo-mercantilism, and international governance. In this discussion, we consider potential reforms that would point towards political democratization within an increasingly cosmopolitan, global context.

Reforms may be introduced in straightforward ways. In purely administrative terms, greater transparency and accountability is required within the governance of national and international football. For example, in cases such as international player transfers or the disbursement of FIFA development grants to football associations, the receipt and distribution of all revenues should be clearly itemized by each party so that any subsequent investigation requires minimal forensic accounting. Mandatory penalties are required for those failing to comply.

The reform of FIFA's deliberative and representative functions could enhance democracy. Currently, the President, General Secretary, and a 24-member Executive Committee wield daily power inside FIFA. FIFA's Congress, which sits twice yearly, elects the Executive on a one-nation-one-vote principle. Despite claiming to be 'truly democratic', FIFA has not confirmed sufficiently democratized grounds for the election of individual congressional members.

To reform, Congress should sit more frequently. The Executive Committee should be established on a strongly rotational basis, and sustain a constitutionally defined independence from the President and General Secretary. The Executive Committee and Congress should expand memberships to encompass grassroots movements, such as women's groups, supporter associations, local football bodies, and match officials. FIFA should not hide behind Swiss financial laws but should become a model of transparency by publishing full accounts.

While football's governing bodies have established new dialogical bodies and deliberative committees, their memberships are typically restricted to familiar political figures with established professional and institutional standing, and their terms of reference are also circumscribed. For example, despite its widely heralded inauguration, FIFA's Task Force ended up being largely concerned with technical issues and solutions like the 'professionalization' of referees, the number of matches in national club competitions, and dates for international fixtures.

The discussion of more systematic reform in football may utilize the disparate arguments of critical theorists and left-liberal political philosophers, notably those with Habermasian influences. A crucial, highly influential intervention by Morgan (1993: 234–7) advocated the democratization of sport along Habermasian lines. Morgan argued that communities of athletes should constructively debate the futures of their disciplines with reference to reason rather than their competitive status and awards. More broadly, the notion of 'cosmopolitan democracy' has received diverse discussion and critical examination across social science (see, for example, Archibugi and Held 1995; Held 1995, 1997, 2004; Archibugi et al. 1998; Linklater 1998; Archibugi 2000; McGrew 2002). For Archibugi (2004: 438), cosmopolitan democracy seeks 'to globalize democracy while, at the same time, democratizing globalization'.

Cosmopolitan democracy is commonly associated with arguments for the universal establishment of democratic principles that have strong institutional bases. Held (2004), for example, sets out eight founding cosmopolitan principles: the equal worth and dignity of all persons, active agency, personal responsibility and accountability, the right to consent and dissent, reflexive and collective decision-making, inclusiveness and subsidiarity, avoiding serious harm alongside the amelioration of urgent needs, and sustainability. These principles would be institutionally supported, notably through a global legal system that advanced universal rights and obligations; a multi-layered political system built upon local and global democratic forums; global taxation and wealth redistribution; and cultural institutions that celebrated difference while underscoring the 'shared fates' of peoples from local to global levels. A 'transnational civil society' would, for Held, constitute a new public sphere that provided the lifeblood for democratic institutions.

In theory, football could represent a highly fruitful domain within which these models of cosmopolitan democracy might receive further disquisition and application. Held's cosmopolitan principles would put much more substance into FIFA's rather anodyne claims about the safeguarding of football, by enhancing democracy, tackling corruption, and ensuring basic sporting needs were globally secured. Institutionally, the model might point towards a tougher global legal framework while enabling a redistributive financial system that assisted developing football nations.

The UK offers some illustrations of broadened political participation in football. For example, 'Supporter Trusts' are democratic organizations that enable fans to influence the running of their clubs. Following the introduction of government funding in 2000, more than 140 Trusts had been established by the year 2006 with a combined membership of over 150,000. The 'Barcelona model' remains the ideal for many Trust members wherein each club is effectively owned and controlled by its members/fans rather than by small coteries of shareholders.

To make significant headway, the idea of cosmopolitan democracy needs to resolve some significant problems, of which we would raise three here. First, it is difficult to envisage a cosmopolitan democracy not least because so few writers on the subject provide genuine blueprints or roadmaps. The nearest existing institution to a global government is the United Nations. However, like FIFA, the UN is an *international* entity that is defined by multinational membership; it would require categorical transformation, into a transnational and cosmopolitan entity, to approximate to Held's vision (Nakano 2006).

Second, there are anthropological concerns that the cosmopolitan democracy model, spawned and incubated in the West, is an enlightened form of political ethnocentrism that would function to undermine the distinctiveness of non-Western cultures. For example, the model is perhaps overly concerned with individual rights and obligations, but not the future and integrity of different peoples and cultures. It says little about resolving the complex interrelationships of politics and culture, for example over religion, language, and ethno-nationalism. In football, this problem may be manifested on those occasions when the game's imposition in new settings has directly negative consequences on local cultural forms; it occurs too when non-Western elites seek purposively to model indigenous football cultures according to Western criteria.

Third, notwithstanding references to 'transnational civil society', Held's model emphasizes the *legal–institutional* implementation of cosmopolitanism and democracy. Greater consideration might be given to the everyday socio-cultural construction and enactment of cosmopolitanism and democracy, at the level of *civil society*; that is, to develop grassroots 'democratic cosmopolitanism' rather than institutional 'cosmopolitan democracy'. For Honig (2001: 13), democratic cosmopolitanism refers to 'forms of internationalism that seek not to govern, per se, but rather to widen the resources, energies, and accountability of an emerging international civil society that contests or supports state actions in matters of transnational and local interest such as environmental, economic, military, cultural, and social policies.' From this line of reasoning, democratized institutions are redundant without being ratified and operationalized at the everyday level through popular political engagement. Thus, the democratization of the game's governing bodies would mean little unless, at grassroots level, social engagement in football was symbiotic to political participation. For example, cosmopolitan democracy in football would be exposed if 'supporter movements' had low memberships or featured a small coterie of official representatives.

Concluding Comments

Our analysis here has yielded three broad points on the politics of the football–globalization nexus, relating to specific political themes, the nation state, and socio-political transformation. In outlining these points, we consider also the salience of glocalization processes and the 'duality of glocality' within each one.

First, extending our earlier analysis of neo-liberalism, we have identified two further ideal–typical political themes and ideologies within global football, namely neo-mercantilism and international governance. Football institutions habitually display more than one political theme: for example, national associations harbour neo-mercantile strategies and are engaged with international governance. UEFA's Champions League provides an exemplary study of these different forces at work. In terms of glocality, different balances of convergence and divergence are apparent between specific football societies. Governing bodies expect to be understood as legitimate sovereigns by the game's various stakeholders. Major divergences of interest arise between the neo-mercantile goals of leading football systems and the developmental aspirations of weaker leagues and associations.

Second, football highlights the continuing relevance of national institutions and ideologies in regard to globalization processes. National associations and league systems partly follow nation states in their 'glocal' adaptations both upwards and downwards. As the continuing 'club versus country' problem highlights, national and international governing bodies retain potent powers and some ultimate sanctions that otherwise restrict neo-liberal tendencies in football, such as the threatened schism of TNC clubs from existing systems of governance. In regard to glocalization, again, strategies of containment and standardization are apparent in how systems of national neo-mercantilism and international governance endeavour to accommodate and to rein in the secessionist inclinations of TNC clubs. On the other hand, glocal variation is evidenced in how national and international governing bodies respond to these and other aspects of football's commercialization (and these divergences include the quantity and quality of corrupt practices).

Third, the issue of football's socio-political transformation may well acquire greater acuity in future. The problems of governmental probity (giving rise to corruption) and socio-political representation (or social inclusion) provide a collective impetus for reform. The more general question of democratization across football's governance may be resolved partly through technical reforms, but it should also provoke debates over more fundamental and philosophically informed transformations. The idea of 'cosmopolitan democracy', as advocated in general globalization studies, has some potential, but requires significant conceptual elucidation. Moreover, as a relatively 'top-down' political reform, cosmopolitan democracy should not occlude analysis of more 'bottom-up' strategies.

Debates on these and other types of political transformation in regard to football must pay due cognizance to glocalization processes. Most notably here, there are an increasingly broad range of opportunities for the creation and development of different social formations, such as new social movements, NGOs, or grassroots associations, each of which contains particular sets of 'glocalized' cultures and political strategies. Reform of the game's decision-making bodies needs to accommodate these emergent glocal formations, if only to establish more meaningful connections between decision-making institutions and grassroots social formations.

5

The Social: Transnational Identities and The Global Civil Society

Introduction

We turn our focus now to the social dimensions of globalization. Curiously, many analyses of global change tend to underplay the social dimension, despite this realm arguably underpinning cultural, economic, and political transformations. As Chapter 1 indicated, the social has been pivotal to football's historical globalization. The writing of football's laws, in 1863, was inspired largely by social exigencies, to enable diverse players and teams to play meaningfully according to common criteria. Football's international diffusion was driven by the everyday social relations of British teachers, traders, workers, and military personnel with onlookers and prospective players from overseas. The increasingly complex and contested social relations of various stakeholders have also served to crystallize football's international relations. The game is now a major component of civil society in most nations: while FIFA's estimates of football followers may have problematic methodologies, the game has many millions of registered players, and its mega-events generate some of the largest television viewing figures across most continents.[102]

In recent years, the broad social realm has acquired global sociological prominence in two ways. First, greater consideration has been accorded to the construction of social (or indeed, 'post-social') transnational networks (cf. Knorr-Cetina 2001; Wittel 2001). Indeed, the purest discussion here would explore social network analysis, which has become a key paradigm within sociology (see, for example, Wellman 1999; Freeman 2004), notably through the recent spread of 'actor network theory' (Law and Hassard 1999; Latour 2005). Social network analysis has a long, somewhat obscured genealogy in social science, which is traceable in part to the theory of 'web of group affiliations', advanced by Simmel (1955; originally published in 1922), whose work is considered later in this chapter (Freeman 2004). Holton (2008) has been at the forefront of the interface between network analysis and globalization theory, while

---

[102]While FIFA has claimed that the World Cup final is watched by more than one billion people, it is estimated more accurately to attract 260–400 million viewers (the *Independent*, 29 August 2007). FIFA claimed in 2006 that around 270 million people are 'actively involved' in football as players or officials across the world; the number of registered players is around 38 million (see http://www.fifa.com/mm/document/fifafacts/bcoffsurv/bigcount.stats package_7024.pdf).

the interdisciplinary journal *Global Networks* has published empirically informed investigations of networked transnational formations, notably in regard to migration and new social movements, as well as through our own special edition on sport (Giulianotti and Robertson 2007b). The globalization of football would seem to offer network analysis a particularly ripe field for investigation, although little work has been undertaken thus far.[103]

Second, social scientists have examined the enormous growth and political potentialities of the emerging 'global civil society' since the early 1990s. Much of this research has been undertaken on, and often in concert with, development-focused NGOs and CBOs, as well as with national governments and IGOs such as the IMF and World Bank.

It is worth remarking here, however, that discussions of civil society, whether at national or global levels, fail to discuss sport (cf. Keane 2003; Edwards 2004; Gellner 1994). Even a vast text by one of the world's leading social theorists ignores sport (Alexander 2006a). This omission is, in our view, a serious oversight, as we seek to demonstrate here, given the public role of sporting associations, and sport's significance in building national and transnational social relations.

In the following, we explore football's contribution to the construction of the global social. First, we develop two keywords – transnationalism and connectivity – which are integral to analyses of the social aspects of football's globalization. Second, we look in detail at supporter formations, as particularly colourful, vibrant, and transnational illustrations of the diverse, hybrid, and fluid social identities within football. Third, we explore at length the universalistic social potentialities of football within two general realms: on one hand, concerning the social inclusion of comparatively marginalized identities; and on the other hand, in regard to social development and humanitarianism, as reflected in football's role for NGOs and the wider global civil society.

Part 1   The Social Aspects of Global Football: Transnationalism and Connectivity

The concepts of transnationalism and connectivity have important utility in explicating the social aspects of football and globalization (see Giulianotti and Robertson 2007b). We consider each term here in turn.

Transnationalism reveals the processual aspects of globalization through exploration of the social interconnections and interweaving of individuals and groups across diverse geo-political terrains. Transnationalism is not a new process. For example, football's 'take-off' phase, from the 1870s to the 1920s, displayed intensive transnationalization through exponential growths in social and societal relations between British, European, and Latin American players and spectators. Latterly, more routine transnational experiences and

---

[103]The project developed by Patrick Doreian, employing in part a network analysis to investigate world football, does have real potential.

encounters occur among players, coaches, and spectators, whether at elite, semi-professional, or amateur levels. For example, greater numbers of international football tournaments or club tours are staged during the northern summer months. The annual Norway Cup in Oslo, first held in 1972, is one of the biggest tournaments; in 2005, it featured around 30,000 young players from over 40 nations playing 4000 matches.

Football has also experienced a greater volume and diversity of transnational media content. In the late 1980s, UK television viewers rarely encountered league fixtures involving non-UK clubs. A decade or so later, most European leagues, as well as leading Latin American and Asian tournaments, could be viewed on UK satellite television. Similar arguments may be made for television viewers in most of Western Europe, East Asia, and North and South America. Broadband internet connections and web-television platforms point towards the future availability of almost *any* professional football league. Football clubs and national associations have become media in their own rights, communicating information globally through their websites. Football journalists have developed more extensive transnational ties with colleagues, enabling stronger globality in their reports and articles, particularly regarding player transfers. Some UK newspapers employ football journalists with foreign language skills to enhance their transnational news content. More football journalists are moving abroad to act as freelance foreign correspondents for media corporations in their home nations.[104] In Japan, it has been common since the mid-1990s for players joining European clubs to be followed by a growing entourage of Japanese journalists. However, in Europe, and particularly the UK, the greater numbers of foreign players have meant that national journalists now have weaker everyday social links with football's most newsworthy personalities and 'insider' figures (cf. Giulianotti and Robertson 2007b).

The concept of *connectivity*, which relates closely to transnationalism registers the social electrification of globalization processes. A notable applicant of the term, Tomlinson (1999: 2) argues that 'complex connectivity' pertains within contemporary globalization, such as through 'the rapidly developing and ever-densening network of interconnections and interdependences that characterize modern social life'. However, connectivity is highly uneven and registers major socio-cultural differences and inequalities.

First, connectivity captures the routinization of transnational communication, such as through transport and mediatization, as facilitated by technological developments. Thus, for example, blackberries, wireless internet facilities, and cheap global telephone calls allow sport journalists to exchange greater diversities and volumes of information about players, while players use their own websites to communicate directly with their worldwide fan base.

Connectivity also defines the greater social volume and energy of transnational relations across time and space. Consider, for example, the growth of

---

[104]For groundbreaking work on foreign correspondents in general, see Hannerz (2002, 2004).

international football fixtures. The World Cup finals have expanded from 18 games contested by 13 teams (mainly European and South American) in 1930, to 64 matches involving 32 nations from all continents in 2006. Qualifying rounds now extend over two years and, for the 2006 tournament, featured 847 fixtures attended by over 18 million spectators (*FIFA Activity Report*, 2006: 51). In the European Cup/Champions League, there were 29 fixtures in 1955–6 contested by teams from 16 nations, rising to as many as 237 games in 2002–3 contested by 72 teams from 48 nations. Even in relatively short periods, the numbers of international fixtures have increased massively, rising from 362 to 1066 games between 1991 and 2004.[105] Transnational media and migration patterns have enabled a greater number of friendly internationals to be played in 'neutral' venues, particularly involving non-European teams in Europe. For example, on one night in February 2007, England hosted four international friendlies; five sides (Australia, Brazil, Ghana, Nigeria, South Korea) were non-European, and none was from the UK.

Although some analysts suggest that the extent of media globalization has been exaggerated (Hafez 2007), football provides a compelling case study of intensified global connectivity over the past few decades, facilitated by mass television ownership, satellite and digital communication, and the close ties between media TNCs and governing bodies (cf. Harvey 1989: 293). In 1962, European television stations only broadcast coverage of the Chile World Cup finals after film had been flown home. Eight years later, the Mexico finals were beamed live by satellite across Europe. Television coverage expanded rapidly: in 1986, 166 nations broadcast around 10,000 hours of action; in 1998, 195 nations covered almost 30,000 hours; in 2002, 213 nations broadcast over 41,000 hours; and for 2006, 214 nations watched 73,000 hours (Miles and Rines 2004; *FIFA Magazine*, April 2007). Meanwhile, FIFA has sought to extend its media connectivity in other ways, by having its endorsed weekly programme *Futbol Mundial* shown in over 100 nations by 2005, while 'Beach Soccer' is reported to be broadcast in 170 nations.

Second, we must understand connectivity in relation to its antonym, *disconnectivity*. Disconnected societies have typically endured various political–economic crises, and are relatively incapable of establishing effective points for the transmission or reception of global flows. The connectivity–disconnectivity couplet extends and updates the development–underdevelopment theme prominent during globalization's 'uncertainty phase' from the 1960s to the late 1990s (see Nettl and Robertson 1968: 29; Robertson 1992: 59–60). Reflexivity was integral to the concept of underdevelopment wherein elites in relatively peripheral societies became increasingly conscious of more rapid development in other nations. Reflexivity is also a core aspect of the more generalized phenomenon of disconnectivity. As an experience, disconnection has

---

[105]The rise is uneven, however, and tends to be highest in 'Olympic years', such as 2000 and 2004, when many continental tournaments and World Cup qualifiers are being played (*FIFA Magazine*, March 2006).

strong parallels with Kristeva's (1982) concept of 'abjection'. For Ferguson (1999: 240–1), abjection denotes 'expulsion', being 'thrown down' as well as out; thus, resources or status (or forms of global connectivity) that had been previously held or promised, are abruptly removed or denied.

In football, disconnection has multifarious manifestations, mostly occurring in developing societies where civil war, poverty, unemployment, disease, and forced migration variously conspire to retard the game's domestic infrastructure and transnational integration. Disconnection is also experienced reflexively and comparatively, as football observers and workers in Africa, Latin America, and (since the early 1990s) Eastern Europe come to contrast their deteriorating conditions and standards with the transnational personnel, commercial riches, and competitive records held by Western Europe's leading clubs. We later discuss the ramifications of disconnectivity more fully in regard to football-related development and humanitarian programmes.

Part 2 Transnational Supporter Identities and Practices

Supporter formations provide a rich, diverse, and important focus for analysing transnational social relations and hybrid or glocalized social identities within football. Here, we assess particularly the cultivation of grassroots supporter formations, notably in establishing 'militant' fan subcultures that provide colourful, vocal or, at times, violent backing for their teams. Most European and Latin American fan subcultures differentiate themselves from older, more restrained, 'official' supporter associations that hold more formal relationships with their respective teams.

Supporter formations: transnational variations

The opening issue concerns the opportunity for these grassroots supporter formations actually to emerge. In most liberal democracies and in some old state socialist nations, the legal status of these supporter groups has not been salient, even for many self-identifying hooligan groups that follow clubs, as their association patterns are informal and not founded upon registered memberships. However, in nations such as China where the state closely regulates civil society, separate fan associations may be denied the legal entitlement to develop, for example where municipal authorities decide to limit the number of supporter collectives that may be formed at any one club (White et al. 1996: 150). Such regulations restrict the extent to which European and Latin American grassroots fandoms may be grafted onto the Chinese context.

Significant national and regional variations arise among supporter formations that have emerged across football's civil society since the 1960s. In northern Europe, notably the UK, the most prominent fan subcultures have been football hooligan formations. The UK was also the epicentre of the 'fanzine' (or fan-magazine) movement, from the late 1980s onwards, as supporters inverted their negative labelling within the public sphere, and commented on the ongoing structural transformation of professional football (cf. Haynes 1995). In southern Europe, and in contrast to UK 'terrace culture', militant fans (or *ultràs*) are often formally organized in membership and headquarters, have been more politicized, have attracted a relatively high proportion of female participants, and are strongly committed to producing spectacular, choreographed displays within the stadium (Podaliri and Balestri 1998: 89–93). In Latin America, the *barras bravas* (or *hinchàs*, as they prefer to be named) have often had close political connections to club officials,[106] have more violent relationships with the police, and in Argentina have been associated with relatively high numbers of fatalities (Archetti and Romero 1994; Gil 1998).

These supporter formations have some significant *sui generis* properties in historical and social terms. For example, in Spain, the *penyes* are small supporter associations, originating at Barcelona in the mid-1940s, which are connected closely to clubs and built upon strong forms of member sociability. Some clubs have over 1500 *penyes* worldwide; each reflects its distinctive member profiles, and has its own rituals and modes of association (Ball 2003: 110–11). Younger *ultràs* groups emerged in the early 1980s in conscious differentiation from the older *penyes*. The *ultràs* sought to exploit extended public freedoms in the post-Franco era and were greatly influenced by transnational connectivity, as Spain had hosted the 1982 World Cup finals and so had attracted tens of thousands of foreign supporters (Spaaij and Viñas 2005: 82–3).

In Mexico, much fan differentiation is predicated on the perceived clientelism of the wider society and on the socio-cultural characteristics of specific clubs. For example, Pumas fans claim a youthful social identity, rooted in the club's traditional preference for young players and open, attacking playing styles. Puma fans disparage the cautious and self-interested kinds of support at other clubs, notably America, that mirror the clientelism of Mexican politics and society (Magazine 2001, 2007a).

Additionally, there is much internal diversity *within* the supporter subcultures at many clubs. In Italy, leading clubs often feature two or more *ultràs* movements with varied socio-political characteristics (Roversi 1992: 56–8). In France, the Marseille club has featured six *ultràs* groups, ranging from the relatively suburban and middle-class Dodgers to the more ethnically mixed Winners (the *Independent*, 28 February 2000).

There is significant transnational evidence of a 'common diversity' across fan subcultures in terms of their practices and identities. In regard to team rivalries, for example, most clubs and national teams converge on the principle of having intense, antonymic rivals. Even in Asian societies, where oppositional solidarities tend to contravene deeper cultural values, fan groups and some football officials have sought to stoke team enmities in order to enliven domestic games.

---

[106]For example, River Plate fans were understood to have received combined monthly perks to the value of US$20,000 by 2007.

However, the socio-cultural content of rivalries can vary significantly. Class, regionalism, ethno-nationalism, ethno-religion, and civic or local chauvinisms are all evident to some degree. Many classic football rivalries are commonly conceived in class or financial terms: for example, in Latin America, we have River–Boca (Buenos Aires), Fluminense–Flamengo (Rio), Universitario–Alianza (Lima), and Olimpia–Cerro Porteño (Asuncion); the first-named teams being in some ways symbolic of wealthy or ruling elites, the second-named with the 'popular classes'.[107] Rivalries may also differentiate clubs in terms of local identity and national/transnational power: for example, in Munich (1860–Bayern), Manchester (City–United), and Madrid (Atletico–Real). In Italy, civic or regional rivalries are strong (e.g. Milan–Internazionale, Sampdoria–Genoa, Palermo–Messina), extending to North–South oppositions across the *mezzogiorno*. In Spain, ethno-national rivalries are also prominent (for instance, Real Madrid against Barcelona against Athletic Bilbao),[108] while the ethno-religious rivalries of Celtic and Rangers cannot be omitted. Beyond these kinds of basic 'common diversity', however, sociological or anthropological analysis helps to excavate deeper layers of social practice and cultural communitas, bringing out the relatively rich and indeed unique meanings and identities that flavour and enliven each opposition.

Further common diversity relates to the contested globalization of the 'hooligan' identity. A term of uncertain social origin, 'hooligan' has been transferred from English to global football contexts to label negatively the practices and identities of particular supporter minorities (Pearson 1983; Giulianotti 1994). However, on the heterogenization side, fan 'hooliganism' is often associated with a manifold and disparate range of behaviours, identities, and contexts. In Latin America and in southern Europe, unlike the north, some fan groups have intimidated or physically attacked their own players if the team has failed to perform adequately in fixtures. We noted in Chapter 3 the fatality levels among Latin American players and fans, particularly Colombia and Argentina, which are far higher than in European nations.

---

[107]Over time, there has been less empirical evidence for these stratified divisions among fans. For example, in Brazil, surveys suggest that support for Flamengo and Corinthians (the two classic 'popular class' teams) is dominated by the more populous lower-class groups, yet both clubs attracted over 11 per cent of all football fans among the top two social classes (A and B). Indeed, Corinthians drew proportionately more of their fans (11 per cent) from classes A and B than from classes D and E (10 per cent). The national appeal of both clubs is confirmed by the fact that while Corinthians attract 16 per cent of fans in their native south-east, they are also backed by 9 per cent of fans in the north/centre-west, and 7 per cent of fans in the north-east and the south (IBOPE IPINIAO – OPP231/2003 – www.ibope.com.br/calandraWeb/servlet/Calandra Redirect?temp=5&proj=PortalIBOPE&pub=T&db=caldb&comp=Opini%E3o+P%FAblica&do cid=0CEA28C6DA4B8D7 D83256EA20061B147). Despite such data, the hermeneutics of class-defined rivalry have tended to remain in Brazilian football culture.

[108]The two clubs in Barcelona have an interesting rivalry. FC Barcelona define themselves in strong ethno-national terms, as the representative Catalan team, whereas Español were long viewed as the pro-centrist Castilian side. The differentiation was muddied somewhat when the latter changed their name to the Catalan title, Espanyol, in 1995.

Simmelian forms: supporters, sociability, worlds

The sociological perspective of Georg Simmel provides a particularly rich and illuminating lens for examining transnational fandom, especially in regard to sociability and social forms. First, for Simmel, 'sociability' is a rich sociological phenomenon that, in its 'pure' condition, has 'no ulterior end', and offers people 'an emancipating and saving exhilaration' (Simmel 1949: 261). Sociability features the 'free-playing, interacting interdependence of individuals', and a striving for *equal* social relations that are 'free of any disturbing material accent' (1949: 255–7; Duncan 1959: 104–5). 'Good form' and 'conversation' are intrinsic to strong sociability; the content or talk within conversations is 'a legitimate end in itself', and should be 'interesting, gripping, even significant' (1949: 259). However, Simmel also points us towards the atomizing and individuated aspects of modern urban life, wherein the individual may feel 'lonely and deserted' in social crowds (Simmel 1971: 331, 334). Thus, the 'proto-social' dynamics of strong sociability may be viewed as providing important respite from these alienating experiences.

Second, in his analysis of social forms, Simmel differentiates three kinds of form along diachronic lines. *Preliminary* forms are essentially emergent, amorphous, and 'proto-cultural', and reflect in part the practical response of individuals to their specific circumstances. *Objective* forms may appear at a later stage, when dependency on practical circumstances is removed and when 'autonomization' occurs. *World* forms are a higher mode and operate as 'great forms', 'through which, as it were, each particular part of the content of the world can, or should, pass' (Simmel 1959: 288). World forms thus allow their protagonists 'to shape the totality of contents into a self-contained, irreducible world of experience' (Levine 1971: xvii).

There is much here that applies to football supporter formations. Certainly, where they have emerged and are sustained at grassroots civil society levels, football supporter groups harbour some rich aspects of proto-sociability. In most settings across the world, talk about football is considered legitimate, significant, and is usually a subject for relatively equal dialogue among interlocutors. The specific sociability of supporter subcultures is marked by social atmospheres that are recreational and often exhilarating when the participants are in 'good form' in terms of mixing analytical conversation, humour, and general revelry (cf. Giulianotti 1991, 1995, 1996, 2005c; Eichberg 1992).

Football supporter formations are further illustrative of Simmel's analysis of social forms, and hint towards a recapitulation of individual and collective spectator identities. *Preliminary* forms of fandom arise at the foundation of clubs or during formative moments in football allegiance. In transnational terms, preliminary fandom is still evident among spectators who have relatively restricted or fleeting identification with specific clubs.

Objective fandom is more prominent as part of autonomization processes, wherein patterned or consistent forms of identification occur. Objective fandom arises when individual supporters, followers, and fans sustain their club allegiances beyond the immediate or singular match context, or when collective supporter formations are established and operate beyond the stadium.

The *world* form of fandom is evident in the strongest modes of solidarity, for example when team identification is integral to the general habitus or social life of individuals and social groups. World forms may be partly manufactured by clubs through marketing and media (for example, with television programmes or magazines that allude to global reach and significance). Transnational supporters, through their international location, tend to reflect more fully upon the club's world status and capabilities. Some world forms are attained through the proselytizing powers and ambitions of their protagonists; for example, by seeking global status as the 'best supporters' or the 'best hooligan groups' in the world. Moreover, many fan formations are closely tied to larger societal forms – such as civic, national, ethno-national, or ethno-religious ones – which provide for the construction of broader *weltanschauungen*; clubs like Barcelona (strong Catalan identity), St Pauli (Hamburg club with red/green politics), Livorno (Italian side from leftist town), and Celtic or Rangers (Glasgow teams, with strong ethno-religious identities) are illustrative.[109]

In broad terms, while the proto-social and conversational appeal of football has a strong degree of globality, it may be more problematic for particular clubs to sustain or to develop further their singular 'world forms', given the impacts of increasing transnational mediatization and migration upon supporter cultures. We consider these latter issues more fully in the next section.

Transnational spectator identities: media, migration, and borders

Transnational social relations and more extensive connectivity have been integral to the formation and subsequent development of fan associations and identities in different nations. Regular international travel, migration, and mediatization all contribute to the extension of social contacts and to the hybridization of subcultural identities.

For example, there is a long and complex history of socio-cultural exchanges between the UK and Italy. The early Italian *ultràs* borrowed significantly from UK supporter and youth styles, such as by developing song repertoires and importing Mod, punk, skinhead, and other subcultural identities. In the UK, the 'soccer casual' hooligan style drew in part on the Italian *paninari* youth identity to become increasingly prominent among young British spectators through the early 1980s. As Italian football gained extensive coverage in UK media from the early 1990s onwards, some British supporters borrowed from the *ultràs* in terms of formation name and stadium practices, to generate more vocal and colourful forms of support.[110]

---

[109]Italian *ultràs*, for example, often possess core members who circulate literature and advance arguments regarding national and international affairs. These statements are typically underpinned by definite political–ideological perspectives.

[110]This Italianization was not as extensive as elsewhere, for example, in Algeria, where even players, grounds, and coaches acquired nicknames relating to the Italian game (Amara and Henry 2004).

Japanese football supporter groups make particular use of transnational practices and identities. During the J-League's infancy in the mid-1990s, many fan practices reportedly accorded closely with strong indigenous values regarding public harmony, cordiality, and hierarchy. Unlike most football nations, and often to the astonishment of imported players and coaches, Japanese fans would cheer and chant the names of opposing players and rival fans, celebrate their own team even when it lost, and debris would be dutifully removed from the stands (Birchall 2000: 59–60). As the J-League developed, different Japanese supporter groups started to borrow and to adapt European and Latin American chants, choreography, musical accompaniments, and naming. Thus, the Nippon Ultras fan group started to follow the national team, while the Verdy Kawasaki club was backed by the Camisa 12 (number 12) supporters (in a name taken from the Corinthians of Brazil). Officials at the Urawa Reds club copied European practices to foster more militant fandom; their 'Crazy Calls' supporter group was known for 'deviant' behaviour, such as rebuking poor play, lambasting losing coaches, and occasional incidents of violence and vandalism. Such cases confirm Kelly's (2007: 198) broad observation that in Japan, as in other nations, the everyday social practices of sport spectators can depart markedly from ideological strictures. Hence, when looking at these formations, much anthropological fascination derives from 'savouring this gap between saying and playing'.

Contemporary kinds of national or transnational connectivity, such as migration and mediatization, serve to transform some of the identity-building strategies of football spectators vis-à-vis their favoured clubs or nations. In analysing this process, Giulianotti (2002) has suggested that four ideal types of spectator identity may be discerned in the global game:

- First, the category of *supporters* may be redefined to refer more specifically to those with 'traditional' and 'hot' forms of club identification that are commonly grounded in long-term emotional, personal, and social ties to the team and its stadium. Strong supporter solidarity is often built around the club's local, civic, or ethno-historical identity.
- Second, the category of *followers* refers to those with 'traditional' yet relatively 'cool' forms of club identification. Followers may come to favour a team on account of its particular cultural history and identity, or its types of players; to maintain such backing, followers rely principally upon the electronic media.
- Third, the category of *fans* refers to those with 'consumerist' and 'hot' forms of club identification. Fans engage symbolically with the team and its players through consumer culture and diverse consumption practices. Fans may be geographically removed from the club's home area, though team identification is usually strong.
- Fourth, *flâneurs* adopt a 'consumerist' and 'cool' form of club identification that is typically transient with thin forms of solidarity. *Flâneurs* tend to consume fashionable sport-related products, to favour winning clubs

or celebrity players *qua* global market brands, and to access tickets for the world's prestige fixtures (irrespective of the competing teams). Thus, whereas fans favour *intensive* consumption that is focused on specific clubs, *flâneurs* are more orientated towards *extensive* consumption wherein club-based market attentions are far more fleeting and scattered (cf. Cowen 2002: 109–11).

Flâneurs, followers, and fans are, in that order, dependent upon forms of mediatized connectivity to spark and sustain their football-related consumption or allegiance. Moreover, as national and transnational migratory flows gather pace, the supporter category will feature more diasporic groups, who sustain their allegiances through personal or collective memories, and who come to rely on global media communications in order to maintain or to reactivate deep forms of solidarity.

Substantial academic and public discussion has pointed to the role of national and transnational commercial influences in undermining the local 'supporters' category, and assisting the more market-defined identities and practices of fans and *flâneurs* (cf. Giulianotti 2005b). Indeed, supporters may experience strong disconnection or abjection from the more globalized, commercialized game: at major clubs in England, for example, highly inflated admission prices may be deemed too expensive; tickets for prestige fixtures like Cup finals may be scarce, due to preferential allocation to corporate or wealthy figures; and the social experience of watching matches may be considered too passive or sanitized.

One notable recent development at major tournaments has been the creation of carnival environments for football supporters who are effectively excluded from the stadium. We noted briefly in Chapter 4, for example, the fan parties at the 2006 World Cup finals in Germany; around 18 million fans gathered in different cities to watch fixtures on giant screens and to join in street-party atmospheres. The Berlin 'Fan Mile' during the final match provided the most prominent instance of public *communitas* surrounding football, enabling up to one million spectators to watch and party together, while the stadium itself largely hosted the elites who had accessed tickets. In such circumstances, greater numbers of committed supporters and followers are relegated to these outside public environments while *flâneurs* with stronger economic and social capital are inside stadiums.

The different influences of migration and mediatization can germinate further, specific kinds of transnational spectator identity within football. Two such identities, providing different kinds of 'long-distance love' in football, relate to 'diasporic self-sustaining communities' and 'self-inventing transnational fandoms'.

First, diasporic supporters are typically migrants who maintain allegiances to their 'home' clubs or national sides. Hence, football allegiances to particular clubs or nations undergo forms of 'mini-globalization' along the routes and outposts established by migrant groups. Strong illustrations of diasporic self-sustaining communities emerge at club level, when

Turkish teams play in Germany, and when Mexico or Ireland play in the United States. The intensive connectivity of satellite or digital television, transnational media networks, and broadband 'computer-mediated communication' can revitalize the fandom of these diasporic communities. For example, the leading Scottish clubs, Celtic and (to a lesser extent) Rangers, have over 120 supporters' clubs sprinkled across North America. Most were founded from the mid-1990s onwards to enable fans to gather in pubs to watch live satellite coverage of their team's fixtures, as provided by an Irish-American television network (Giulianotti and Robertson 2005, 2007a). More broadly in North America, transnational networks like ESPN, Fox, GolTV, Azteca America, Globo, and TyC provide diasporic audiences with live or recorded action from leading European and Latin American tournaments, to be viewed in private homes or public spaces like bars and social clubs.[111] These latter settings may be critical for awakening the collective memories and communities of sentiment among relatively dormant supporter diasporas.

Second, self-inventing transnational fandoms arise among football followers with minimal or no biographical attachments to the favoured team or nation. Transnational media connectivity is crucial to the initial conception and maturation of such fandom. In Asia, for example, the English FA Cup final is claimed to reach up to 600 million viewers, around 40 times the UK figure (*Asian Football Business Review*, 27 March 2007). Thus, Manchester United's claim in 2006 to have more than 40 million fans in Asia (with 20 million alone in China) has been dependent upon such extensive television exposure, while Chelsea's bid to reach 100 million Chinese was reliant upon a tie-up deal in 2007 with a major internet portal (*International Herald Tribune*, 23 October 2006; the *Guardian*, 9 January 2007).

In some nations, long-term mass media coverage of foreign leagues can precipitate relatively thick forms of transnational football solidarity. In Norway, by 2003, the official British Football Supporters' Union had over 55,000 members (the vast majority being Norwegian), with stated allegiances towards 45 different clubs. The Norwegian press had reported extensively on English football since the early twentieth century, but crucially, live English fixtures were screened regularly on national television from 1969 until 1995, which served to inspire long-term, long-distance allegiances among Norwegians (Hognestad 2006).

Further research in Finland, Israel, and South Africa has explored other, highly mediatized forms of identification with English clubs (Ben-Porat 2000; Farred 2002; Heinonen 2005). In most circumstances, transnational followers hail particularly from white-collar professional sectors, and some are sufficiently wealthy and committed to travel abroad to watch their favoured side several times each season.

---

[111]For example, GolTV had 11 million subscribers in North America by 2007, its main attraction being live Latin American and European fixtures, notably the Spanish league.

Long-distance affections may also be inspired or consummated when the favoured team visits its 'foreign' backers. We noted in earlier chapters the global summer tours of Europe's TNC clubs.[112] For example, Chelsea have undertaken summer tours in Asia and North America, have established a Chinese-language website, and have engaged with the AFC and Chinese FA to build grassroots player development programmes. However, the role of competitive success in motivating such fandom is reflected in China where Chelsea fans (*flâneurs?*) possess younger demographics than their peers who back Manchester United or Real Madrid (the *Guardian*, 9 January 2007).

The construction of long-distance supporter formations and fluid fan identities, through processes of migration and mediatization, encourages our reflection on the problematic issue of borders. In recent years, the theme of border identities and border thinking has been explored, particularly by Latin American analysts (see García Canclini, 1993, 1995; Mignolo 2000). For García Canclini, border cultures are highly mobile and hybrid, and also precipitate processes of reterritorialization even in locales of rapid social transformation. The sudden urbanization of Tijuana, on the US–Mexico border, is paradigmatic, and is also a harbinger of societal transformation since, as García Canclini posits, 'today all cultures are border cultures' (1995: 261). Similarly, for Mignolo (2000), border thinking (or 'border gnosis') is demonstrated among Latin Americans, especially Chicanos. Border thinking arises from the juxtaposition and confrontation between hegemonic Occidental/Anglo-American thought systems and more marginalized or subjugated types of knowledge or aesthetic code, notably those associated with Hispanic and indigenous peoples. Border societies develop hybrid forms of knowledge that gain particular expression, for example, in the social practices and perspectives of Chicano migrants in southern American states.

When applied to football, the notion of 'border territory' takes on two particular forms, each of which reflects diverging concentrations and patterns of socio-cultural interchange. First, *border ecumenes* arise where relatively long-standing and increasing levels of football and other transcultural exchange still occur. For example, modern UK football has always possessed a border ecumene involving the four 'Home Nations', most notably for Scots who have played and watched the game in England since the late nineteenth century. Other border ecumenes arise on the continent, in bi- and multi-lingual regions, where culturally hybrid forms of football allegiance may arise, such as for Basque teams across southern France and northern Spain. Some border ecumenes may be defined much more explicitly in socio-cultural rather than territorial

---

[112]Chelsea reported in 2006 their aspiration to be the world's biggest team by 2014. The Abramovich regime has enabled Chelsea to become the most popular foreign side in Russia, hence when playing against the CSKA side in Moscow in November 2004, 80 per cent of tickets for visiting supporters were reserved for Russians who were backing the English side.

terms, through extensive reciprocity between particular cities, regions, or nations. For example, at club level, particular bonds have existed between the Barcelona club and Dutch football since Cruyff's transfer to Spain in the early 1970s. A broader border ecumene exists between European nations and old imperial outposts, for example between Portugal and Lusophone societies, resulting notably in transfers of Brazilian, Angolan, and Mozambican players to Portuguese clubs.

Border ecumenes that are defined in territorial terms have major political ramifications, notably for nation states. We noted in earlier chapters the strong resistance of football's governing bodies towards planned cross-border movements by clubs for financial reasons. However, when intense political and civil society pressures combine, a fraying or fragmenting of border divisions is frequently threatened. These kinds of pressure have enabled some Northern Irish clubs to play in leagues in the Republic of Ireland; or, at international level, lie behind Israel's membership of UEFA.

Second, *border identities* emerge territorially or symbolically within border spaces, and are consciously defined by their molten hybridity. In football, such identities cluster around clubs that have been founded in relatively new urban settings, in zones of high migration, or in fresh football territories. For example, new clubs may function to surmount senses of social disconnectivity that migrants otherwise experience within strange surroundings. Across the world, but particularly in Latin America, many clubs were founded around the turn of the twentieth century by British expatriates who were seeking to provide themselves with forms of socio-cultural reterritorialization in distant lands; games and their associated societies offered these settlers ideal ways of securing reterritorialization. Through the early twentieth century, clubs like Palmeiras (the Italian club in São Paulo) or Vasco da Gama (the Portuguese club in Rio) were built up by European migrants. In post-war Australia, European migrants established numerous clubs that served indirectly to ease assimilation (Hay 2001); later, British migrants turned to support new clubs in the emerging national league, most notably Perth Glory (Brabazon 1998). In the past decade, in the United States, border football identities have been evident at clubs like the New York Red Bulls, which has an ethnically diverse and relatively new 'core' support, and at LA Galaxy, which attracts a good Latino support; and in Spain at the Malaga club, which attracts a significant backing from British expatriates who chant songs in English.

Overall, supporter formations provide one of the richest zones for exploring the vibrant social transformations across football's global civil society. Supporter relations are marked by some intensive patterns of transnational sociability that, in Simmelian terms, extend to the construction of 'world' forms. Transnational connectivity is highlighted through the socio-cultural exchanges of names, practices, and rituals that occur among supporters across a global terrain. 'Militant' supporter formations illustrate the 'duality of glocality', or 'common diversity' across cultures, for example in terms of their sharing generally the idea of intense rivalries with particular clubs, while being differentiated through their distinctive socio-cultural contents. Migration, mediatization, and football's massive commercial growth all underpin the construction of fresh football identities, and new kinds of relationship between different types of spectator. Our theorizations of *flâneur* spectators, 'diasporic self-sustaining communities', 'self-inventing transnational fandoms', and border ecumenes or identities, all point towards new kinds of football allegiance that are increasingly important within the social dimensions of the global game. Part of this transformation is played out through socio-political issues, regarding the marginalization or 'disconnection' of localist supporter identities in the context of football's greater transnationalization.

Part 3   Football and Universalism: Identities, Development, and Global Civil Society

The transnational social dimensions of football now encompass strongly normative and political domains concerning the game's *universalistic* possibilities, in terms of promoting greater global consciousness, tackling social conflicts and forms of disconnectivity, and building a global civil society. Thus, at a juncture in which, as Robertson (1992: 183; 2007d) argues, the world has become 'for itself', football as well as other sports may be understood as crucial cultural mediums in shaping such strong senses of universalistic globality. Here, we highlight three crucial dimensions of the football–universalism nexus: first, we explore *identity* themes; second, we examine relationships between northern and southern hemispheres in regard to *development*; third, these discussions facilitate our analysis of the intersections of *football and peace* within the global civil society.

Transnational civil society: identities – race/ethnicity, gender, sexuality

Football has long been a domain for transnational struggles over social inclusion in regard to 'race' and ethnicity, and gender, and has in more recent times encompassed the cultural politics of sexuality. We discussed the historical details of these continuing cultural citizenship struggles in Chapter 1; here, we note the growing importance and diversification of such debates relative to the game's transnational development.

Since the late 1990s, football's major institutions have been more active in tackling racial discrimination within civil society. In Europe, for example, UEFA has penalized some national associations and clubs for racism among supporters at international fixtures. International conferences and NGOs have been established to tackle racism. For example, the Football Against Racism in Europe (FARE) network was founded in 1999, and has been largely financed by the EU, national governments, and UEFA; by 2007, FARE was organizing anti-racism action weeks in 37 European nations, aided by leading football personalities.

National differences on the politics of 'race' are sometimes noticeable. In the UK, the public abuse of non-white players was particularly nasty for a long period, from at least the early 1960s (when the brilliant South African Albert Johanneson emerged at Leeds United) to the late 1980s. Aided by strong grassroots movements among players and supporters, racist abuse has been largely eradicated from most stadiums, although, higher up within UK football, whites still dominate the game's decision-making roles. On the European mainland, in the south and particularly the east, racist abuse of players is far more prominent, as highlighted, for example, when black England players were abused systematically at a friendly fixture in Madrid in November 2004, and in Italy in November 2005 where the Ivorian international Marco Zoro stopped play to protest against the racism of Internazionale supporters. More broadly, an EU-funded study in 2002 found that just over 10 per cent of European supporter group websites contained forms of racism, largely of the 'latent' variety.[113] In the post-Communist nations, vocal crowd racism has been a recurring problem, and should be interpreted in the context of the relative disconnection, or indeed abjection, of these societies within and beyond international football competition. In recent years, UEFA has widened its definition of unacceptable 'discriminatory' social practices to include long-standing forms of religious abuse; thus, Scotland's Rangers club were investigated and fined for anti-Catholic chants by supporters at international fixtures in 2006 and 2007.

The exact parameters of 'racism' are set to be probed in further ways. For example, the argument that club teams should possess a 'backbone' of national players is perceived, by some, to be duly protective of the domestic game, but by others to be a racist and xenophobic policy. Additionally, as a UEFA member, Israel's treatment of its Arab population, and its continuing occupation of invaded territories, may provide some fresh domains for anti-discriminatory discourses and campaigns within football, notably among new social movements (cf. Philo and Berry 2004: 34–40).

Turning to gender issues, women's football was very strong in some nations during the early twentieth century, but long periods of systematic institutional, social, and symbolic exclusion subsequently followed. Latterly, the women's game has made enormous advances since the 1980s: at elite level, the women's World Cup finals, first contested in 1991, featured 32 fixtures at the 2003 tournament which were broadcast to 144 nations (*FIFA Magazine*, March 2007), while at the everyday level, by 2006, FIFA estimated that there were over 30 million female players worldwide, mostly in the child or youth categories (cf. Roberts 2004: 87).[114] Women now feature prominently in European and North American media coverage of football tournaments, and female consumers are an important, fresh market for sport-related industries.

---

[113]See http://eumc.europa.eu/eumc/material/pub/football/Football.pdf
[114]See www.fifa.com/en/comp/committee/0,2440,77-1882028-U19W-2004,00.html

However, a disjuncture remains between the numerical participation and cultural recognition of women within football. Leading European football officials still employ sexist stereotyping when discussing the women's game's transnational growth. For example, FIFA's Sepp Blatter called for a 'more female aesthetic' in women's football, with players donning 'more feminine clothes' like 'tighter shorts'.[115] UEFA President Lennart Johansson suggested that companies should exploit images of the typical 'sweaty, lovely looking girl playing on the ground, with the rainy weather'.[116]

Women's football participation in non-Western settings, notably Islamic societies, has inspired civil rights struggles and advances. In Iran, women have contravened national laws by forcing their way into stadiums, and by removing their headscarves to celebrate international victories. In Saudi Arabia, the government lifted a ban on cross-gender public relations to enable Swedish women to attend a friendly international fixture (*World Soccer*, March 2006). In Jordan in 2005, a women's international futsal tournament comprised teams from across the Arab world; matches were broadcast live on Al-Jazeera and covered in detail by the Arab press.

Western institutions have provided direct support. In post-Taliban Afghanistan, German coaches have been particularly active in promoting football and other sports, with women and girls accounting for approximately 30 per cent of participants (*FIFA Magazine*, December 2005). Additionally, the IFAB, which oversees the global rules of football, decreed that women players should not wear the *hijab* during matches – a decision contested by some Muslim Canadian players on the grounds of a perceived human rights violation.[117]

Latterly, football's sexual politics have broadened to include gay and lesbian participation. Separate gay and lesbian clubs and associations have been established, with the New York Ramblers club, founded in 1980, being among the earliest. In the UK, the Gay Football Supporters' Network was founded in 1989, and the first gay club, Stonewall FC, was established in London in 1991. Alternative social forms of transnational connectivity have enabled these communities to counteract everyday marginalization. By 2007, the International Gay and Lesbian Football Association featured over 30 member clubs drawn from North America, Europe, Latin America, Australasia, and China.

Some football-related NGOs and social movements have sought to counter the game's 'heteronormative' and homophobic cultures. In the UK, homophobic abuse at matches has been criminalized, and anti-discriminatory campaigns have been initiated to promote gay and lesbian social inclusion. The sexualization of football players in English consumer culture has

---

[115]See news.bbc.co.uk/sport1/hi/football/3402519.stm
[116]See http://news.bbc.co.uk/sport1/hi/football/women/4102440.stm
[117]See www.ctv.ca/servlet/ArticleNews/story/CTVNews/20070303/soccer_headscarves_070303?s_name=&no_ads=

widened to accommodate the 'gay gaze' (cf. Cashmore and Parker 2003). Yet all football nations converge over the process by which gay professional players typically hide their sexuality from team-mates and supporters in order to safeguard their careers.

In general terms, football's civil society has witnessed significant citizenship struggles, particularly in developed nations, to engage social identities that have endured disconnectivity or even abjection within and beyond the game. As the domains of gender and race demonstrate, processes of greater social inclusion and connectivity have been relatively uneven and are prone to be undermined by regressive practices among key decision-makers.

Global civil society – development and universalism

Much recent research and development work explores football's potential contribution to social universalism at grassroots and transnational levels. Here, we examine the broader historical and transnational contexts for the emergence of these debates and policy initiatives before exploring in detail their football-focused manifestation.

First, the football–universalism interface connects to the thematization of a *global civil society*. If we define civil society in Hegelian terms – as all social life between state and the family – then football and other sports appear as increasingly important domains. While the general idea of a global civil society invariably points towards stronger transsocietal connectivity, the future format is highly contested by different ideological and institutional forces.[118] For example, a 'neo-liberal' civil society would feature, as its key constituents, voluntary NGOs and the 'corporate social responsibility' (CSR) divisions in TNCs, and would function to ameliorate the social damage wrought by free-market policies. A radicalized or 'activist' civil society may emerge instead that is buttressed in part by new social movements which press for the radical redistribution of power and stronger participatory democracy; the World Social Forum, and its vision of 'planetary citizenship', is an obvious illustration (cf. Fisher and Ponniah 2003; Kaldor 2003).

Second, the football–universalism nexus inspires critical reflection upon *human and citizenship rights*. We live increasingly within an 'age of human rights', as Bobbio (1996) has indicated, marked at least since 1948 by a proliferation of legislation, conventions, and declarations at national and international levels. Across the *longue durée*, the discourse of rights has been gradually extended to encompass hitherto marginalized or excluded groups such as women, the working classes, and a diversity of ethnic minorities (cf. Habermas 2001b). Some nation states and INGOs locate sport within this 'culture of rights' with reference to personal freedom and self-development (cf. Kidd and Donnelly 2000; Giulianotti and McArdle 2006). Football's inclusion of previously marginalized groups, as adumbrated above, reflects

---

[118]See, for example, Walzer (1997), Kaldor (2003), Keane (2003), Amoore and Langley (2004), Anheier et al. (2004), Baker and Chandler (2004), Alexander (2006b).

sport's contribution to extending citizenship rights. The promotion of football by various NGOs within traumatized regions is conveyed, in part, through the ethos that all people, and in particular children, share the 'right to play', irrespective of circumstance. A further illustration is provided by the Homeless World Cup, an annual tournament which, by 2006, featured 48 national teams of players aiming to 'create better and brighter lives', with sponsorship from the UN, Nike, CNN, and various other bodies.[119]

Third, NGOs and CBOs – whether at international, national, or local levels – are pivotal to the emerging global civil society and transnationalization of human rights. Some estimates put NGO numbers at around 60,000 for the year 2003,[120] while the World Bank reports that by 2000 around US$11–12 billion in foreign aid was channelled through CBOs.[121] Given the social consequences of transnational neo-liberal policies, NGOs have fulfilled important quasi-state functions in basic welfare provisions within developing nations. Their transnational frameworks and proximities to donor nations enable international NGOs to press northern regimes and their citizens for greater world focus upon the global poor.

The systemic role of NGOs is not without problems. Some northern NGOs may appear, at best, as humane fronts for Western development or at worst as the unelected 'handmaidens' of free-market globalization (cf. Kaldor 2003). NGOs lack the democratic mandates of elected governments to initiate social policies in developing nations; they may also evade sanction for breaking national laws or local customs. NGOs have often failed to utilize indigenous knowledge, and to empower citizens at grassroots levels to take ownership of relevant projects (cf. Fisher 1997; Shaw-Bond 2000). Indeed, some analysts have critiqued the way in which some development work, and associated NGOs, including sport-focused ones, largely function to construct self-reliant, market-orientated, neo-liberal subjects, and thus reproduce forms of colonial relation between the Global North and South (cf. Heron 2007; Darnell 2008). These observations are highly salient to sport, not least because governing bodies are themselves classified as NGOs. Football provides NGOs with a powerful and highly popular medium for engaging with local peoples, and so tends to avoid problems that may otherwise occur regarding the external imposition of alien cultural practices upon client groups in the Global South.

Fourth, the football–universalism theme has provided a symbolic and practical space for the public advertisement of *corporate social responsibility*. Some TNCs, notably in sport merchandise, have been publicized supporters of conventions and movements like the UN Global Compact, founded in 2000, to advance 'corporate citizenship' in regard to human rights,

---

[119]See www.homelessworldcup.org/content/tournament

[120]See www.lse.ac.uk/Depts/global/Publications/Yearbooks/2004/DataProgramme2004.pdf

[121]See http://web.worldbank.org/WBSITE/EXTERNAL/TOPICS/CBO/0,,contentMDK:20101499~menuPK:244752~pagePK:220503~piPK:220476~theSitePK:228717,00.html

labour rights, and environmental sustainability; the Global Alliance for Workers and Communities, which links companies with NGOs to improve labour conditions and training; and the Fair Labor Association, an American organization founded in 1996 to establish and monitor global labour standards.

The highly effective campaigns of new social movements played a crucial role in inspiring these and other new compacts. Trumpeting their 'social responsibility', various sport TNCs have produced self-reports on labour practices in their production plants. Nike's 2005 self-report – featuring around 700 factories, and some 650,000 workers worldwide – criticized conditions in 25–50 per cent of Asian production plants, wherein many workers were subjected to physical and sexual abuse, meagre wages, few breaks or days off, and pressure to undertake long overtime.

Some analysts have suggested somewhat hopefully that TNCs like Nike are in the vanguard of an emergent 'third age of corporate responsibility'. The first age involved philanthropy to aid community projects; the second risk management and protective PR machines. The third age, it is claimed, marries social responsibility and business instrumentality: TNCs that protect worker rights and promote community assistance gain improved performances in return (*Financial Times*, 20 April 2005). However, other analysts would indicate that CSR is in large part a public relations exercise, noting that oppressive labour relations continue in developing nations.

The case of football production demonstrates the largely unfinished work within the game in regard to humanizing industrial conditions in developing nations. By 2005, around 80 per cent of the world's annual output of 40 million footballs was manufactured in the city of Sialkot, Pakistan. A 1996 UN study had estimated that over 7000 children worked in Sialkot making footballs. Initiatives by various international organizations, such as the UN, FIFA, and ILO, eradicated much of this practice. Yet adolescents and adults employed in ball-making still face low wages, at around €25 per month, while child labour may well have been diverted into other industries.

Returning to the broad issue of global civil society and human rights, leading governmental bodies and NGOs have manoeuvred politically to promote universalist policies through sport. At the 2002 Winter Olympics in Salt Lake City, the UN Secretary-General, Kofi Annan, argued that governments, NGOs, and local communities should employ sport 'systematically' to alleviate poverty, disease, and conflict. A year later, a major conference involving key institutions and decision-makers was convened in Switzerland. The subsequent 'Magglingen Declaration on Sport and Development' was endorsed by the United Nations, and strongly informed much sport-related policy (Giulianotti 2004b).[122] A UN inter-agency taskforce on sport was followed by the General Assembly establishing 2005 as the International Year of Sport and Physical Education. Adolf Ogi, former President of Switzerland, was appointed as the Secretary-General's Special

---

[122]See www.sportanddev.org/en/about/history.htm

Adviser on Sport for Development and Peace. Football and other sports thus became integral to the social, political, and cultural missions of the UN, notably in war-torn regions, embodying the global organization's commitment to greater engagement with grassroots civil society.

In the post-war period, the involvement of football's governing bodies with development missions has had two historical periods. First, in the 1960s, non-European football elites experienced forms of underdevelopment and disconnection from the advanced sporting world, notably Europe, and most turned to back João Havelange's successful candidature for FIFA President in 1974 (cf. Nettl and Robertson 1968; Sugden and Tomlinson 1998). In return, from 1975 onwards, Havelange utilized sponsor revenues from major TNCs, notably Adidas and Coca-Cola, to fund early football development programmes under the stewardship of Sepp Blatter.

A second, markedly more expansive and expensive phase of development commenced when Blatter succeeded Havelange in 1998. In 1999, the *Goal* programme was launched, providing national football associations with up to US$400,000 to build headquarters and additional infrastructure. From 1999 to 2006, the Financial Assistance Programme (FAP) distributed US$250,000 annually to each member association to fund local development; by 2005, at least 10 per cent was allocated to women's football. Later FIFA programmes prioritized the development of human capital; for example, *FUTURO III* was orientated towards 'teaching the teachers', notably in sport management, coaching, refereeing, and medicine. Commercial work was also prominent, notably in the *Com-Unity* programme which promoted stronger links between football associations and the wider civil society, particularly business and sponsors.

Since the early 1970s, FIFA has contributed to partnerships with various IGOs and NGOs. SOS Children's Villages, which has projects in over 130 countries, has been a prominent FIFA partner since 1994. By 2006, FIFA had listed over 100 global players (current or former) as SOS ambassadors, including Weah (Liberia), Blanc and Pires (France), Klinsmann (Germany), Sanchez (Mexico), and Okocha (Nigeria); in 2006, FIFA donated €25 million to this NGO to finance six new villages. Other partnerships have been forged with UNICEF, WHO, and the ILO. In line with the 2002 Monterey agreement by developed nations, which commits 0.7 per cent of national GDP to international aid, FIFA has announced that it will spend that percentage of its revenues on social development programmes. More critical analysts submit that, as a not-for-profit international NGO that accrues billions in commercial revenues, FIFA should be contributing rather more to help the majority of its members.

Some of FIFA's public campaigns and donations explicitly address local issues and problems. For example, in southern Africa, FIFA links with various governmental and non-governmental organizations to improve HIV/AIDS awareness.[123] Following the Asian Tsunami, a FIFA/UEFA charity match was contested in

---

[123]For example, FIFA declared that the Under-20 World Cup in Canada in 2007 would aim to raise US$2 million to challenge HIV/AIDS in southern Africa

February 2005 and helped raise over US$10 million for projects in the worst affected nations. Further work has been undertaken in Kashmir, following the 2005 earthquake that killed around 100,000 people. Other NGOs or projects to gain FIFA contributions include streetfootballworld, the Special Olympics, Play Soccer (to aid children's education and sport in Africa), and Caritas (for female sport in Afghanistan).

In recent years, FIFA has sought to exercise more direct influence upon its financial contributions to humanitarian programmes. FIFA and streetfootballworld came together to establish the 'Football for Hope' programme wherein, from 2006 to 2015, grassroots projects were to be implemented in over 100 nations, with Africa given priority. The programme seeks to act in accordance with the Millennium Development Goals.

While its practical and financial engagement with development has strengthened considerably, so too has FIFA's ideological work in advancing its universalist appearance. However, FIFA's favoured slogans on these themes lend themselves to critical sociological scrutiny. First, FIFA has announced its commitment to 'building the house of football' as a home to the global 'FIFA family'; watchwords thereof include universality, quality, democracy, solidarity and trust (*FIFA*, 2004: 12–13). However, only recently has FIFA's budgeting come under close scrutiny; we noted too in Chapter 4 the various allegations of corruption and maladministration that surround leading football officials. While development-related contributions are to be welcomed, such outlay is often overshadowed by FIFA's other expenditure: consider the US$80 million 'divorce' settlement with Mastercard, or the £5 million spent by FIFA's elite over six weeks in France at the 1998 World Cup finals, or the US$200 million construction costs of the new headquarters in Zurich (Yallop 1999: 295).

Second, FIFA has employed the 'Fair Play' slogan to appeal to universalistic sporting values that are to be protected by the global governing body; thus, FIFA distributes annual prizes to players, supporters, and organizations that embody this ethos. However, the 'Fair Play' legend requires some historical demythologizing. It has been utilized to appeal nostalgically to an imagined 'golden age' of 'honest' sport that never fully existed. It was also deployed to smooth British techniques of social engineering through sport: at national levels, it was used to mould boys through the 'controlled confrontation' of games; and at international level, 'fair play' was integral to the ethnocentric 'civilizing mission' of British games, which aimed to inculcate 'muscular Christianity' across the colonies (Mangan 1998: 182–3). In more recent times, how 'fair play' translates into playing techniques is disputed by many football nations; indeed, the term tends to mask rather than to reveal the colonial and cross-cultural complexities that underlie simple messages about football's universalism.

Third, the legend 'Think globally, act locally' has been the motto for the 2002 and 2006 World Cup finals, though it does have a far older history, notably through association with environmental movements since the 1970s (Tomlinson 1999: 21). The legend connotes that global issues may be addressed through local actions, while everyday problems have global origins and so may require transnational resolution (Urry and McNaughten 1998). However, the slogan does have some debilitating features. First, it still obfuscates political relationships between the two levels: global citizens may be moved to think about and to help the 'local', but not necessarily in the way that 'local' people would favour. Second, to recall our arguments in Chapter 1, the slogan underplays the dynamic, mobile, and hybrid qualities of the local, and elides the problematic definition of locality. Third, also extending earlier arguments, the slogan makes a somewhat simplistic analytical division between local and global, which may inadvertently serve to abolish the local (Robertson 1992: 177). Given these problems, 'Think globally, act locally' appears more as an anodyne form of 'globe talk' than as a serious praxis for global citizens.

FIFA has not been the only football institution to advance sport and development initiatives. In 1996, UEFA and CAF founded the cross-Meridian Project, building closer continental ties (including political ones), and helping to 'professionalize' African players, coaches, and management. UEFA's Hat-Trick programme was founded in August 2003 to finance development projects across the 53 member associations; €450 million was earmarked for sharing over 2008–12.

Elite players have forged some noteworthy connections with development and aid organizations. Ronaldo, Zidane, and Drogba have been prominent UNDP 'Goodwill Ambassadors', and an annual 'Match Against Poverty' since 2003 has promoted the Millennium Development Goals, notably the aim of halving world poverty by 2015. Charitable foundations have been founded by numerous players, notably transnational Latin American talents. Jorginho (Bayern Munich and Brazil) founded a school for 1200 Brazilian children, financed by centres in Brazil and Germany. Jürgen Klinsmann's Agapedia foundation aids children in Bulgaria, Germany, Moldova, and Romania. José Luis Chilavert (Paraguay, various European and South American teams) runs an eye clinic in Asuncion and sponsors the care and education of 600 children from the Chaco region. Juan Pablo Sorin (Argentina, various European and South American teams) helps to finance schools and a hospital in north-east Argentina, and has compiled a book on social deprivation and injustice in his country.

Nations with strong internationalist backgrounds figure prominently in sport-related development. Norway's Ministry of Foreign Affairs and national aid organizations contribute financially to the national football association's (NFF) work on various international programmes, such as in the Balkans, Vietnam, and Zambia. The Ministry and the NFF play key roles in organizing the Norway Cup, discussed earlier; many participating teams have their expenses paid by the hosts. Norwegian aid agencies like NORAD and the Strømme Foundation have contributed large sums to the renowned Mathare Youth Sports Association (MYSA) in Kenya. MYSA was founded in 1987 and by 2003 had grown into a major local NGO with approximately 14,000 members and around 1000 football teams. Crucially, MYSA is committed to high levels of local decision-making and leadership to avoid dependency relationships upon northern donors (cf. Hognestad and Tollisen 2004).

We have discussed in some detail the links with NGOs, but football has also produced alternative formations within the emerging global civil society, notably grassroots social movements. Some social movements possess transnational kinds of solidarity, and may even extend across sports: for example, formations that have exposed the exploitative labour practices of TNCs in East Asia, or other movements among athletes through the 1980s and 1990s which protested against forms of racism and sexism. Yet, as Italian football reminds us, the political complexions of these transnational social movements can be very varied and need not be particularly universalistic. Certainly, for example, the Italian club Internazionale has established ties with the Zapatista rebels in Mexico by financing development projects in the Chiapas region, while team players have voiced their support. Yet fans at many Italian clubs – including Internazionale – have also been associated with neo-fascist movements and engaged in the overt racist abuse of non-white players.[124]

Overall, however, in defining the dominant participants and model of the future global civil society, it seems likely that, in football as in other fields of social life, the neo-liberal/NGO model will continue to hold the upper hand over the activist/new social movement model. We have noted already the exponential numerical growth of NGOs in recent years. As NGOs themselves, football's governing bodies have strongly commercialized the game, with extensive connectivity to transnational business groups and corporations. Indicatively perhaps, FIFA has its own CSR division, and Blatter addressed the World Economic Forum in Davos in 2006, to state that football and sport in general can have a positive influence on the world. Football's leading officials, however, have yet to contribute to that alternative transnational movement, the World Social Forum.

As some analysts have noted, new social movements are often 'tamed' into becoming NGOs, in order to extend their political impact beyond the streets and to secure careers for their emergent elites. The schism in the German Green movement, between *fundis* and *realos*, was an early illustration of this process with the pragmatic latter group emerging as victors (Wallerstein 2001: 266). Some evidence for the taming of new social movements, through stronger connectivity with established political institutions and frameworks, might also be found in football. In the UK, for example, critical fan social movements emerged at many clubs in the late 1980s, in part by founding 'fanzines' and alternative supporter associations. Processes of institutionalized 'taming' occurred, as some fanzines adopted a more professional and business-like structure, while some fan movements were gradually incorporated into formal entities and national bodies (for instance,

---

[124]Lazio fans have also courted notoriety by unfurling anti-Semitic banners and, in 2000, a tribute to the assassinated Serbian warlord and alleged war criminal, Arkan.

the Football Supporters' Federation, founded in 2002; or 'Supporter Trusts') with whom the relevant authorities could do business.

A similar 'taming' might be observed in the foundation of 'progressive' football-related NGOs, such as FARE, which tend to feature employees with strong activist credentials, but which are institutionally committed to campaigns for social citizenship and inclusion rather than more radical reforms of the game's governing structures or commercialist ethos. Again, it certainly remains to be seen whether the more activist movements in football will explore broader transnational networks, for example by contributing to future 'World Social Forums'.

One final point for consideration concerns the possibility that new social movements in football or sport more generally may connect in part to particular kinds of nationalistic or transnational politics. The specific position of China is especially salient here with regard to sport and human rights. The 2008 Beijing Olympics – in which the football tournament played a significant part – witnessed attempts by nation states, new social movements, and NGOs to counter China's global rebranding by highlighting the host nation's human rights record regarding restrictions on individual and collective liberties, involvement in the Darfur region, the violent suppression of dissent in Tibet, and support for the Mugabe regime in Zimbabwe. As China's economic expansion continues, and greater involvement is secured in football's global political economy, to the possible extent that European clubs are invested in or even bought by Chinese citizens or corporations, so new frontiers of mobilization and dissent may be established within the game by new social movements or NGOs on the global issue of human rights.

Global civil society – football and peace

In recent years, much research and development work has explored football's specific contribution in war-torn regions for aiding conflict resolution, peace-building, and resocialization of traumatized peoples. UN Secretary-General Kofi Annan crystallized this view in January 2006 when, on a visit to FIFA's Headquarters, he observed: 'Sport has an incredible capacity to work as a catalyst for positive change in the world and I can't think of anything that can bring people together like football. For 90 minutes at a time, people become one nation' (FIFA 2006: 29).

We should, however, exercise initial caution when evangelizing or essentializing these 'functions' of sport. First, there are countless historical counter-examples of serious social breakdown within football: spectator and policing violence provide recurring illustrations, with football-centred rioting an important flashpoint for the outbreak of the Yugoslav civil war (Lalic and Vrcan 1998).[125] More broadly, as the former UNHCR has indicated, sport is one domain in which human rights are often contravened

---

[125]Many violent supporter subcultures were transferred from stadiums into the rival military forces on the Serbian and Croatian sides.

(David 2004). For example, sport systems have a particularly weak record in protecting athletes from physical and mental forms of abuse, including excessive sport-related 'labour' among children, normalized doping of competitors, and 'quick fix' medical treatment for injuries (Brackenridge 2004; Donnelly and Petherick 2004; Houlihan 2004; Schneider 2004).

Second, vocal proponents of the contemporary football–peace theme should beware of the possibility of repeating earlier types of error in social policy. Through much of the twentieth century, a lot of sport-centred policy in industrialized nations sought to use physical exercise for disciplinary and governmental ends, in particular to divert young people and the lower classes from perceived delinquent or 'licentious' temptations such as alcohol, drugs, promiscuity, and deviant youth practices. However, despite their latter-day revival by the UK's Labour government to promote education and crime-reduction initiatives, there is little hard evidence to confirm that these sport-flavoured social policies have a great deal of success (cf. Robins 1992). Thus, it may be that IGOs and NGOs, with their sport-driven programmes, may risk making similar mistakes in southern societies, with an additional twist of post-colonial paternalism in dealing with their client groups.

These initial problems and dangers may be largely offset by IGOs and NGOs if sufficient knowledge of and engagement with indigenous groups is secured. Informed consent and project ownership are crucial issues on this point. NGOs have much to gain in terms of legitimacy and potential successes if they are able and willing to implement post-Fordist, devolved, or 'glocalist' working practices, which mandate close liaison with local communities, and the training of indigenous peoples to run projects with broad decision-making autonomy.

The 'Open Fun Football Schools' (OFFS) provide one prominent illustration of football–peace initiatives (see Gasser and Levinsen 2004). The OFFS are organized by a Danish NGO (Cross Cultures Project Association) and receive support *inter alia* from the Norwegian Football Federation and UEFA. The OFFS bring together children from different ethnic groups, particularly those divided by major conflicts, to play football and to enjoy general sport together. Local coaches are trained to foster the festive, 'sport for all' ethos of OFFS, while building self-confidence, imagination, social skills, and bonds among participants. OFFS were first established in the post-civil war environment of the former Yugoslavia. By 2004, around 4000 local leaders and coaches had organized over 230 schools for almost 50,000 children; the OFFS were subsequently introduced in the Middle East.

Football–peace initiatives may be introduced in locations with long-standing military tensions or histories of extensive violence. For example, in Korea, where North–South diplomacy is often tense and the border is reputedly the most fortified area in the world, the two national football teams have contested 'reunification' or 'peace' fixtures on a periodic basis since 1990. The fixture in Seoul in September 2002 was marked by intensive symbolic displays of national unity throughout the game, with players from both teams holding aloft a flag showing a unified Korea. In the Middle

East, football projects have sought to traverse ethno-religious and political divides through sporting contact.

In Colombia, the 'Football for Peace' project was established in 1996 by a German doctoral student to draw young people from surrounding cultures of violence, to explore how conflicts may be resolved peacefully through play. The project was transferred back to Germany to counteract right-wing influences, and subsequently inspired the streetfootballworld NGO that established work on a systematic international basis.

The war-torn states of West Africa provide some of the most acute circumstances in which the peace-building possibilities of football may be critically explored. Most war combatants have been children and young people with at least some prior football experience. Richards' (1997) pioneering anthropological analysis in Sierra Leone concluded that football constitutes one rare domain in which young people socialize and compete in relatively rule-governed ways, and that the game may aid the resocializing of those brutalized by warfare. Richards observed that local teams and associations had introduced disciplinary codes for unruly spectators or players who otherwise threatened the viability of matches. Latterly, in line with sport's rising status on development agendas, IGOs and NGOs have sponsored sporting initiatives across West Africa, in order to capture the energies and ethical codes of young people who are at risk of falling into military combat. In Liberia, for example, where civil war raged for 15 years, the UN has backed numerous sport initiatives, including a five-week nationwide sporting festival in March 2007.

Aid missions in these locations face three key problems that also confront other football–peace initiatives (cf. Armstrong 2004, 2007). First, NGO engagement needs to be long-term and tailored to local needs. Some critics indicate that NGOs are too instrumental, highly centralized, and myopic in their development strategies. Thus, for example, local people may be suddenly 'swamped' with sport gifts or publicity; but, after a short period, the development workers disappear, the sport resources evaporate, and little is achieved in terms of continuing support. In this way, NGO engagement may give local populations a 'shock therapy' of connectivity with global civil society, only to lapse quickly back into disconnectivity; more nuanced, carefully resourced, and extensive engagement would prove more successful.

Second, football will solve little unless the deeper structural problems that underpin these conflicts are addressed, such as the ending of poverty, famine, or the illegal occupation of territories. If these solutions are not found, then football's practices and symbols may end up being integrated back into the everyday cultures of violent domination.

Third, a complicating factor concerns the social tensions and contradictions that may arise between NGOs, CBOs, and other involved parties at institutional and grassroots levels. The problem centres here on a tendency to prioritize social and political connections between major decision-makers on the donor and receiving sides, rather than to focus on social connectivity at the grassroots levels. As an important aspect of 'global civil society', football–peace initiatives need to focus on the local level. Thus, indigenous peoples must be classified not as mere 'recipients' of aid, but as full participants in terms of formulating, administering, and 'owning' the relevant projects.

Concluding Comments

In this chapter, we have sought to contribute theoretically and substantively to the renewal of academic discussion on the social aspects of globalization. We argued that the concepts of transnationalism and connectivity facilitate theorization of socio-global processes, notably in regard to highlighting issues of social 'disconnection' or exclusion from globalization, and also in registering the interdependency of trends towards convergence and divergence across societies. Diverse football supporter groups, notably involving youth subcultures, reveal particularly complex and varied forms of transnational identity and exchange. In Simmelian terms, football is one of the strongest realms in popular culture to facilitate transnational kinds of proto-sociality, and provides an important field for the greater coherence of social identities, including the articulation of 'world' forms. We noted too that processes of mediatization and migration are impacting directly upon spectator solidarities, for example in the development of *flâneur* identities, alongside the stronger emergence of 'diasporic', 'self-inventing', and border fandoms at both club and national-team levels. The rise of these new spectator identities is coterminous with the growing senses and experiences of 'disconnection' endured by more established supporters.

We considered in some detail the highly prominent question of football's interrelationship with social universalism. Social identities relating to gender, ethnicity, and sexuality have been central to those transnational struggles that challenge forms of disconnectivity or exclusion within the global game. In recent years, the football–global civil society nexus has acquired an especially strong relevance in regard to themes of development, human rights, corporate responsibility, and peace. Many IGOs, national governments, and NGOs have founded partnerships with football's major institutions and figureheads to construct development programmes and to establish peace-building initiatives in conflict zones. Arguably, the game's leading decision-makers could contribute more financially to these programmes, and cement closer ties to movements like the World Social Forum rather than the World Economic Forum. Football is particularly prominent among the many sports that are engaged in peace-building initiatives, which are most effective when sustained participation occurs within conflict zones. In this way, the game is considered highly useful in reconnecting fractured societies with routine, rule-governed, peaceable kinds of social life.

We would argue that these various components of the football–universalism nexus are underpinned in part by the development of new citizenship issues from the 1970s onwards. In other words, a *tertiary mobilization* of socio-political identity appears to have been occurring. The first mobilization involved the detachment and realignment of primordial loyalties, such as from religion to nation state. The second mobilization witnessed the confirmation of individuals as legal, political, and social citizens (cf. Marshall 1950). The third phase encompasses the rights and duties of the second phase, but also enters new territory, by fostering 'a conception of the individual as human, with rights and needs (perhaps, ultimately, duties) which are not solely societal'. Thus, tertiary mobilization 'relativizes citizenly involvement', to produce new kinds of relationship and differentiation between the individual, the 'concrete society', and humankind (Robertson and Chirico 1985). Potentially, this tertiary mobilization of citizenship may prioritize humankind; or, to answer an earlier consideration, it may centralize the question of how humankind might go from 'in itself' to 'for itself'. Important research problems thus open up for sport sociologists in regard to how football allows these tertiary conceptions of sociopolitical identity to be explored and concretized.

Robertson (1992: 78–9) has argued that four 'images of world order' may be discerned in regard to globalization. These are *Global Gemeinschaft 1 and 2*, and *Global Gesellschaft 1 and 2*. Each of these images of world order stresses a particular elemental reference point, whether it is individuals, national societies, world system, or humankind. Most saliently here, *Global Gemeinschaft 2* stresses humankind as its 'pivotal ingredient', and this specific image of world order has two versions: *centralized* and *decentralized*. The centralized version of *Global Gemeinschaft 2* advocates the foundation of a kind of global village that is bound together by a 'globewide Durkheimian conscience collective'; the decentralized version anticipates a rather softer type of political connectivity, enabling a more pluralistic framework for a world community to emerge.

In football, the centralized version of a *global gemeinschaft* is idealized especially in the rhetoric of major transnational institutions, such as when governing bodies, IGOs, and sport-related TNCs allude to a 'global football family' that is bound together by a common passion and, by extension, a universal commitment to the game's sovereign institutions, ethics, images, and consumer products. However, we would posit that the decentralized version more accurately fits the picture of football's civil society that we have painted here. The decentralized version appreciates the possibility, indeed the necessity, of sustained difference within the game and wider global civil society. In this way, we are also able to recognize that the seductive, Simmelian, proto-social forms of sociability surrounding football also possess different cultural manifestations. And we further recognize that, while football may be utilized for development and peace-building projects, the social and societal identities in the game will continue to evolve in divergent ways and through varied connections, rather than to converge upon a single, unifying socio-cultural model.

Finally, the inevitable influence of *realpolitik* in regard to the global civil society must be considered. One concern for football must be the possibility that the game will be utilized by northern nation states and NGOs as a particularly seductive cultural mechanism for the exercise of 'soft power' or 'soft imperialism' in war-torn regions or among 'problematic' communities. A strong ideological claim of the game's governing bodies – which goes largely unchallenged in most public spheres – is that football is a unique cultural form that seems to transcend many ethno-religious, ethno-national, and civilizational divisions, such as in the Balkans, West Africa, or the Middle East. Yet the asociological claim that football is somehow above politics will generate deeper public scepticism as the game becomes increasingly and directly engaged in the making of a 'global civil society'. Football's transcultural status would be severely shaken if it were to be utilized systematically – particularly by outside agencies, and with minimal grassroots consultation – to promote political settlements or ideologies that are at one with the policies of dominant nations and IGOs. The game's governing bodies may adopt some initial practical strategies in order to circumvent this possibility. Most obviously, governing bodies should be highly watchful in the relationships that are established with IGOs, NGOs, and TNCs, and should work in close partnerships with local peoples when implementing football-related projects. More potently, the game should contribute towards the strengthening of a two-way dialogue between local communities at grassroots levels and powerful nation states, TNCs, NGOs, and IGOs.

Epilogue

As we noted in the Prologue, in writing this book, our aims have been two-fold: first, we have aimed to place the analysis of football squarely within the academic mainstream, and second, we have sought to advance understanding of globalization processes through close investigation of the global game.

We trust that by now, the reader is well enough informed about football's global significance, whether in terms of its expanding cultural significance, financial value, or political status. Examination of the global game has also enabled us to advance a variety of concepts – including duality of glocality, hard/soft Americanization, exceptional nationalism, Americolonization, and dis/connectivity – that may be readily transferred into studies of other realms of globalization.

Here, our intention is to advance these aims further by developing a theoretical model of the key global themes within football. We do so by integrating and expanding arguments from our earlier chapters.[126]

Mapping the Global Game

The four global themes that we set out in earlier chapters were *neo-liberalism*, *neo-mercantilism*, *international governance*, and *global civil society*. In developing our model, we have integrated these four themes within the 'global field', as initially set out by Robertson (1992) and discussed in Chapter 1. The global field consists in four 'elemental reference points' which, to reiterate, are *individual selves*, *national societies*, *international relations*, and *humankind*. Each of our four themes is connected to one of these elemental reference points. Thus, neo-liberalism links to the individual, neo-mercantilism to national societies, international governance to international relations, and global civil society to humankind.

In broad terms, the global field reveals the different pushes and pulls experienced by individuals and social groups within the context of contemporary globalization. For example, in recent times, football supporters in Europe or Latin America have been pulled variously towards individualistic cultures of global celebrity and consumerism that surround elite players or sporting products; towards national societies through strong forms of 'exceptional nationalism' during major football tournaments; towards

---

[126]The model provided here will be outlined more fully as the 'global football field' in future work.

NEO-MERCANTILISM	NEO-LIBERALISM
National society	*Individuals*
GLOBAL CIVIL SOCIETY	INTERNATIONAL GOVERNANCE
Humankind	*International relations*

Figure 6.1   *The global field and associated themes*

greater reflexivity over the international politics of world football, and how arising conflicts influence the game at everyday levels; and towards a stronger, cosmopolitan appreciation of the benefits of multiculturalism, as illustrated by the embrace of non-national players at league clubs or by widespread interest in foreign football systems.

We set out below the four relationships of political themes and elemental reference points. These relationships are also depicted in Figure 1.

Neo-liberalism/individuals

Neo-liberal political–economic strategies are strongly associated with advancing the interests of the individual 'free agent' across the global marketplace. Historically, neo-liberalism has been particularly influential within football through the uncertainty and millennial phases, notably since the late 1980s, following deregulation of the media sector and various international markets.

In the millennial phase, the thematization of individuals has moved towards issues of regulation and risk management. In football, individual spectators are both regulated through more orchestrated and intensive security strategies, and moulded through particular authorized fan identities. Various institutions, including intergovernmental bodies and TNCs, engage role-model players to endorse diverse social policies ranging from local education initiatives to the alleviation of global poverty. Alternatively, risk-taking or 'excessive' behaviour is also brought into sharper public focus, notably through the nightlife tastes of some elite players or the occasional eruptions of spectator disorder.

In institutional terms, neo-liberalism in football is strongly associated with major TNCs, notably elite clubs, media networks, and the game's key sponsors, which gain most from economic deregulation and which seek to appeal to the 'footloose global consumer'. The implementation of neo-liberal principles in football would enable elite clubs to function more fully as TNCs in terms of branding, player recruitment, and exploring the option of breakaway league systems.

The relationship of neo-liberalism to processes of cosmopolitanization and glocalization is double-edged. On one hand, the free movement of players, merchandise, and television coverage of national leagues has created increasingly transnational and multicultural football experiences at everyday levels. Local and national societies also have more opportunities to place themselves on the world stage, and to engage critically with other cultural practices and belief systems through football.

On the other hand, neo-liberalism has a significant elective affinity with relatively instrumental, market-centred strategies that are associated with thin cosmopolitanism or corporate-driven types of glocalization. For example, individuals are more likely to accept their classification as global football consumers, and to hold relatively weak, *flâneur*-type social solidarity towards clubs or players. This process is accelerated by the ways in which TNC clubs increasingly adapt their public images to appeal to these transnational football consumers.

The neo-liberalism–individual relationship harbours some inherent dangers. The free-market, consumerist ethos is difficult to reconcile with the collectivist values that are consciously sustained at most clubs and national sides. The tendency of neo-liberalism to produce market cartels – such as, in theory, a European league dominated or controlled by a few clubs – runs counter both to the 'uncertainty of outcome' principles that make sport highly marketable, and to the traditional promotion/relegation system which adds further layers of competitive complexity. Free markets often exacerbate competitive inequalities within or between nations and regions, and stoke financial turbulence as more clubs or league systems fall into debt and decline.

We envisage that social divisions and conflicts surrounding commodification will be manifested more acutely within football. The distribution of revenues – notably television income, access to tickets, and elite players – will be contested at national and international levels, in part as a way of challenging perceived pathologies in football, such as socio-economic exclusion from stadiums, growing competitive gulfs between clubs, and weaker structures of feeling between supporters and teams.

At the elite level, football's commercial dimensions will become more globalized and transcultural. Clubs in Western Europe will see a wider range of international ownership and investment, notably from Asia, to go alongside growing East European and American involvement. Given the additional revenues released by wealthy football oligarchs, leagues such as those in Germany and France will struggle to resist the competitive commercial pressure to adopt UK or Italian models of club ownership.

Emerging TNCs from Asia will play a more prominent role in football sponsorship. Clubs and associations will advance the opportunity for closer vertical integration with media corporations, as more football institutions seek to maximize direct revenues from the live broadcasting of fixtures and tournaments. Meanwhile, the elite game and its players will be more intensively integrated within mainstream consumer and celebrity culture, thereby further sharpening divisions with players at semi-professional and amateur levels.

Neo-mercantilism/national society

Neo-mercantile political–economic strategies are strongly associated with national football systems. Historically, neo-mercantilism in football intensified through the twentieth century as the power of national associations and league systems was cemented, while national teams gained potent representative significance. In recent years, expansionist neo-mercantile strategies have been best illustrated by the global televising of Western European leagues, most obviously the EPL, and in Russia by the influence of state and national industries in building up the domestic sport system.

In the contemporary, millennial phase of globalization, national football industries and the nation state have combined particularly over themes of governance, risk-management, and social control. The free market in players, spectator allegiances, and media–sport contracts has sparked recurring debates over the long-term viability of established national leagues. In the post-9/11 context, national governments that host football mega-events have taken on enormous security responsibilities and budgets.

At first glance, neo-mercantilism has a significant correlation with contemporary processes of banal *and* exceptionalism nationalism. For example, the EPL has become part of the everyday mediasphere of many nations, while heightened national identification erupts periodically during international mega-events. Neo-mercantilism corresponds too with the glocalisation processes identified by urban studies analysts, as national football institutions 'upscale' to transnational partnerships with TNC clubs or media networks.

More subtly, national societies and identities are concretized further through critical engagements in multicultural contexts. For example, 'rooted' forms of cosmopolitanism and glocalization demonstrate how national particularities may be sharpened and revivified as part of a critical openness towards other cultures.

The neo-mercantilism–national society relationship harbours some inherent weaknesses and problems. Intensive nationalism may be actuated through aggressive or violent antagonisms towards other societies. Evermore powerful national football empires may emerge from the zero-sum struggle between neo-mercantile forces. Greater disconnectivity may bedevil the national football systems in many 'emerging' nations, as Asian and African peoples come to favour glamorous international leagues over depleted indigenous tournaments.

We envisage that football will continue to crystallize many of the forces and conflicts surrounding the nation. As its transnational significance increases, football will be a more important domain in which national societies pursue global status or, in some instances, the right to establish autonomous nation states. The deterritorialization of elite national league systems will become increasingly politicized, most notably as the game's developing nations seek to counteract their virtual penetration by Europe's football industries.

The influences of Americanization and 'Asianization' upon national football systems will be more closely scrutinized and contested (cf. Crothers

2007; Tsuda 2007). On one hand, elite European leagues will tailor their televised products to suit the tastes of international markets and, we expect, will also explore further opportunities to stage competitive fixtures in these new settings. On the other hand, North American and Asian leagues will endeavour to compete against these globalized football systems by nurturing their own multicultural, indigenous competitions with a greater array of star players and coaches, alongside inflated commercial and media revenues.

International relations/international governance

The close interrelationships of the two internationals – relations and governance – are confirmed in institutional terms, as IGOs in football such as FIFA and UEFA have sought to control and to shape the game's multipolar complexity.

Football's international governance has expanded enormously through the twentieth century, as membership of continental and global bodies has risen inexorably, thereby producing complex transnational political matrices. In the millennial period, these international institutions will experience further struggles between economically powerful and weaker forces within football, while risk-focused issues regarding security and the game's 'carbon footprints' will have growing salience for mega-events.

The future internal structure of football's governing bodies will influence significantly the likely outcome of these processes. The gradual modification of governing bodies would ensure *realpolitik* remained the heartbeat of football's international society, with a greater propensity towards more instrumental, thin variants of cosmopolitanism. More radical restructuring would require more political engagement with more stakeholders, particularly at grassroots level, and would reflect a thicker form of political cosmopolitanism, though it is difficult to envision exactly how this new framework would operate.

International governance does harbour some significant weaknesses and dangers. Internally, though unlikely in the short term, football's governing bodies need to strengthen their status by tackling allegations of corruption, patronage, and lack of transparency more robustly. Governing bodies may be incapable of integrating the heterogeneity of competing interests and aspirations across the widening spectrum of stakeholders. Moreover, given the game's intensive commodification, the European Union may interpret as spurious the governing bodies' claim that football should retain an essentially non-economic, 'special status'.

Greater political influence will continue to be exerted by less established football regions, particularly North America, the Far East, and the Global South, with consequences for the allocation of World Cup final places and the right to host the game's mega-events. Potential challenges will linger over the special membership status of the UK's four national associations inside FIFA. Political conflicts between elite clubs and smaller national associations will also become more acute within the international governing bodies.

Global civil society/humankind

The fourth and final interrelationship connects the political–economic theme of global civil society with the elemental reference point of humankind. The global civil society promotes ideas regarding a common world humanity and shared transnational fate. Numerous IGOs, NGOs, new social movements, TNCs, and nation states have sought to connect football with principles and issues associated with the global civil society, such as peace-building, development, democratization, social inclusion, and social responsibility.

Football's global civil society may be said to have had a lengthy incubation, encompassing 'the right to play' struggles of marginalized social groups such as the male working-classes, women, and non-whites in different contexts. Development and humanitarian programmes have crystallized through the engagement of football's leading institutions with NGOs and IGOs since the early 1970s.

At first glance, the global civil society is the most likely of all four themes to embrace the universalistic possibilities of transnationalism and cross-cultural exchange. 'Ethical glocalism', with its concern for normative issues surrounding the local–global interface, is most easily located inside this quadrant. However, a broad range of cosmopolitanisms may still be evidenced: *thin* cosmopolitanism across international institutions, through discourses on the 'global football family'; *rooted* cosmopolitanism, as supporters and players gel strong partisanship and generalized appreciation of technical artistry; and *thick* cosmopolitanism, through full engagements with the differences that undergird other football cultures.

The global civil society harbours several tensions or problems. As with international relations, it contains a wide range of competing and potentially irreconcilable institutional forces. In real terms, highly influential institutions within global civil society – notably IGOs, TNCs (through CSR), and pragmatic NGOs – have significant or stronger ties to alternative political–economic themes that are discussed here. Those split loyalties will inevitably impact upon the type of global civil society that is realized within football.

We envisage that the global civil society will witness further transnational convergence on issues of social inclusion. For example, greater pressures will be exerted by international governing bodies, corporations, and NGOs for convergence between nations and regions on the themes of race and gender. The extension of social inclusion strategies to the realm of sexuality will occur, though this process will be relatively slow and driven on initially by social movements and some NGOs principally in Western Europe.

Stronger critical reflexivity will be exercised by academics, social movements, and critical NGOs, towards two issues pertaining to the global civil society: first, the social effects of extensive surveillance and securitization in football contexts, especially mega-events in the Global North; and second, testing the real value of football-related projects in the promotion of peace, development, and human rights, especially in the Global South.

The global civil society will become a greatly enlarged realm in terms of the volume and variety of participating institutions and associated projects. In turn, it is likely to become an increasingly contested realm. TNCs and some sporting federations, under the banner of CSR, have sought to implement particular development and inclusive programmes that are rather weaker than some NGOs or social movements would prefer. Conversely, more radical, external NGOs and social movements will probe human rights and social development issues within football and other sports. These latter, diverse forces may cohere and mobilize within shared political spaces such as the World Social Forum.

Football and other sports will become increasingly prominent domains in which 'appeals to humankind' are made by diverse social forces. The build-up to the Beijing Olympics in 2008 was paradigmatic, as nationalist movements, human rights groups, and global celebrities spotlighted the Chinese government's record on various domestic and international issues, Tibet, arms trading in the Darfur region, and support for Mugabe in Zimbabwe. At the everyday level, liberal media, NGOs, and new social movements will continue to extend the politics of football into humankind issues, for example when publicizing the backgrounds of international investors and sponsors within the European game.

Domains of contestation in global football

As we have indicated, significant tensions and conflicts often arise within and between the four political–economic themes. Each quadrant contains competing forces that seek to shape or to dominate that specific theme, most obviously TNC clubs (neo-liberalism), national associations and league systems (neo-mercantilism), national and continental associations (international relations), and various forces ranging from radical social movements to corporate PR departments (global civil society).

Tensions also arise in the institutional relationships that engage the themes. Thus, for example, the neo-liberalism/neo-mercantilism relationship involves clashes between elite clubs and national associations, notably on the 'club versus country' issue; the international governance–global civil society witnesses some tensions between global federations and critical NGOs, notably over corruption or development issues; and, the neo-liberalism–international governance relationship contains struggles between elite clubs and federations over issues like international fixture schedules.

When we consider some of global football's more contentious issues, all four thematic forces are evidently contesting the outcome. For example, the broad issue of distributive justice at the World Cup finals involves the allocation of match tickets, revenues, and tournament places, and thus engages the competing interests of national governments and associations (neo-mercantilism); elite clubs, media, and merchandise TNCs (neo-liberalism); continental governing bodies (international governance); and NGOs and supporter groups (global civil society). As with many other issues, global civil society has relatively weaker influence than the other political–economic themes.

Global Football's Future?

As we have indicated, the 'world game' of football will experience a range of internal and external pressures in future years.[127] Many of these pressures will crystallize the increasingly prominent themes of globalization through the twenty-first century, such as the interplay of surveillance/transparency, the complex opening and closing of national societies, greater multiculturalism and polyethnicity within nations, and the creation of more diverse forms of cosmopolitanism and glocalization.

Among the game's individual spectators, we envisage that the status differentiation between 'supporters' and 'consumers' will sharpen, and underpin conflicts over resource allocations. Meanwhile, football attendance and related consumption will become increasingly important domains for the implementation of 'dataveillance' systems, whether by nation states for the purposes of monitoring citizens, or by commercial organizations to enhance marketing techniques. For some national societies – particularly those hosting mega-events like European finals – football may function to open the nation state in formal ways, for example by easing tourist entry requirements. Additionally, consumer 'piracy' may become more prominent and difficult to police at the transnational level, for example as individual viewers evade national pay-TV networks by freely accessing live matches through foreign internet platforms.

Everyday cosmopolitanism within football clubs and national societies will intensify as the transnational circulation of players will increase further, well into the 2010s. Endeavours by FIFA to restrict the participation of 'non-national' players in fixtures, even if implemented, would still be jeopardized by the reassertion of European labour laws, and might boomerang as nations respond through the 'naturalization' of many more foreign stars.

Issues of Asianization and Americanization will acquire greater magnitude, for example as struggles intensify to host the World Cup finals from 2018 onwards. Longer-term influences may be evidenced, however, if India and China join the United States and Japan in developing elite league systems that are more able to attract leading players and to challenge established tournaments in Europe and South America. Elsewhere, particularly if the credit crunch has long-term global impacts, accumulated wealth in the Gulf states and Russia may be a fresh source of financial support for the global game, notably in elite club ownership, sponsorships, and the hosting

---

[127]We should point out that, while we have used the phrases 'global game' or 'world game' to designate football, we recognize that in the USA, such terms have long been connected to indigenous sports and to associated events (witness, for example, claims to 'world' championships for the final games of the American football or baseball seasons).

of mega-events. Meanwhile, the struggles between different sporting leagues and federations, including football, will become more intense, either as they encroach into each other's apparent territory, or pursue expansion into rich new markets, especially in Asia.

We envisage greater pressure being exerted on governing bodies and major sponsors to substantiate their grandiloquent universalistic statements on football, such as through more extensive funding of development and humanitarian programmes. One possible focus might be on whether football's governing bodies can be pressed into standardizing the sole usage and endorsement of 'fair trade' products, particularly equipment and kits, during showpiece tournaments.

More broadly, football will increasingly become a public domain in which the parameters of cosmopolitanism are explored. Individuals and social groups will pursue, and be expected to establish, different mixtures of intensive particularity (such as partisan fan identification with clubs or nations), instrumental interests in transnational processes (such as appreciating only foreigners at specific clubs) and deeper, thicker variants of cosmopolitanism. At the same time, football will continue to offer the full gamut of particularities in terms of identity: to supporters who claim territorial meanings for their clubs that are either archaic, residual, or dominant in historical terms; to those who, through a blend of migration and mediatization, have rather more deterritorialized and imagined ties to their sides; and to others who, in creating or entering new towns and cities, seek to reterritorialize themselves socially by founding representative teams.

To these points, we would add that there are three realms which deserve closer inspection in regard to the nexus of globalization processes and football in the twenty-first century. First, the role of gender in shaping the 'global game' will become more significant. In this book, we have highlighted in particular women's endeavours to gain full participatory roles inside football, both in historical terms and as part of the making of global civil society. While these struggles continue, more attention may be turned towards women's growing and diverse influences upon the game in economic, political, and cultural terms. In this regard, sociological analyses of the globalization of football would need to extend beyond more general sociologies of global processes, since the latter have tended hitherto to pay relatively little attention to gender issues.

Second, the sociological fields of race, ethnicity, post-colonialism, and post-imperialism will acquire greater salience in the globalization of football. Here, we have emphasized the relevance of these fields. We envisage that this broad realm may be extended in manifold ways by analysts of football, such as through detailed ethnographies from the 'Global South', studies of Asian and African diasporas in the Global North, or the theoretical elaboration of 'subaltern studies' in relation to the global game (cf. Chaturvedi 2000).

Third, the interface between sociological studies of the body and of globalization offers some intriguing opportunities for analysts of football. We have indicated already how cross-cultural tensions and balances – in terms of convergence and divergence, or the 'duality of glocality' – are revealed by the way in which different societies come to nurture particular technical skills and to develop specific corporeal interpretations of the game. Future research may yield further findings on how the medicalization of football is manifested transnationally, such as in regard to techniques of treatment or discourses of risk surrounding player injuries. Moreover, we need also to address the possible impacts and influences of prosthetics and the 'post-human' condition within football, and to set these emergent analyses within the context of transnational processes (cf. Haraway 1991; Shilling 2008; Turner 2008).

Finally, we may reflect on how social scientists might approach the study of these and other processes within global fields such as football. What research techniques and analytical strategies are most appropriate for investigating these complex transnational phenomena?

To answer this methodological question, we return to explore the possibilities of our keyword, glocalization. Here, we seek to echo and to extend Holton's (2005: 191, 2008: 199–200) argument that sociologists should employ 'methodological glocalism' when conducting contemporary social research. In our view, methodological glocalism contains two components that underpin the research process. First, glocalization features the 'duality of glocality', and thus requires sociologists to recognize and to explore in methodological and ontological terms the possibilities of transnational convergence and divergence among social groups and societies. Second, the multi-scalar aspect of glocalization processes must also be acknowledged within the research process; in other words, researchers need to recognize the interrelations between, as well as the making and remaking of, the local, regional, national, international, and transnational realms.

Methodological glocalism stands in some contrast to 'methodological cosmopolitanism' (Beck and Sznaider 2006; Beck 2007). The latter is explicitly constructed in opposition to what Martins (1974) had long ago termed the principle of 'methodological nationalism', to the extent that Beck and his colleagues dismiss the national as a sociological 'zombie category'. Conversely, methodological glocalism requires us to adopt an open stance towards the possibilities of the national and the nation state, as one of many scalar categories that are consciously constructed and transformed by social actors.

But ultimately, we insist that what requires full recognition, whether in method or in theory, is the central transnational and sociological status of football itself. If our fellow social scientists are serious about understanding globalization in the twenty-first century, then all of us need to look far more closely at *the* global cultural form that transfixes and fascinates so many diverse societies and so many millions of the world's citizens.

References

Alabarces, P. and M.G. Rodríguez (2000) 'Football and Fatherland: The Crisis of National Representation in Argentinian Soccer', in G.P.T. Finn and R. Giulianotti (eds) *Football Culture: Local Contests, Global Visions*, London: Frank Cass.

Alabarces, P., R. Coelho, and J. Sanguinetti (2001) 'Treacheries and Traditions in Argentinian Football Styles: The Story of Estudiantes de La Plata', in G. Armstrong and R. Giulianotti (eds) *Fear and Loathing in World Football*, Oxford: Berg.

Alegi, P. (2004) *Laduma! Soccer, Politics, and Society in South Africa*, Scottsville: University of KwaZulu-Natal Press.

Alexander, J. (2006a) *The Civil Sphere*, Oxford: Oxford University Press.

Alexander, J. (2006b) 'Global Civil Society', *Theory, Culture & Society*, 23: 521–4.

Amable, B. (2004) *The Diversity of Modern Capitalism*, Oxford: Oxford University Press.

Amara, M. and I. Henry (2004) 'Between Globalization and Local "Modernity": The Diffusion and Modernization of Football in Algeria', *Soccer & Society*, 5(1): 1–26.

Amoore, L. and P. Langley (2004) 'Ambiguities of Global Civil Society', *Review of International Studies*, 30: 89–110.

Anderson, B. (1983) *Imagined Communities*, London: Verso.

Andreff, W. (2004) 'The Taxation of Player Moves from Developing Countries', in R. Fort and J. Fizel (eds) *International Sports Economics Comparisons*, Westport: Praeger.

Andreff, W. and P. Staudohar (2000) 'The Evolving European Model of Sport Professional Finance', *Journal of Sports Economics*, 1(3): 257–76.

Andreff W. and P. Staudohar (2002) 'European and US Sports Business Models', in C. Barros, M. Ibrahimo and S. Szymanski (ed.) *Transatlantic Sport: The Comparative Economics of North American and European Sports*, Cheltenham: Edward Elgar.

Andrews, D.L. (2001) *Michael Jordan, Inc.*, Albany, NY: SUNY Press.

Andrews, D.L. and S.J. Jackson (eds) (2001) *Sport Stars: The Cultural Politics of Sporting Celebrity*, London: Routledge.

Anheier, H.K., M. Kaldor and M. Glasius (eds) (2004) *Global Civil Society 2004/5*, London: Sage.

Appadurai, A. (1995) 'Playing with Modernity: The Decolonization of Indian Cricket', in C.A. Breckenridge (ed.) *Consuming Modernity*, Minneapolis, MN: University of Minnesota Press.

Appadurai, A. (1998) *Modernity at Large*, Minneapolis, MN: University of Minnesota Press.

Appiah, K.A. (1997) 'Cosmopolitan Patriots', *Critical Inquiry*, 23: 617–39.

Arbena, J. (2000) 'Meaning and Joy in Latin American Sports', *International Review for the Sociology of Sport*, 35: 83–91.

Archetti, E. (1996) 'In Search of National Identity: Argentinian Football and Europe', in J.A. Mangan (ed.) *Tribal Identities: Nationalism, Europe, Sport*, London: Frank Cass.

Archetti, E. (1998a) *Masculinities*, Oxford: Berg.

Archetti, E. (1998b) 'The *Potrero* and the *Pibe*: Territory and Belonging in the Mythical Account of Argentinian Football', in N. Lovell (ed.) *Locality and Belonging*, London: Routledge.

Archetti, E. and A. Romero (1994) 'Death and Violence in Argentinian Football', in R. Giulianotti, N. Bonney and M. Hepworth (eds) *Football, Violence and Social Identity*, London: Routledge.

Archibugi, D. (2000) 'Cosmopolitical Democracy', *New Left Review*, 4: 137–50.

Archibugi, D. (2004) 'Cosmopolitan Democracy and its Critics: A Review', *European Journal of International Relations*, 10(3): 437–73.

Archibugi, D. and D. Held (eds) (1995) *Cosmopolitan Democracy: An Agenda for a New World Order*, Cambridge: Polity.

Archibugi, D., D. Held and M. Köhler (eds) (1998) *Re-imagining Political Community: Studies in Cosmopolitan Democracy*, Stanford, CA: Stanford University Press.

Armstrong, G. (2004) 'The Lords of Misrule: Football and the Rights of the Child in Liberia, West Africa', *Sport in Society*, 7(3): 473–502.

Armstrong, G. (2007) 'The Global Footballer and the Local War-Zone: George Weah and Transnational Networks in Liberia, West Africa', *Global Networks*, 7(2): 230–47.

Armstrong, G. and R. Giulianotti (eds) (1997) *Entering the Field: New Perspectives on World Football*, Oxford: Berg.

Armstrong, G. and R. Giulianotti (eds) (1998a) *Football, Cultures, Identities*, Basingstoke: Macmillan.

Armstrong, G. and R. Giulianotti (1998b) 'From Another Angle: Surveillance and Football Hooligans', in C. Norris, G. Armstrong and J. Moran (eds) *Surveillance, CCTV and Social Control*, Aldershot: Avebury/Gower.

Armstrong, G. and R. Giulianotti (eds) (2001) *Fear and Loathing in World Football*, Oxford: Berg.

Armstrong, G. and R. Giulianotti (eds) (2004) *Football in Africa*, Basingstoke: Palgrave.

Arnason, J. (1991) 'Modernity as a Project and as a Field of Tension,' in A. Honneth and H. Joas (eds) *Communicative Action*, Cambridge: Polity.

Arnason, J.P. (2001) 'The Multiplication of Modernity', in E. Ben Rafael and Y. Sternberg (eds) *Identity, Culture and Globalization*, Leiden: Brill.

Ascari, G. and P. Gagnepain (2006) 'Spanish Football', *Journal of Sports Economics*, 7: 76–89.

Ascherson, N. (2002) *Stone Voices: The Search for Scotland*, London: Granta.

Axford, B. (1995) *The Global System: Economics, Politics and Culture*, Oxford: Polity.

Back, L., J. Solomos and T. Crabbe (2001) *The Changing Face of Football: Racism, Identity and Multiculture in the English Game*, Oxford: Berg.

Baker, G. and D. Chandler (eds) (2004) *Global Civil Society: Contested Futures*, London: Routledge.

Baldacchino, G. (2002) 'A Nationless State? Malta, National Identity and the EU', *West European Politics*, 25(4): 191–206.

Bale, J. and J. Sang (1996) *Kenyan Running*, London: Frank Cass.

Ball, P. (2003) *Morbo: The Story of Spanish Football*, London: WSC Books.

Banks, S. (2002) *Going Down: Football in Crisis*, Edinburgh: Mainstream.

Barber, B. (1992) 'Jihad versus McWorld', *Atlantic Monthly*, March.

Barber, B. (1996) *Jihad vs McWorld*, New York: Ballantine.

Baroncelli, A. and U. Lago (2006) 'Italian Football', *Journal of Sports Economics*, 7: 13–28.

Barros, C.P. (2006) 'Portuguese Football', *Journal of Sports Economics*, 7: 96–104.

Bartlett, C.A. and S. Ghoshal (1989) *Managing Across Borders: The Transnational Solution*, Cambridge, MA: Harvard Business School Press.

Beck, P.J. (1999) *Scoring for Britain: International Football and International Politics, 1900–39*, London: Frank Cass.

Beck, P.J. (2003) 'The Relevance of the "Irrelevant": Football as a Missing Dimension in the Study of British Relations with Germany', *International Affairs*, 79(2): 387–411.

Beck, U. (1999) *World Risk Society*, Cambridge: Polity.

Beck, U. (2000) *What is Globalization?*, Cambridge: Polity.

Beck, U. (2004) 'Rooted Cosmopolitanism: Emerging from a Rivalry of Distinctions', in U. Beck, N. Sznaider and R. Winter (eds) *Global America? The Cultural Consequences of Globalization?* Liverpool: Liverpool University Press.

Beck, U. (2006) *Cosmopolitan Vision*, Cambridge: Polity.

Beck, U. (2007) 'The Cosmopolitan Condition', *Theory, Culture & Society*, 24(7–8): 286–90.

Beck, U. and N. Sznaider (2006) 'Unpacking Cosmopolitanism for the Social Sciences: A Research Agenda', *British Journal of Sociology*, 57(1): 1–23.

Bellos, A. (2002) *Futebol: The Brazilian Way of Life*, London: Bloomsbury.

Ben-Porat, A. (2000) 'Overseas Sweetheart: Israeli Fans of English Football', *Journal of Sport & Social Issues*, 24(4): 344–50.

Berger, P. (1986) *The Capitalist Revolution*, New York: Basic Books.

Berger, S. and R. Dore (eds) (1999) *National Diversity and Global Capitalism*, Ithaca, NY: Cornell University Press.

Besson, R., R. Poli and L. Ravenel (2008) *Demographic Study of Footballers in Europe*, Neuchâtel: CIES.

Beyer, P. (1994) *Religion and Globalization*, London: Sage.

Beyria, F. (2005) 'France vs Algeria: Soccer Drama as an Identity Analyzer', paper to the conference *Putting Pierre Bourdieu to Work*, University of California, Berkeley, 12–13 May.

Billig, M. (1995) *Banal Nationalism*, London: Sage.

Birchall, J. (2000) *Ultra Nippon: How Japan Reinvented Football*, London: Headline.

Birley, D. (1993) *Sport and the Making of Britain*, Manchester: Manchester University Press.

Birley, D. (1995) *Playing the Game: Sport and British Society 1910-45*, Manchester: Manchester University Press.

Blatter, J. (2004) 'From Spaces of Place to Spaces of Flows?', *International Journal of Urban and Regional Research*, 28(3): 530–48.

Bobbio, N. (1996) *The Age of Rights*, Cambridge: Polity.

Bougheas, S. and P. Downward (2003) 'The Economics of Professional Sports Leagues: Some Insights on the Reform of Transfer Markets', *Journal of Sports Economics*, 4: 87–107.

Bourdieu, P. (1998) 'The Essence of Neo-liberalism', *Le Monde Diplomatique*, December.

Bourdieu, P. (1999) *Acts of Resistance: Against the Tyranny of the Market*, New York: New Press.

Bower, T. (2003) *Broken Dreams*, London: Pocket Books.

Boyle, R. and R. Haynes (2004) *Football in the New Media Age*, London: Routledge.

Brabazon, T. (1998) 'What's the Story Morning Glory? Perth Glory and the Imagining of Englishness', *Sporting Traditions* 14(2): 53–66.

Brackenridge, C. (2004) 'Women and Children First?', *Sport in Society*, 7(3): 322–37.

Breckenridge, C.A., S. Pollock, H.K. Bhabha and D. Chakrabarty (eds) (2002) *Cosmopolitanism*, Durham, NC: Duke University Press.

Brenner, N. (1998) 'Global Cities, Glocal States: Global City Formation and State Territorial Restructuring in Contemporary Europe', *Review of International Political Economy*, 5(1): 1–37.

Brenner, N. (1999) 'Globalisation as Reterritorialisation: The Re-scaling of Urban Governance in the European Union', *Urban Studies*, 36(3): 431–51.

Brenner, N. (2004) 'Urban Governance and the Production of New State Spaces in Western Europe, 1960–2000', *Review of International Political Economy*, 11(3): 447–88.

Brick, C. (2001) 'Can't Live With Them, Can't Live Without Them: Reflections on Manchester United', in G. Armstrong and R. Giulianotti (eds) *Fear and Loathing in World Football*, Oxford: Berg.

Brohm, J.-M. (1978) *Sport: A Prison of Measured Time*, London: Pluto.

Bromberger, C. (1994) 'Foreign Footballers, Cultural Dreams and Community Identity in some North-Western Mediterranean Countries', in J. Bale and J. Maguire (eds) *The Global Sports Arena*, London: Cass.

Bromberger, C. (1995) 'Football as World-View and as Ritual', *French Cultural Studies*, 6: 293–311.

Brown, A. (ed.) (1998) *Fanatics!* London: Routledge.

Brown, M. and S. Seaton (1999) *Christmas Truce*, London: Pan.

Brus, A. and E. Trangbaek (2003) 'Asserting the Right to Play: Women's Football in Denmark', *Soccer & Society*, 4(2/3): 95–111.

Buraimo, B., R. Simmons and S. Szymanski (2006) 'England', *Journal of Sports Economics*, 7(1), 29–46.

Burawoy, M. et al. (2000) *Global Ethnography: Forces, Connections and Imaginations in a Postmodern World*, Berkeley, CA: University of California Press.

Burns, J. (1999) *Barça: A People's Passion*, London: Bloomsbury.

Canclini, N.G. (1993) *Transforming Identity: Popular Culture in Mexico*, Austin, TX: University of Texas Press.

Canclini, N.G. (1995) *Hybrid Cultures*, Minneapolis, MN: Minnesota University Press.

Carrington, B. (1998) 'Football's Coming Home, But Whose Home and Do We Want It? Nation, Football and the Politics of Exclusion', in A. Brown (ed.) *Fanatics!* London: Routledge.

Carvalho, J.D., S. Stein, and S.C. Stokes (1984) 'Soccer and Social Change in Early Twentieth Century Peru', *Studies in Latin American Popular Culture*, 3: 17–27.

Cashmore, E. and A. Parker (2003) 'One David Beckham?', *Sociology of Sport Journal*, 20(3): 214–31.

Castells, M. (1997) *The Power of Identity*, Oxford: Blackwell.

Chang, H.-J. (1998) 'Transnational Corporations and Strategic Industrial Policy', in R. Kozul–Wright and R. Rowthorn (eds) *Transnational Corporations and the Global Economy*, Basingstoke: Palgrave.

Chang, K.J. (2002) *Kicking Away the Ladder*, London: Anthem.

Chaturvedi, V. (ed.) (2000) *Mapping Subaltern Studies and the Postcolonial*, London: Verso.

Chiba, N., O. Ebihara and S. Morino (2001) 'Globalization, Naturalization and Identity: The Case of Borderless Elite Athletes in Japan', *International Review for the Sociology of Sport*, 36(2): 203–21.

Clifford, J. (1997) *Routes: Travel and Translation in the Late Twentieth Century*, Cambridge: Harvard University Press.

Cohen, R. and P. Kennedy (2000) *Global Sociology*, Basingstoke: Palgrave.

Conn, D. (1997) *The Football Business*, Edinburgh: Mainstream.

Conn, D. (2005) *The Beautiful Game? Searching for the Soul of Football*, London: Yellow Jersey.

Connell, R.W. (2005) 'Globalization, Imperialism, and Masculinities', in M.S. Kimmel, J. Hearn and R.W. Connell (eds) *Handbook of Studies on Men and Masculinities*, Thousand Oaks, CA: Sage.

Connell, R.W. (2007) 'The Northern Theory of Globalization', *Sociological Theory*, 25(4): 368–85.

Cowen, T. (2002) *Creative Destruction*, Princeton, NJ: Princeton University Press.

Crolley, L. and V. Duke (2007) 'La Crisis y el fútbol: economic change and political continuity in Argentine football', in R. Miller and L. Crolley (eds) *Football in the Americas: fútbol fútebol, soccer*, London: Institute for the Study of the Americas.

Crothers, L. (2007) *Globalization and American Popular Culture*, Lanham, MD: Rowman & Littlefield.

Cvetkovich, A. and D. Kellner (1997) *Articulating the Global and the Local: Globalization and Cultural Studies*, Boulder, CO: Westview.

Dallmayr, F. (1998) *Alternative Visions: Paths in the Global Village*, Lanham, MD: Rowman & Littlefield.

DaMatta, R. (1991) *Carnivals, Rogues and Heroes: An Interpretation of the Brazilian Dilemma*, Notre Dame: Notre Dame University Press.

Danforth, L. (2001) 'Is the "World Game" an "Ethnic Game" or an Aussie Game? Narrating the Nation in Australian Soccer', *American Ethnologist*, 28(2): 363–87.

Darnell, S. (2008) *Changing the World Through Sport and Play: A Post-Colonial Analysis of Canadian Volunteers within the 'Sport for Development and Peace' Movement*, unpublished PhD thesis, Graduate Department of Exercise Sciences, University of Toronto.

David, P. (2004) *Human Rights in Youth Sport*, London: Routledge.

De Biasi, R. and P. Lanfranchi (1997) 'The Importance of Difference: Football Identities in Italy', in G. Armstrong and R. Giulianotti (eds) *Entering the Field: New Perspectives on World Football*, Oxford: Berg.

De Melo, L.M. (2007) 'Brazilian Football: Technical Success and Economic Failure', in R. Miller and L. Crolley (eds) *Football in the Americas: Fútbol, Futebol, Soccer*, London: Institute for the Study of the Americas.

Dejonghe, T. and H. Vandeweghe (2006) 'Belgian Football', *Journal of Sports Economics*, 7(1): 105–13.

Delanty, G. (2006) 'The Cosmopolitan Imagination: Critical Cosmopolitanism and Social Theory', *British Journal of Sociology*, 57(1): 25–47.

Del Burgo, M. (1995) 'Don't Stop the Carnival: Football in the Societies of Latin America', in S. Wagg (ed.) *Giving the Game Away: Football, Politics and Culture on Five Continents*, London: Leicester University Press.

Delgado, F. (1999) 'Sport and Politics: Major League Soccer, Constitution and (The) Latino Audience(s)', *International Review for the Sociology of Sport*, 23(1): 41–54.

Deloitte (2004a) *Annual Review of Football*, London: Deloitte.

Deloitte (2004b) *Football Money League 2003/2004*, London: Deloitte.

Deloitte (2007a) *Annual Review of Football Finance*, London: Deloitte.

Deloitte (2007b) *Football Money League*, London: Deloitte.

Deloitte (2008) *Annual Review of Football Finance*, London: Deloitte.

Dicken, P. and Y. Miyamachi (1998) '"From Noodles to Satellites": The Changing Geography of the Japanese Sogo Shosha', *Transactions of the Institute of British Geographers*, 23(1): 55–78.

Dine, P. (2002) 'France, Algeria and Sport: From Colonisation to Globalisation', *Modern and Contemporary France*, 10(4): 495–506.

Dobson, S. and J. Goddard (2001) *The Economics of Football*, Cambridge: Cambridge University Press.

Donnelly, P. and L. Petherick (2004) 'Worker's Playtime? Child Labour at the Extremes of the Sporting Spectrum', *Sport in Society*, 7(3): 301–21.

Dore, R. (2000) 'Will Global Capitalism be Anglo-Saxon Capitalism?', *New Left Review*, 6, November–December: 101–19.

Dore, R., W. Lazonick and M. O'Sullivan (1999) 'Varieties of Capitalism in the Twentieth Century', *Oxford Review of Economic Policy*, 15(4): 102–20.

Doremus, P., W.W. Keller, L.W. Pauly and S. Reich (1999) *The Myth of the Global Corporation*, Princeton: Princeton University Press.

Downing, D. (1999) *Passovotchka: Moscow Dynamo in Britain 1945*, London: Bloomsbury.

Duke, V. and L. Crolley (1996) 'Football Spectator Behaviour in Argentina: A Case of Separate Evolution', *Sociological Review*, 44: 272–93.

Duncan, H.D. (1959) 'Simmel's Image of Society', in K.H. Wolff (ed.) *Essays on Sociology, Philosophy and Aesthetics by Georg Simmel et al.*, Ohio: Ohio State University Press.

Eagleton, T. (2006) 'Homo Loquax: Talking Bodies', *Globalizations*, 3(1): 1–4.

Edelman, R. (1993) *Serious Fun: A History of Spectator Sports in the USSR*, New York: Oxford University Press.

Edelman, R. and J. Riordan (1994) 'USSR/Russia and the World Cup: Come On You Reds!', in J. Sugden and A. Tomlinson (eds) *Hosts and Champions*, Aldershot: Arena.

Edwards, M. (2004) *Civil Society*, Cambridge: Polity.

Eichberg, H. (1992) 'Crisis and Grace: Soccer in Denmark', *Scandinavian Journal of Medicine and Science in Sport*, 2(3): 119–28.

Eick, V. and E. Töpfer (2008) 'The Human- and Hard-ware of Policing Neoliberal Sport Events', paper to the conference *Security and Surveillance at Mega Sport Events*, Durham University, 25 April.

Eisenberg, C. (1991) 'Football in Germany. Beginnings, 1890–1914', *International Journal of the History of Sport*, 8(2): 205–20.

Eisenstadt, S.N. (2003) *Comparative Civilizations and Multiple Modernities*, Leiden: Brill.

Elias, N. and E. Dunning (1986) *Quest for Excitement*, Oxford: Blackwell.

Escobar, G. (1969) 'The Role of Sports in the Penetration of Urban Culture to the Rural Areas of Peru', *Kroeber Anthropological Society Papers*, 40: 72–81.

Euchner, C.C. (1993) *Playing the Field: Why Sports Teams Move and Cities Fight to Keep Them*, Baltimore, MD: John Hopkins University Press.

Falk, R. (2005) 'Reimagining the Governance of Globalization', in R.P. Appelbaum and W.I. Robinson (eds) *Critical Globalization Studies*, London: Routledge.

Farred, G. (2002) 'Long Distance Love: Growing Up a Liverpool Football Club Fan', *Journal of Sport & Social Issues*, 26(4): 6–24.

Fasting, K. (2003) 'Small Country – Big Results: Women's Football in Norway', *Soccer and Society*, 4(2/3): 149–61.

Ferguson, J. (1999) *Expectations of Modernity: Myths and Meanings of Urban Life on the Zambian Copperbelt*, Berkeley, CA: University of California Press.

Ferguson, J. (2006) *Global Shadows: Africa in the Neoliberal World Order*, Durham, NC: Duke University Press.

FIFA (2004) *World Report on Football Development*, Zurich: FIFA.

FIFA (2006) *FIFA Activity Report 2006*, Zurich: FIFA.

Fine, R. (2007) *Cosmopolitanism*, London: Routledge.

Finn, G.P.T. and P. Dimeo (1998) 'Scottish Racism, Scottish Identities: The Case of Partick Thistle', in A. Brown (ed.) *Fanatics!* London: Routledge.

Fisher, M. and T. Ponniah (eds) (2003) *Another World is Possible*, London: Zed Books.

Fisher, W.F. (1997) 'Doing Good? The Politics and Antipolitics of NGO Practices', *Annual Review of Anthropology*, 26: 439–64.

Foer, F. (2004) *How Soccer Explains the World*, New York: Harper Collins.

Frank, A.G. (1967) *Capitalism and Underdevelopment in Latin America*, New York: Monthly Review.

Freeman, L.C. (2004) *The Development of Social Network Analysis: A Study in the Sociology of Science*, Vancouver: Empirical Press.

Freire, P. (1970) *Pedagogy of the Oppressed*, New York: Continuum.

Freyre, G. (1963) *The Mansions and the Shanties*, London: Weidenfield & Nicolson.

Frick, B. and J. Prinz (2006) 'Crisis? What Crisis? Football in Germany', *Journal of Sports Economics*, 7: 60–75.

Friedman, J. (1999) 'Indigenous Struggles and the Discreet Charm of the Bourgeoisie', *Journal of World-Systems Research*, 5(2): 391–411.

Friedman, J. (2003) *Cultural Identity and Global Process*, London: Sage.

Frykholm, P. (1997) 'Soccer and Social Identity in Pre-Revolutionary Moscow', *Journal of Sport History*, 24(2): 143–54.

Gasser, P.K. and A. Levinsen (2004) 'Breaking Post-War Ice: Open Fun Football Schools in Bosnia and Herzegovina', *Sport in Society*, 7(3): 457–72.

Gay, J. (1974) *Poetry and Prose, Vol. I* (ed. V.A. Dearing), Oxford: Clarendon.

Gay, P. (2007) *Modernism: The Lure of Heresay – From Baudelaire to Beckett and Beyond*, London: Heinemann.

Gellner, E. (1983) *Nations and Nationalism*, Ithaca, NY: Cornell University Press.

Gellner, E. (1994) *Conditions of Liberty: Civil Society and Its Rivals*, London: Allen Lane.

Gertler, M. (1992) 'Flexibility Revisited: Districts, Nation-states and the Forces of Production', *Transactions of the Institute of British Geographers*, 17: 259–78.

Gibney, M. (2003) 'Introduction', in M. Gibney (ed.) *Globalizing Rights*, Oxford: Oxford University Press.

Giddens, A. (1990) *The Consequences of Modernity*, Cambridge: Polity.

Gil, G.J. (1998) *Fútbol e Identidades Locales*, Madrid: Mino y Dávila.

Gil, G.J. (2002) 'Soccer and Kinship in Argentina: The Mother's Brother and the Heritage of Identity', *Soccer and Society*, 3(3): 11–25.

Gilbert, A. (2007) 'From Dreams to Reality: The Economics and Geography of Football Success', in R. Miller and L. Crolley (eds) *Football in the Americas: Fútbol, Futebol, Soccer*, London: Institute for the Study of the Americas.

Gilpin, R. (2001) *Global Political Economy*, Princeton: Princeton University Press.

Giulianotti, R. (1991) 'Scotland's Tartan Army in Italy: The Case for the Carnivalesque', *Sociological Review*, 39(3): 503–30.

Giulianotti, R. (1994) 'Social Identity and Public Order: Political and Academic Discourses on Football Violence', in R. Giulianotti, N. Bonney and M. Hepworth (eds) *Football, Violence and Social Identity*, London: Routledge.

Giulianotti, R. (1995) 'Football and the Politics of Carnival: An Ethnographic Study of Scottish Fans in Sweden', *International Review for the Sociology of Sport*, 30(2): 191–224.

Giulianotti, R. (1996) 'Back to the Future: An Ethnography of Ireland's Football Fans at the 1994 World Cup Finals in the USA', *International Review for the Sociology of Sport*, 31(3): 323–48.

Giulianotti, R. (1999a) *Football: A Sociology of the Global Game*, Cambridge: Polity.

Giulianotti, R. (1999b) 'Built by the Two Valeras: Football Culture and National Identity in Uruguay', *Culture, Sport, Society*, 2(3): 134–154.

Giulianotti, R. (2002) 'Supporters, Followers, Fans and *Flaneurs*: A Taxonomy of Spectator Identities in World Football', *Journal of Sport and Social Issues*, 26(1): 25–46.

Giulianotti, R. (2003) 'Celtic, the UEFA Cup Final and the Condition of Scottish Club Football: Notes and Recommendations from Seville', *Journal of Sport and Social Issues*, 27(3): 207–14.

Giulianotti, R. (2004a) 'Football in Zimbabwe: Between Colonialism, Independence and Globalization', in G. Armstrong and R. Giulianotti (eds) *Football in Africa*, Basingstoke: Macmillan.

Giulianotti, R. (2004b) 'Human Rights, Globalization and Sentimental Education: The Case of Sport', *Sport in Society*, 7(3): 355–69.

Giulianotti, R. (2005a) 'Towards a Critical Anthropology of Voice: The Politics and Poets of Popular Culture, Scotland and Football', *Critique of Anthropology*, 25(4): 339–60.

Giulianotti, R. (2005b) 'Sports Spectators and the Social Consequences of Commodification: Critical Perspectives from Scottish Football', *Journal of Sport and Social Issues*, 29(4): 386–410.

Giulianotti, R. (2005c) 'The Sociability of Sport: Scotland Football Supporters as Interpreted through the Sociology of Georg Simmel', *International Review for the Sociology of Sport*, 40(3): 289–306.

Giulianotti, R. (2007) 'Das Britische Fussball-Labor: Überwachung, Gouvernementalität und Neomerkantilismus', in V. Eick, J. Sambale and E. Töpfer (eds) *Kontrollierte Urbanität*, Berlin: Transcript Verlag.

Giulianotti, R. and G. Armstrong (2004) 'Drama, Fields and Metaphors: An Introduction to Football in Africa', in G. Armstrong and R. Giulianotti (eds) *Football in Africa*, Palgrave: Macmillan.

Giulianotti, R. and D. McArdle (eds) (2006) *Sport, Civil Liberties and Human Rights*, London: Routledge.

Giulianotti, R. and R. Robertson (2005) 'Glocalization, Globalization and Migration: The Case of Scottish Football Supporters in North America', *International Sociology*, 21(2): 171–98.

Giulianotti, R. and R. Robertson (2007a) 'Forms of Glocalization: Globalization and the Migration Strategies of Scottish Football Fans in North America', *Sociology*, 41(1): 133–52.

Giulianotti, R. and R. Robertson (2007b) 'Recovering the Social: Globalization, Football and Transnationalism', *Global Networks*, 7(2): 144–86.

Giulianotti, R. and J. Williams (eds) (1994) *Game without Frontiers: Football, Identity and Modernity*, Aldershot: Arena.

Goldblatt, D. (2004) *Football Yearbook 2004–5: The Complete Guide to the World Game*, London: DK.

Goldblatt, D. (2006) *The Ball is Round: A Global History of Football*, London: Viking.

Gorn, E.J. and W. Goldstein (1993) *A Brief History of American Sports*, New York: Hill and Wang.

Gouguet, J.J. and D. Primault (2006) 'The French Exception', *Journal of Sport Economics*, 7(1): 47–59.

Goulstone, J. (1974) *Modern Sport*, Bexleyheath.

Goulstone, J. (2000) 'The Working-Class Origins of Modern Football', *International Journal of the History of Sport*, 17: 135–43.

Grow, R. (1998) 'From Gum Trees to Goalposts, 1858–1876', in R. Hess and B. Stewart (eds) *More Than A Game: An Unauthorised History of Australian Rules Football*, Melbourne: Melbourne University Press.

Guttmann, A. (1994) *Games and Empires: Modern Sports and Cultural Imperialism*, New York: Columbia University Press.

Guttmann, A. and L. Thompson (2001) *Japanese Sports: A History*, Honolulu: Hawaii University Press.

Habermas, J. (2001a) 'Why Europe Needs a Constitution', *New Left Review*, September–October, 11: 5–26.

Habermas, J. (2001b) *The Postnational Constellation*, Cambridge: Polity.

Hafez, K. (2007) *The Myth of Media Globalization*, Cambridge: Polity.

Hagemann, A. (2008) 'From Stadium to Fanzone: The Architecture of Control', paper to the conference *Security and Surveillance at Mega Sport Events*, Durham University, 25 April.

Hamelink, C.J. (1983) *Cultural Autonomy in Global Communication*, London: Longman.

Hamelink, C.J. (1994) *The Politics of World Communication: A Human Rights Perspective*, London: Sage.

Hamelink, C.J. (1995) *World Communication: Disempowerment and Self-Empowerment*, London: Zed Books.

Hannerz, U. (1990) 'Cosmopolitans and Locals in World Culture', in M. Featherstone (ed.) *Global Culture*, London: Sage.

Hannerz, U. (1992) *Cultural Complexity: Studies in the Social Organization of Meaning*, New York: Columbia University Press.

179

Hannerz, U. (1996) *Transnational Connections*, London: Routledge.

Hannerz, U. (2002) 'Among the Foreign Correspondents: Reflections on Anthropological Styles and Audiences', *Ethnos* 67: 57–74.

Hannerz, U. (2004) *Foreign News: Exploring the World of Foreign Correspondents*, Chicago: University of Chicago Press.

Hanzan, B.A. (1987) 'Sport as an Instrument of Political Expansion: The Soviet Union in Africa', in W.J. Baker and J.A. Mangan (eds) *Sport in Africa*, New York: Holmes and Meier.

Haraway, D. (1991) *Simians, Cyborgs and Women: The Reinvention of Nature*, London: Routledge.

Hare, G. (2003). *Football in France: A Cultural History*, Oxford: Berg.

Hargreaves, J. (1986) *Sport, Power and Culture*, Cambridge: Polity.

Harmes, A. (2001) 'Mass Investment Culture', *NLR* 9, May–June: 103–24.

Hart, S. (1998) 'The Future for Brands', in S. Hart and J. Murphy (eds) *Brands: The New Wealth Creators*, Harmondsworth: Macmillan.

Haruna, M. and S.A. Abdullahi (1991) 'The "Soccer Craze" and Club Formation among Hausa Youth in Kano, Nigeria', *Kano Studies* (special issue on football).

Harvey, A. (2001) '"An Epoch in the Annals of National Sport": Football in Sheffield and the Creation of Modern Soccer and Rugby', *International Journal of the History of Sport*, 18(4): 53–87.

Harvey, A. (2005) *Football: The First Hundred Years – The Untold Story*, London: Routledge.

Harvey, D. (1989) *The Condition of Postmodernity*, Oxford: Blackwell.

Harvey, D. (2005) *A Brief History of Neo-liberalism*, Oxford: Oxford University Press.

Hay, R. (2001) '"Those Bloody Croatians": Croatian Soccer Teams, Ethnicity and Violence in Australia, 1950–99', in G. Armstrong and R. Giulianotti (eds) *Fear and Loathing in World Football*, Oxford: Berg.

Haynes, R. (1995) *The Football Imagination*, Aldershot: Arena.

Heinonen, H. (2005) *Jalkapallon Lumo*, Jyvaskyla: Atena.

Helal, R.G. (1994) *The Brazilian Soccer Crisis as a Sociological Problem*, unpublished PhD thesis, Department of Sociology, New York University.

Held, D. (1995) *Democracy and the Global Order*, Cambridge: Polity.

Held, D. (1997) 'Globalization and Cosmopolitan Democracy', *Peace Review*, 9(3): 309–17.

Held, D. (2004) *Global Covenant: The Social Democratic Alternative to the Washington Consensus*, Cambridge: Polity.

Henderson, R.W. (2001) *Ball, Bat and Bishop: The Origin of Ball Games*, Champaign, IL: University of Illinois Press.

Heron, B. (2007) *Desire for Development: Whiteness, Gender, and the Helping Imperative*, Waterloo, ONT: Wilfrid Laurier University Press.

Hesse-Lichtenberger, U. (2002) *Tor! The Story of German Football*, London: WSC Books.

Hesselmann, M. and R. Ide (2006) 'A Tale of Two Germanys: Football Culture and National Identity in the GDR', in A. Tomlinson and C. Young (eds) *German Football: History, Culture, Society and the World Cup 2006*, London: Routledge.

Hettne, B. (2005) 'Beyond the New Regionalism', *New Political Economy*, 10(4): 543–71.

Hill, D. (1989) *Out of His Skin: The John Barnes Phenomenon*, London: Faber.

Hirst, P. and G. Thompson (1999) *Globalization in Question*, 2nd edition, Cambridge: Polity.

Hjelm, J. and E. Olofsson (2003) 'A Breakthrough: Women's Football in Sweden', *Soccer and Society*, 4(2/3): 182–204.

Hobsbawm, E. (1983) 'Mass-Producing Traditions: Europe 1870–1914', in E. Hobsbawm and T. Ranger (eds) (1983) *The Invention of Traditions*, Cambridge: Cambridge University Press.

Hobsbawm, E. (1990) *Nations and Nationalism since 1780*, Cambridge: Cambridge University Press.

Hognestad, H. (2006) 'Transnational Passions: A Statistical Study of Norwegian Football Supporters', *Soccer & Society*, 7(4): 439–62.

Hognestad, H. and A. Tollisen (2004) 'Playing Against Deprivation: Football and Development in Kenya', in G. Armstrong and R. Giulianotti (eds) *Football in Africa*, Basingstoke: Palgrave.

Holmes, M. (1994) 'Symbols of National Identity and Sport: The Case of the Irish Football Team', *Irish Political Studies*, 9: 81–98.

Holt, R. (1989) *Sport and the British: A Modern History*, Oxford: Oxford University Press.

Holton, R.J. (1998) *Globalization and the Nation-State*, Basingstoke: Macmillan.

Holton, R.J. (2005) *Making Globalization*, Basingstoke: Palgrave.

Holton, R.J. (2008) *Global Networks*, Basingstoke: Palgrave.

Hong, F. and J.A. Mangan (2003) 'Will the "Iron Roses" Bloom Forever? Women's Football in China: Changes and Challenges', *Soccer and Society*, 4(2/3): 47–66.

Honig, B. (2001) *Democracy and the Foreigner*, Princeton: Princeton University Press.

Hopkins, A.G. (ed.) (2002) *Globalization in World History*, London: Pimlico.

Horak, R. and W. Maderthaner (1996) 'A Culture of Urban Cosmopolitanism: Uridil and Sindelar as Viennese Coffee-house Heroes', *International Journal of the History of Sport*, 13(1): 139–55.

Horton, E. (1997) *Moving the Goalposts*, Edinburgh: Mainstream.

Houlihan, B. (2004) 'Civil Rights, Doping Control and the World Anti-Doping Code', *Sport in Society*, 7(3): 420–37.

Huntington, S.P. (1993) 'The Clash of Civilizations?', *Foreign Affairs*, 72(3): 44–57.

Igbinovia, P. (1985) 'Soccer Hooliganism in Black Africa', *International Journal of Offender Therapy and Comparative Criminology*, 29: 135–46.

Ikeda, S. (1996) 'World Production', in T.K. Hopkins, I. Wallerstein et al., *The Age of Transition: Trajectory of the World-System 1945–2025*, London: Zed Books.

Imlach, G. (2005) *My Father and Other Working-Class Football Heroes*, London: Yellow Jersey Press.

Inglis, S. (1990) *The Football Grounds of Europe*, London: HarperCollinsWillow.

Jennings, A. (2007) *Foul! The Secret World of FIFA*, London: CollinsWillow.

Jessop, B. and N.L. Sum (2000) 'An Entrepreneurial City in Action: Hong Kong's Emerging Strategies in and for (Inter)Urban Competition', *Urban Studies*, 37: 2287–313.

Jewell, R.T. and D.J. Molina (2005) 'An Evaluation of the Relationship between Hispanics and Major League Soccer', *Journal of Sports Economics*, 6(2): 160–77.

Johnson, C. (2004) *The Sorrows of Empire: Militarism, Secrecy, and the End of the Republic*, New York: Metropolitan Books.

Jones, K. (2007) 'Building the Women's United Soccer Association: A Successful League of Their Own?', in R. Miller and L. Crolley (eds) *Football in the Americas: Fútbol, Futebol, Soccer*, London: Institute for the Study of the Americas.

Jones, M. (2008) *Skin Tight: An Anatomy of Cosmetic Surgery*, Oxford: Berg.

Jong-Young, L. (2004) 'The Development of Football in Korea', in W. Manzenreiter and J. Horne (eds) *Japan, Korea and the 2002 World Cup*, London: Routledge.

Kaldor, M. (2003) *Global Civil Society*, Cambridge: Polity.

Kapferer, J.-N. (1992) *Strategic Brand Management*, London: Kogan Page.

Kapur, D. and J. McHale (2005) *Give Us Your Best and Brightest*, Washington: Brookings Institute.

Katz, D. (1994) *Just Do It: The Nike Spirit in the Corporate World*, Holbrook, MA: Adams.

Katz, E. and T. Liebes (1993) *The Export of Meaning: Cross-Cultural Readings of 'Dallas'*, 2nd edition, Cambridge: Cambridge University Press.

Kay, G. (1975) *Development and Underdevelopment*, London: Macmillan.

Keane, J. (2003) *Global Civil Society?*, Cambridge: Cambridge University Press.

Kelly, W.W. (2007) 'Is Baseball a Global Sport? America's "National Pastime" as Global Field and International Sport', *Global Networks*, 7(2): 187–201.

Kidd, B. and P. Donnelly (2000) 'Human Rights in Sports', *International Review for the Sociology of Sport*, 35(2): 131–48.

King, C. (2004) *Offside Racism: Playing the White Man*, London: Routledge.

Knorr-Cetina, K. (2001) 'Postsocial Relations: Theorizing Sociality in a Postsocial Environment', in G. Ritzer and B. Smart (eds) *Handbook of Social Theory*, London: Sage.

Korr, C. and M. Close (2008) *More Than Just A Game: Football v. Apartheid*, London: Collins.

Krasner, S. (1993) 'Westphalia and all That', in J. Goldstein and R. Keohane (eds) *Ideas and Foreign Policy*, Ithaca, NY: Cornell University Press.

Kristeva, J. (1982) *Powers of Horror: An Essay on Abjection*, New York: Columbia University Press.

Kuper, S. (1994) *Football Against the Enemy*, London: Orion.

Lago, U., R. Simmons and S. Szymanski (2006) 'The Financial Crisis in European Football: An Introduction', *Journal of Sports Economics*, 7: 3–12.

Lagos, G. (1963) *International Stratification and Underdeveloped Countries*, Chapel Hill, NC: The University of North Carolina Press.

Lalic, D. and S. Vrcan (1998) 'From Ends to Trenches and Back: Football in the Former Yugoslavia', in G. Armstrong and R. Giulianotti (eds) *Football, Cultures, Identities*, Basingstoke: Macmillan.

Landau, E. (2007) 'Brazilian Football: The Missed Opportunity of 1997–2000', in R. Miller and L. Crolley (eds) *Football in the Americas: Fútbol, Futebol, Soccer*, London: Institute for the Study of the Americas.

Lane, J.F. (2003) 'Neo-Liberalism as Imposition and Invasion: Problems in Bourdieu's Politics', *French Cultural Studies*, 14: 323–35.

Lanfranchi, P. (ed.) (1992) *Il Calcio e Il Suo Publicco*, Napoli: ESI.

Lanfranchi, P. and M. Taylor (1999) *Moving with the Ball*, Oxford: Berg.

Lanfranchi, P. and A. Wahl (1996) 'The Immigrant as Hero: Kopka, Mekloufi and French Football', *International Journal of the History of Sport*, 13(1): 114–27.

Lanfranchi, P., C. Eisenberg, T. Mason and A. Wahl (2004) *100 Years of Football: The FIFA Centennial Book*, London: Weidenfeld & Nicolson.

Latouche, S. (1996) *The Westernization of the World*, Cambridge: Polity.

Latour, B. (2005) *Reassembling the Social: An Introduction to Actor Network Theory*, Oxford: Clarendon.

Law, J. and J. Hassard (eds) (1999) *Actor Network Theory and After*, Oxford: Blackwell.

Lechner, F. (2005) 'Religious Rejections of Globalization', in M. Juergensmeyer (ed.) *Religion and Global Civil Society*, Oxford: Oxford University Press.

Lechner, F. (2007) 'Imagined Communities in the Global Game: Soccer and the Development of Dutch National Identity', *Global Networks*, 7(2): 215–29.

Leite Lopes, J.S. (1997) 'Successes and Contradictions in "Multiracial" Brazilian Football', in G. Armstrong and R. Giulianotti (eds) *Entering the Field: New Perspectives on World Football*, Oxford: Berg.

Leite Lopes, J.S. (1999) 'The Brazilian Style of Football and its Dilemmas', in G. Armstrong and R. Giulianotti (eds) *Football, Cultures and Identities*, Basingstoke: Macmillan.

Leite Lopes, J.S. (2000) 'Class, Ethnicity, and Color in the Making of Brazilian Football', *Daedalus*, 129: 239–70.

Leseth, A. (1997) 'The Use of *Juju* in Football: Sport and Witchcraft in Tanzania', in G. Armstrong and R. Giulianotti (eds) *Entering the Field: New Perspectives on World Football*, Oxford: Berg.

Lever, J. (1969) 'Soccer: Opium of the Brazilian People', *Trans-Action*, 7: 36–43.

Lever, J. (1983) *Soccer Madness*, Chicago: University of Chicago Press.

Levine, D.N. (1971) 'Introduction', to G. Simmel, *On Individuality and Social Forms: Selected Writings*, in D.N. Levine (ed.), Chicago: University of Chicago Press.

Levine, R.M. (1980) 'Sport and Society: The Case of Brazilian *Futebol*', *Luso-Brazilian Review*, 17(2): 233–52.

Levi-Strauss, C. (1966) *The Savage Mind*, Chicago: University of Chicago Press.

Linklater, A. (1998) *The Transformation of Political Community*, Cambridge: Polity.

Little, C. (2002) 'The Forgotten Game? A Reassessment of the Place of Soccer within New Zealand Society, Sport and Historiography', *Soccer and Society*, 3(2): 38–50.

Lodziak, C. (1966) *Understanding Soccer Tactics*, London: Faber and Faber.

Lucifora, C. and R. Simmons (2003) 'Superstar Effects in Sport: Evidence from Italian Soccer', *Journal of Sports Economics*, 4(1): 35–55.

MacClancy, J. (1996) 'Nationalism at Play: The Basques of Vizcaya and Athletic Bilbao', in J. MacClancy (ed.) *Sport, Identity and Ethnicity*, Oxford: Berg.

Maffesoli, M. (1996) *The Time of the Tribes*, London: Sage.

Magazine, R. (2001) '"The Colours Make Me Sick": America FC and Upward Mobility in Mexico', in G. Armstrong and R. Giulianotti (eds) *Fear and Loathing in World Football*, Oxford: Berg.

Magazine, R. (2007a) 'Football Fandom and Identity in Mexico', in R. Miller and L. Crolley (eds) *Football in the Americas: Fútbol, Futebol, Soccer*, London: Institute for the Study of the Americas.

Magazine, R. (2007b) *Golden and Blue Like My Heart: Masculinity, Youth and Power Among Soccer Fans in Mexico City*, Tucson: University of Arizona Press.

Magoun, F.P. Jr. (1938) *History of Football: From the Beginnings to 1871*, Bochum-Langendreer: Verlag Heinrich Pöppinghaus.

Mair, A. (1997) 'Strategic Localization: The Myth of the Postnational Enterprise', in K. Cox (ed.) *Spaces of Globalization: Reasserting the Power of the Local*, London: Guilford.

Majumdar, B. and K. Bandyopadhyay (2005) 'From Recreation to Competition: Early History of Indian Football', *Soccer & Society*, 6(2/3): 124–41.

Manela, E. (2007) *The Wilsonian Moment: Self-Determination and the International Origins of Anti-Colonial Nationalism*, New York: Oxford University Press.

Mangan, J.A. (1981) *Athleticism in the Victorian and Edwardian Public School*, Cambridge: Cambridge University Press.

Mangan, J.A. (1998) *The Games Ethic and Imperialism: Aspects of the Diffusion of an Ideal*, London: Frank Cass.

Mangan, J.A. (2001) 'Soccer as Moral Training: Missionary Intentions and Imperial Legacies', *Soccer & Society*, 2(2): 41–56.

Markovits, A.S and S.L. Hellerman (2001) *Offside: Soccer and American Exceptionalism*, Princeton: Princeton University Press.

Marling, W.H. (2006) *How American Is Globalization?*, Baltimore, MD: Johns Hopkins.

Marschik, M. (1998) 'Offside: The Development of Women's Football in Austria', *Football Studies*, 1(2): 69–88.

Marschik, M. (2001) 'Mitropa: Representations of Central Europe in Football', *International Review for the Sociology of Sport*, 36(1): 7–23.

Marshall, T.H. (1950) *Citizenship and Social Class, and Other Essays*, Cambridge: Cambridge University Press.

Martin, C.R. and J.L. Reeves (2001) 'The Whole World Isn't Watching (But We Thought They Were): The Super Bowl and United States Solipsism', *Culture, Sport, Society*, 4(2): 213–36.

Martin, P. (1991) 'Colonialism, Youth and Football in French Equatorial Africa', *International Journal of the History of Sport*, 8(1): 56–71.

Martins, H. (1974) 'Time and Theory in Sociology', in J. Rex (ed.) *Approaches to Sociology*, London: Routledge & Kegan Paul.

Mason, T. (1980) *Association Football and English Society 1863–1915*, Brighton: Harvester.

Mason, T. (1995) *Passion of the People? Football in South America*, London: Verso.

Mason, T. (1996) 'Football – Sport of the North?', in J. Hill and J. Williams (eds) (1996) *Sport and Identity in the North of England*, Edinburgh: Edinburgh University Press.

Mazwai, T. (2003) *Thirty Years of South African Soccer*, Cape Town: Sunbird.

McCrone, D. (1992) *Understanding Scotland: The Sociology of a Stateless Nation*, London: Routledge.

McCrone, D., A. Morris and R. Kiely (1995) *Scotland the Brand*, Edinburgh: Edinburgh University Press.

McGovern, P. (2002) 'Globalization or Internationalization? Foreign Footballers in the English League, 1946–1995', *Sociology*, 36(1): 23–42.

McGrew, A.G. (2002) 'Liberal Internationalism: Between Realism and Cosmopolitanism', in A.G. McGrew and D. Held (eds) *Governing Globalization: Power, Authority and Global Governance*, Cambridge: Polity.

McLuhan, M. (1964) *Understanding Media: The Extensions of Man*, London: Routledge and Kegan Paul.

McLuhan, M. and Q. Fiore (1989) *The Medium is the Massage*, New York: Touchstone.

McNeill, W.H. (1986) *Polyethnicity and National Unity in World History*, Toronto: University of Toronto Press.

Meisl, W. (1955) *Soccer Revolution*, London: Phoenix.

Menary, S. (2007) *Outcasts! The Lands That FIFA Forgot*, London: Know the Score.

Merkel, U. (2000) 'The Hidden Social and Political History of the German Football Association, 1900–1950', *Soccer & Society*, 1(2): 167–86.

Meyer, J.W., J. Boli, G.M. Thomas and F.O. Ramirez (1997) 'World Society and the Nation-State', *American Journal of Sociology*, 103(1): 144–81.

Mignolo, W. (2000) *Local Histories/Global Designs*, Princeton: Princeton University Press.

Mikos, L. (2006) 'German Football – A Media Economic Survey: The Impact of KirchMedia on Football and Television in Germany', in A. Tomlinson and C. Young (eds) *German Football: History, Culture, Society and the World Cup 2006*, London: Routledge.

Miles, L. and S. Rines (2004) *Football Sponsorship and Commerce*, London: International Marketing Reports.

Miller, R. (2007) 'Introduction', in R. Miller and L. Crolley (eds) *Football in the Americas: Fútbol, Futebol, Soccer*, London: Institute for the Study of the Americas.

Miller, T., G. Lawrence, J. McKay and D. Rowe (1999) 'Modifying the Sign: Sport and Globalization', *Social Text*, 17(3): 15–33.

Millward, P. (2006) 'Networks, Power and Revenue in Contemporary Football: An Analysis of G14', *International Review of Modern Sociology*, 32(2): 199–216.

Moffett, S. (2003) *Japanese Rules*, London: Yellow Jersey.

Mooij, M. de (1997) *Global Marketing and Advertising*, London: Sage.

Mora y Araujo, M. (2007) 'Round Pegs in Square Holes? The Adaptation of South American Players to the Premiership', in R. Miller and L. Crolley (eds) *Football in the Americas: Fútbol, Futebol, Soccer*, London: Institute for the Study of the Americas.

Morgan, W. J. (1993) *Leftist Theories of Sport*, Urbana, IL: University of Illinois Press.

Morgan, W.J. (1995) 'Cosmopolitanism, Olympism, and Nationalism: A Critical Interpretation of Coubertin's Ideal of International Sporting Life', *Olympika*, IV: 79–92.

Mosely, P. (1994) 'Balkan Politics in Australian Soccer', in *ASSH Studies in Sports History No.10: Ethnicity and Soccer in Australia*, ASSH/University of Western Sydney: Macarthur.

Murray, W. (1996) *The World's Game: A History of Soccer*, Urbana and Chicago, IL: University of Illinois Press.

Nairn, T. (1977) *The Break-Up of Britain*, London: NLR Books.

Nakano, T. (2006) 'A Critique of Held's Cosmopolitan Democracy', *Contemporary Political Theory*, 5(1): 33–51.

Nauright, J. (1999) 'Bhola Lethu: Football in Urban South Africa', in G. Armstrong and R. Giulianotti (eds) *Football, Cultures and Identities*, Basingstoke: Macmillan.

Neale, W. (1964) 'The Peculiar Economics of Professional Sport', *Quarterly Journal of Economics*, 78: 1–14.

Nettl, J.P. and R. Robertson (1968) *International Systems and the Modernization of Societies*, New York: Basic.

Newsham, G.J. (1994) *In a League of their Own! Dick, Kerr Ladies Football Club 1917–1965*, Chorley: Pride of Place Publishing.

Niezen, R. (2003) *The Origins of Indigenism*, Berkeley, CA: University of California Press.

Nkwi, P.N. and B. Vidacs (1997) 'Football: Politics and Power in Cameroon', in G. Armstrong and R. Giulianotti (eds) *Entering the Field: New Perspectives on World Football*, Oxford: Berg.

O'Donnell, H. (1994) 'Mapping the Mythical: A Geopolitics of National Sporting Stereotypes', *Discourse & Society*, 5(3): 345–80.

Ohmae, K. (1990) *The Borderless World: Power and Strategy in the Interlinked Economy*, London: Collins.

Ohmae, K. (1993) 'The Rise of the Region State', *Foreign Affairs*, 72(2): 78–87.

Ohmae, K. (1995) *The End of the Nation State*, New York: Free Press.

Okay, C. (2002) 'The Introduction, Early Development and Historiography of Soccer in Turkey: 1890–1914', *Soccer & Society*, 3(3): 1–10.

Oxford Dictionary of New Words (1991) compiled by S. Tulloch. Oxford: Oxford University Press.

Pearson, G. (1983) *Hooligan: A History of Respectable Fears*, Basingstoke: Macmillan.

Perkin, H. (1989) 'Teaching the Nations How to Play', *International Journal of the History of Sport*, 6(2): 145–55.

Perkins, D.H. et al. (2001) *Economics of Development*, New York: Norton.

Perlmutter, H.V. (1972) 'The Development of Nations, Unions and Firms as Worldwide Institutions', in H. Gunter (ed.) *Transnational Industrial Relations*, New York: St. Martin's Press.

Petras, J. and H. Veltmeyer (2001) *Globalization Unmasked: Imperialism in the Twenty-first Century*, London: Zed.

Pfister, G. (2003) 'The Challenges of Women's Football in East and West Germany: A Comparative Study', *Soccer & Society*, 4(2/3): 128–48.

PFPO (Professional Football Players Observatory) (2008) *The PFPO's Champions League Report 2007–2008*, Besançon: PFPO.

Philo, G. and M. Berry (2004) *Bad News from Israel*, London: Pluto.

Pieterse, J.N. (1995) 'Globalization as Hybridization', in M. Featherstone, S. Lash and R. Robertson (eds) *Global Modernities*, London: Sage.

Pieterse, J.N. (2004) 'Hyperpower Exceptionalism: Globalization the American Way', in U. Beck, N. Sznaider and R. Winter (eds) *Global America? The Cultural Consequences of Globalization*, Liverpool: Liverpool University Press.

Pieterse, J.N. (2007) *Ethnicities and Global Multiculture*, Lanham, MD: Rowman and Littlefield.

Podaliri, C. and C. Balestri (1998) 'The *Ultràs*, Racism and Football Culture in Italy', in A. Brown (ed.) *Fanatics!* London: Routledge.

Poli, R. and L. Ravenel (2006) *Annual Review of the European Football Players' Labour Market*, Neuchâtel: CIES.

Pollock, S. (2000) 'Cosmopolitan and Vernacular in History', *Public Culture*, 12(3): 591–625.

Pujol, F. and P. Garcia del Barrio (2006) 'Report on Media Value of Professional European Football', September, University of Navarra.

Rachman, G. (2007) 'Beautiful Game, Lousy Business: The Problems of Latin American Football', in R. Miller and L. Crolley (eds) *Football in the Americas: Fútbol, Futebol, Soccer*, London: Institute for the Study of the Americas.

Richards, P. (1997) 'Soccer and Violence in War-Torn Africa: Soccer and Social Rehabilitation in Sierra Leone', in G. Armstrong and R. Giulianotti (eds) *Entering the Field*, Oxford: Berg.

Rigauer, B. (1981) *Sport and Work*, New York: Columbia University Press.

Ritzer, G. (2003) 'Rethinking Globalization: Glocalization/Grobalization and Something/Nothing', *Sociological Theory*, 21(3): 193–209.

Ritzer, G. (2004) *The Globalization of Nothing*, Thousand Oaks, CA: Pine Forge.

Roberts, K. (2004) *The Leisure Industries*, Basingstoke: Palgrave.

Robertson, R. (1985) 'The Relativization of Societies: Modern Religion and Globalization', in T. Robbins et al. (eds) *Cults, Culture & The Law*, Chico, CA: Scholars Press.

Robertson, R. (1990a) 'After Nostalgia? Wilful Nostalgia and the Phases of Globalization', in B.S. Turner (ed.) *Theories of Modernity and Postmodernity*, London: Sage.

Robertson, R. (1990b) 'Mapping the Global Condition: Globalization as the Central Concept', *Theory, Culture & Society*, 7: 15–30.

Robertson, R. (1992) *Globalization: Social Theory and Global Culture*, London: Sage.

Robertson, R. (1994) 'Globalisation or Glocalisation?', *Journal of International Communication*, 1(1): 33–52.

Robertson, R. (1995) 'Glocalization: Time–Space and Homogeneity–Heterogeneity', in M. Featherstone, S. Lash and R. Robertson (eds) *Global Modernities*, London: Sage.

Robertson, R. (1998a) 'The New Global History: History in a Global Age', *Cultural Values*, 2 (2 & 3): 368–84.

Robertson, R. (1998b) 'Identidad Nacional y Globalizacion: Falacias Contemporaneas', *Revista Mexicana de Sociologia*, 1(enero-marzo): 3–19.

Robertson, R. (2001) 'Globalization Theory 2000+: Major Problematics', in G. Ritzer and B. Smart (eds) *Handbook of Social Theory*, London: Sage.

Robertson, R. (2004) 'Rethinking Americanization', in U. Beck, N. Sznaider and R. Winter (eds) *Global America? The Cultural Consequences of Globalization?* Liverpool: Liverpool University Press.

Robertson, R. (2007a) 'Open Societies, Closed Minds? Exploring the Ubiquity of Suspicion and Voyeurism', *Globalizations*, 4(3): 399–416.

Robertson, R. (2007b) 'Global Millennialism: A Postmortem on Secularization', in P. Beyer and L. Beaman (eds) *Religion, Globalization and Society*, Leiden: Brill.

Robertson, R. (2007c) 'Glocalization', in R. Robertson and J.A. Scholte (eds) *Encyclopedia of Globalization*, vol. 2, London: Routledge.

Robertson, R. (2007d) 'Globalization, Culture and', in R. Robertson and J.A. Scholte (eds) *Encyclopedia of Globalization*, London: Routledge.

Robertson, R. and J.A. Chirico (1985) 'Humanity, Globalization and Worldwide Religious Resurgence', *Sociological Analysis*, 46: 219–42.

Robertson, R. and R. Giulianotti (2006) 'Fútbol, Globalización y Glocalización: un análisis sociológico del juego mundial', *Revista Internacional di Sociología* LXIV, Number 45: 9–35.

Robertson, R. and J.A. Scholte (eds) (2007) *Encyclopedia of Globalization*, London: Routledge.

Robertson, R. and K.E. White (eds) (2003a) *Globalization: Critical Concepts in Sociology* (six volumes), London: Routledge.

Robertson, R. and K.E. White (2003b) 'Globalization: An Overview', in R. Robertson and K.E. White (eds) *Globalization: Critical Concepts in Sociology* (six volumes), London: Routledge.

Robertson, R. and K.E. White (2004) 'La Glocalizzazione Rivisitata ed Elaborata', in F. Sedda (ed.) *Glocal*, Roma: Luca Sossella Editore.

Robins, D. (1992) *Sport as Prevention: The Role of Sport in Crime Prevention Programmes Aimed at Young People*, University of Oxford: Centre for Criminological Research.

Robinson, W.I. (2002) 'Capitalist Globalization and the Transnationalization of the State', in M. Rupert and H. Smith (eds) *Historical Materialism and Globalization*, London: Routledge.

Robinson, W.I. (2004) 'Global Crisis and Latin America', *Bulletin of Latin American Research*, 23(2): 135–53.

Rogers, E. (1962) *Diffusion of Innovations*, New York: Free Press.

Rosen, S. (1981) 'The Economics of Superstars', *American Economic Review*, 76(4): 845–58.

Rosenau, J. (1990) *Turbulence in World Politics: A Theory of Change and Continuity*, Princeton, NJ: Princeton University Press.

Rosenau, J. (1997) *Along the Domestic–Foreign Frontier: Exploring Governance in a Turbulent World*, Cambridge: Cambridge University Press.

Rosenau, J. (2003) *Distant Proximities: Dynamics Beyond Globalization*, Princeton, NJ: Princeton University Press.

Rostow, W.W. (1960) *The Stages of Economic Growth: A Non-Communist Manifesto*, Cambridge: Cambridge University Press.

Rothacher, A. (ed.) (2004) *Corporate Cultures and Global Brands*, Hackensack, NJ: World Scientific Publishing.

Roversi, A. (1992) *Calcio, Tifo e Violenza*, Bologna: Il Mulino.

Rowe, D. (2003) 'Sport and the Repudiation of the Global', *International Review for the Sociology of Sport*, 38(3): 281–94.

Rowe, D. (2004) 'Watching Brief: Cultural Citizenship and Viewing Rights', *Sport in Society*, 7(3): 385–402.

Rumford, C. (ed.) (2007) *Cosmopolitanism and Europe*, Liverpool: Liverpool University Press.

Russell, D. (1997) *Football and the English: A Social and Cultural History of English Football, 1863–1995*, Carnegie: Preston.

Said, E. (1995) *Orientalism*, Harmondsworth: Penguin.

Sassoon, D. (2002) 'On Cultural Markets', *New Left Review*, 17, September–October: 113–26.

Schafer, W. (2006) 'Regional Globality: An Oxymoron or a Focal Point for Globalization Research?', paper to the conference *The Global Futures of World Regions: The New Asias and the Vision of East Asian Sociology*, Seoul, Korea, 28–9 September.

Scher, A. (1996) *La Patria Deportista*, Buenos Aires: Planeta.

Schiller, H.I. (1969) *Mass Communications and American Empire*, Boston: Beacon.

Schiller, H.I. (1976) *Communication and Cultural Domination*, Armonk, NY: M.E. Sharpe.

Schneider, A.J. (2004) 'Privacy, Confidentiality and Human Rights in Sport', *Sport in Society*, 7(3): 438–56.

Scholte, J.A. (2005) *Globalization*, 2nd edition, Basingstoke: Palgrave.

Shaw-Bond, M. (2000) 'The Backlash Against NGOs', *Prospect*, April: 51–6.

Shilling, C. (2008) *Changing Bodies: Habit, Crisis and Creativity*, London: Sage.

Simmel, G. (1949) 'The Sociology of Sociability', trans. E.C. Hughes, *American Journal of Sociology*, 55(3): 254–61.

Simmel, G. (1955) *Conflict and the Web of Group Affiliations*, New York: Free Press.

Simmel, G. (1959) *Essays on Sociology, Philosophy and Aesthetics by Georg Simmel et al.*, edited by K.H. Wolff, Columbus, OH: Ohio State University Press.

Simmel, G. (1971) *On Individuality and Social Forms: Selected Writings*, edited by D.N. Levine, Chicago: University of Chicago Press.

Sklair, L. (1995) *Sociology of the Global System*, 2nd edition, Baltimore, MD: John Hopkins University Press.

Sklair, L. (2001) *The Transnational Capitalist Class*, Oxford: Blackwell.

Sklair, L. (2002) *Globalization*, 3rd edition, Oxford: Oxford University Press.

Smart, B. (2005) *The Sport Star*, London: Sage

Smith, A. (1986) *The Ethnic Origins of Nations*, Oxford: Blackwell.

Smith, A. (1990) 'Towards a Global Culture?', in M. Featherstone (ed.) *Global Culture: Nationalism, Globalization and Modernity*, London: Sage.

Smith, A. (1994) *Canada: An American Nation?*, Montreal: MQUP.

Smith, P. (1997) *Millennial Dreams: Contemporary Culture and Capital in the North*, London: Verso.

Solberg, H.A. and C. Gratton (2004) 'Would European Soccer Clubs Benefit from Playing in a Super League', *Soccer & Society*, 5(1): 61–81.

Sorek, T. (2007) *Arab Soccer in a Jewish State*, Cambridge: Cambridge University Press.

Spaaij, R. and C. Viñas (2005) 'Passion, Politics and Violence: A Socio-Historical Analysis of Spanish *Ultras*', *Soccer & Society*, 6(1): 79–96.

Stauth, G. and B.S. Turner (1988) *Nietzsche's Dance: Resentment, Reciprocity and Resistance in Social Life*, Oxford: Blackwell.

Steel, C. (2008) *Hungry City: How Food Shapes our Lives*, London: Chatto & Windus.

Stiglitz, J. (2002) *Globalization and Its Discontents*, New York: Norton.

Stiglitz, J. (2006) *Making Globalization Work*, Harmondsworth: Penguin.

Stokes, M. (1996) '"Strong as a Turk": Power, Performance and Representation in Turkish Wrestling', in J. MacClancy (ed.) *Sport, Identity and Ethnicity*, Oxford: Berg.

Strange, S. (1994) *The Retreat of the State: The Diffusion of Power in the World Economy*, Cambridge: Cambridge University Press.

Stuart, O. (1996) 'Players, Workers, Protestors: Social Change and Soccer in Colonial Zimbabwe', in J. MacClancy (ed.) *Sport, Identity and Ethnicity*, Oxford: Berg.

Sugden, J. and A. Tomlinson (eds) (1994) *Hosts and Champions*, Aldershot: Arena.

Sugden, J. and A. Tomlinson (1998) *FIFA and the Contest for World Football*, Cambridge: Polity.

Swyngedouw, E. (1992) 'The Mammon Quest: "Glocalization", Interspatial Competition and the Monetary Order: The Construction of New Scales', in M. Dunford and G. Kafkalis (eds) *Cities and Regions in the New Europe: The Global–Local Interplay and Spatial Development Strategies*, London: Belhaven Press.

Swyngedouw, E. (1997) 'Neither Global nor Local: "Glocalization" and the Politics of Scale', in K. Cox (ed.) *Spaces of Globalization*, New York: Guilford Press.

Swyngedouw, E. (2004) 'Globalisation or Glocalisation? Networks, Territories and Re-Scaling', *Cambridge Review of International Affairs*, 17(1): 25–48.

Szymanski, S. and T. Kuypers (2000) *Winners and Losers: The Business Strategy of Football*, London: Penguin.

Taylor, C. (1998) *The Beautiful Game: A Journey Through Latin American Football*, London: Weidenfeld & Nicolson.

Taylor, I. (1987) 'Putting the Boot into a Working Class Sport: British Soccer after Bradford and Brussels', *Sociology of Sport Journal*, 4: 171–91.

Therborn, G. (1995) 'Routes to/through Modernity', in M. Featherstone, S. Lash and R. Robertson (eds) *Global Modernities*, London: Sage.

Therborn, G. (2000) 'Globalizations: Dimensions, Historical Waves, Regional Effects, Normative Governance', *International Sociology*, 15(2): 151–79.

Tomlinson, J. (1991) *Cultural Imperialism: A Critical Introduction*, London: Pinter.

Tomlinson, J. (1999) *Globalization and Culture*, Cambridge: Polity.

Tomlinson, J. (2007) *The Culture of Speed*, London: Sage.

Tranter, N. (1998) *Sport, Economy and Society in Britain, 1750–1914*, Cambridge: Cambridge University Press.

Tsuda, T.G. (2007) 'When Minorities Migrate: The Racialization of the Japanese Brazilians in Brazil and Japan', in R.S. Parrenas and L.C.D. Siu (eds) *Asian Diasporas: New Formations, New Conceptions*, Palo Alto, CA: Stanford University Press.

Tuastad, D. (1997) 'The Political Role of Football for Palestinians in Jordan', in G. Armstrong and R. Giulianotti (eds) *Entering the Field: New Perspectives on World Football*, Oxford: Berg.

Turner, B.S. (2008) *Body and Society*, 3rd edition, London: Sage.

Urry, J. and P. McNaughten (1998) *Contested Natures*, London: Routledge.

Vergès, F. (2001) 'Vertigo and Emancipation, Creole Cosmopolitanism and Cultural Politics', *Theory, Culture & Society*, 18: 169–83.

Vertovec, S. and R. Cohen (eds) (2002) *Conceiving Cosmopolitanism: Theory, Context and Practice*, Oxford: Oxford University Press.

Veseth, M. (2005) *Globaloney: Unraveling the Myths of Globalization*, Lanham, MD: Rowman & Littlefield.

Vinnai, G. (1973) *Football Mania*, London: Ocean.

Votre, S. and L. Mourão (2003) 'Women's Football in Brazil: Progress and Problems', *Soccer & Society*, 4(2/3): 254–67.

Wagg, S. (ed.) (2004) *British Football and Social Exclusion*, London: Routledge.

Wagner, P. (2000) 'Modernity – One or Many?', in J. Blau (ed.) *The Blackwell Companion to Sociology*, Oxford: Blackwell.

Walby, S. (1999) 'The New Regulatory State: The Social Powers of the European Union', *British Journal of Sociology*, 50(1): 118–40.

Walby, S. (2003) 'The Myth of the Nation-State: Theorizing Society and Polities in a Global Era', *Sociology*, 37(1): 531–48.

Wallerstein, I. (1974) *The Modern World System: Capitalist Agriculture and the Origins of the European World Economy in the Sixteenth Century*, New York: Academic Press.

Wallerstein, I. (2000) *The Essential Wallerstein*, New York: New Press.

Wallerstein, I. (2001) *The Decline of American Power*, New York: New Press.

Walsh, A.J. and R. Giulianotti (2001) 'This Sporting Mammon! A Moral Critique of the Commodification of Sport', *Journal of the Philosophy of Sport*, 28: 53–77.

Walsh, A.J. and R. Giulianotti (2006) *Ethics, Money and Sport*, London: Routledge.

Walton, J. (2001) 'Basque Football Rivalries in the Twentieth Century', in G. Armstrong and R. Giulianotti (eds) *Fear and Loathing in World Football*, Oxford: Berg.

Walvin, J. (1975) *The People's Game*, London: Allen Lane.

Walvin, J. (1994) *The People's Game: The History of Football Revisited*, Edinburgh: Mainstream.

Walvin, J. (2001) *The People's Game: The History of Football Revisited*, Edinburgh: Mainstream.

Walzer, M. (ed.) (1997) *Toward a Global Civil Society*, Oxford: Berghahn.

Wangerin, D. (2006) *Soccer in a Football World: The Story of America's Forgotten Game*, London: WSC Books.

Watson, J. (ed.) (1997) *Golden Arches East: McDonald's in East Asia*, Palo Alto, CA: Stanford University Press.

Weatherhill, S. (2000) 'Resisting the Pressures of "Americanization": The Influence of European Community Law on the "European Sport Model"', in S. Greenfield and G. Osborn (eds) *Law and Sport in Contemporary Society*, London: Frank Cass.

Weber, M. (1958) 'Politics as a Vocation', in H.H. Gerth and C.W. Mills (eds) *From Max Weber: Essays in Sociology*, Oxford: Oxford University Press.

Weiss, L. (1997) 'Globalization and the Myth of the Powerless State', *New Left Review*, 225: 3–27.

Wellman, B. (ed.) (1999) *Networks in the Global Village*, Boulder, CO: Westview.

Westad, O.A. (2005) *The Global Cold War*, Cambridge: Cambridge University Press.

Whannel, G. (1992) *Fields in Vision*, London: Routledge.

White, G., J. Howell and S. Xiaoyuan (1996) *In Search of Civil Society: Market Reform and Social Change in Contemporary China*, Oxford: Clarendon Press.

Wilber, C.K. (ed.) (1970) *The Political Economy of Development and Underdevelopment*, New York: Random House.

Wilkesmann, U. and D. Blutner (2002) 'Going Public: The Organizational Restructuring of German Football Clubs', *Soccer & Society*, 3(2): 19–37.

Wilkins, M. (1998) 'Multinational Corporations: A Historical Account', in R. Kozul-Wright and R. Rowthorn (eds) *Transnational Corporations and the Global Economy*, Basingstoke: Palgrave.

Williams, J. (2003) 'The Fastest Growing Sport? Women's Football in England', *Soccer & Society*, 4(2/3): 112–27.

Williams, J., S. Hopkins and C. Long (2001) *Passing Rhythms: Liverpool FC and the Transformation of Football*, Oxford: Berg.

Wittel, A. (2001) 'Toward a Network Sociality', *Theory, Culture & Society*, 18(6): 51–76.

Wong, L.L. and R. Trumper (2002) 'Global Celebrity Athletes and Nationalism: Fútbol, Hockey, and the Representation of Nation', *Journal of Sport & Social Issues*, 26: 168–94.

Wood, D. (2007) 'Arriba Peru! The Role of Football in the Formation of a Peruvian National Culture', in R. Miller and L. Crolley (eds) *Football in the Americas: Fútbol, Futebol, Soccer*, London: Institute for the Study of the Americas.

Woolridge, J. (2002) 'Mapping the Stars: Stardom in English Professional Football, 1890–1916', *Soccer & Society*, 3(2): 51–69.

Yallop, D. (1999) *How They Stole The Game*, London: Poetic Publishing.

Žižek, S. (2002) *Welcome to the Desert of the Real*, London: Verso.

Index

Please note that page references to footnotes will be followed by the letter 'n'

Index